Work From Home

50

Ways to Make

Money Online Analyzed

By

Michael Ezeanaka

www.MichaelEzeanaka.com

Copyright ©2019

All rights reserved. Except as permitted under the U.S. Copyright Act of 1976, the scanning, uploading and distribution of this book via the Internet or via any other means without the express permission of the author is illegal and punishable by law. Please purchase only authorized electronic editions, and do not participate in or encourage electronic piracy of copyrighted material.

Disclaimer

This publication is designed to provide competent and reliable information regarding the subject matter covered. However, it is sold with the understanding that the author is not engaged in rendering investment or other professional advice. Laws and practices often vary from state to state and country to country and if investment or other expert assistance is required, the services of a professional should be sought. The author specifically disclaims any liability that is incurred from the use or application of the contents of this book.

Books In The Business and Money Series	
Series #	Book Title
1	Affiliate Marketing
2	Passive Income Ideas
3	Affiliate Marketing + Passive Income Ideas (2-in-1 Bundle)
4	Facebook Advertising
5	Dropshipping
6	Dropshipping + Facebook Advertising (2-in-1 Bundle)
7	Real Estate Investing For Beginners
8	Credit Cards and Credit Repair Secrets
9	Real Estate Investing And Credit Repair (2-in-1 Bundle)
10	Passive Income With Affiliate Marketing (2nd Edition)
11	Passive Income With Dividend Investing

The kindle edition will be available to you for FREE when you purchase the paperback version from Amazon.com (The US Store)

Download The Audio Versions Along With The Complementary PDF Document For **FREE** from Amazon.com or Audible.com

Business Scorecard

How would you like to download a scorecard that neatly summarizes, in alphabetical order, each business model's score across 4 areas – simplicity, passivity, scalability and competitiveness? If you want it, a PDF version of the card is hosted on my website and can be downloaded for free. However, a password is required to unlock the download. Follow the steps below to retrieve the password!

Steps to take

1. The password consists of 8 characters (all lower case)
2. Here is the incomplete password: d-n-u-b-
3. The second, fourth, sixth and eight character of the password is missing and is located in random pages of this book.
4. Read this book carefully to locate and retrieve them (they're so obvious you can't miss them).
5. Once you have the complete password then go to www.MichaelEzeanaka.com
6. Navigate to Free Stuff > Ebooks/Audiobooks > Business Scorecard
7. Enter the password, download the scorecard and enjoy!

Table of Contents

Books In The Business and Money Series 3

Business Scorecard 4

Introduction 16

What is Passive Income? 17

Success Mindset 18
    Taking Responsibility for Your Success and Failures 18
    Adopting an Abundance Mindset 19
    Mapping Out a Course of Action 19

50 Online Businesses Analyzed 19

Business #1 21
    Amazon Kindle Direct Publishing 21
        Ratings Based on Our Criteria 22
        Tips for Success 22
        Frequently Asked Questions and Answers 23
        Myth Busters About Kindle Direct Publishing 24

Business #2 26
    Amazon FBA (Fulfilled by Amazon) 26
        Ratings Based on Our Criteria 26
        Tips For Success 27
        Frequently Asked Questions and Answers 28
        Myth Busters About Amazon FBA 30

Business #3 32
    Blogging 32
        Ratings Based on Our Criteria 32
        Tips for Success 33
        Frequently Asked Questions and Answers 33
        Myth Busters About Blogging 35

Business #4 36
    Domain Flipping 36
        Ratings Based on Our Criteria 36
        Tips for Success 37
        Frequently Asked Questions and Answers 38
        Myth Busters About Domain Flipping 39

Business #5 41
    Shopify 41
        Ratings Based on Our Criteria 42
        Tips For Success 42
        Frequently Asked Questions and Answers 43
        Myth Busters About Selling on Shopify 44

Business #6 46
    Freelancing as a Virtual Assistant 46

- Ratings Based on Our Criteria 46
- Tips on How to Be Successful as a Virtual Assistant 47
- Frequently Asked Questions and Answers 48
- Myth Busters About Working as a Virtual Assistant 49

Business #7 51
Affiliate Marketing 51
- Ratings Based on Our Criteria 51
- Tips on How to Be Successful in Affiliate Marketing 52
- Frequently Asked Questions and Answers 53
- Myth Busters About Affiliate Marketing 54

Business #8 56
Dropshipping 56
- Ratings Based on Our Criteria 56
- Tips For Success 57
- Frequently Asked Questions and Answers 58
- Myth Busters About Dropshipping 59

Business #9 61
Create Online Courses 61
- Ratings Based on Our Criteria 61
- Tips For Success 62
- Frequently Asked Questions and Answers 63
- Myth Busters About Creating Online Courses 64

Business #10 66
Build an Application 66
- Ratings Based on Our Criteria 66
- Tips For Success 67
- Frequently Asked Questions and Answers 68
- Myth Busters About Building and Making Money from Apps 69

Business #11 70
Online Consultancy 70
- Ratings Based on Our Criteria 70
- Tips For Success 71
- Frequently Asked Questions and Answers 72
- Myth Busters About Online Consultancy 73

Business #12 75
Online Surveys 75
- Ratings Based on Our Criteria 75
- Tips For Success 76
- Frequently Asked Questions and Answers 77
- Myth Busters About Online Surveys 78

Business #13 79
Online Auctions 79
- Ratings Based on Our Criteria 79
- Tips For Success 79
- Frequently Asked Questions and Answers 80
- Myth Busters About Selling in Auction Sites 81

Business #14 83
Cryptocurrency 83
- Ratings Based on Our Criteria 83
- Tips For Success 83
- Frequently Asked Questions and Answers 84
- Myth Busters about Trading Cryptocurrencies 85

Business #15 87
Commodities Trading 87
- Ratings Based on Our Criteria 87
- Tips For Success 87
- Frequently Asked Questions and Answers 88
- Myth Busters about Trading Commodities 89

Business #16 91
Make YouTube Videos 91
- Ratings Based on Our Criteria 91
- Tips For Success 92
- Frequently Asked Questions and Answers 93
- Myth Busters About Making Money on YouTube 94

Business #17 97
Social Media Influencer 97
- Ratings Based on Our Criteria 97
- Tips For Success 98
- Frequently Asked Questions and Answers 99
- Myth Busters about Being a Social Media Influencer 100

Business #18 102
Photography – Royalty from Photographs 102
- Ratings Based on Our Criteria 102
- Tips For Success 103
- Frequently Asked Questions and Answers 103
- Myth Busters about Stock Photography 104

Business #19 106
Real Estate - REITS 106
- Ratings Based on Our Criteria 106
- Tips For Success 106
- Frequently Asked Questions and Answers 107
- Myth Busters about Real Estate and REITS 108

Business #20 110
Become a Business Silent Partner 110
- Ratings Based on Our Criteria 110
- Tips For Success 110
- Frequently Asked Questions and Answers 111
- Myth Busters about Silent Partners in Business 112

Business #21 113
Rent Out Unused Space with AirBnb 113
- Ratings Based on Our Criteria 113
- Tips For Success 113

    Frequently Asked Questions and Answers 114
    Myth Busters about Renting Out Space in Airbnb 114

Business #22 116
Invest in a Lending Club 116
    Ratings Based on Our Criteria 116
    Tips For Success 116
    Frequently Asked Questions and Answers 117
    Myth Busters about Investing in Lending Club 118

Business #23 120
Get Cash Back Rewards on Credit Cards 120
    Ratings Based on Our Criteria 120
    Tips For Success 120
    Frequently Asked Questions and Answers 121
    Myth Busters about Using Cashback Credit Cards 122

Business #24 124
Create a Comparison Website 124
    Ratings Based on Our Criteria 124
    Tips For Success 125
    Frequently Asked Questions and Answers 125
    Myth Busters about Building a Comparison Website 126

Business #25 128
Create a Software Program 128
    Ratings Based on Our Criteria 128
    Tips For Success 128
    Frequently Asked Questions and Answers 129
    Myth Busters about Software Development 130

Business #26 132
Buy and Rent Out Expensive Equipment 132
    Ratings Based on Our Criteria 132
    Tips For Success 133
    Frequently Asked Questions and Answers 133
    Myth Busters about Renting Out Equipment 134

Business #27 136
Buy an Existing Online Business 136
    Ratings Based on Our Criteria 136
    Tips For Success 136
    Myths About Buying An Existing Business 137

Business #28 138
License Out Your Smart Ideas and Earn Royalties 138
    Ratings Based on Our Criteria 138
    Tips For Success 139
    Myths About Licensing Your Ideas 139

Business #29 141
Invent Something, Have It Patented, and Earn Royalties 141

Business #30 142

Franchise a Business 142
   Ratings Based on Our Criteria 142
   Tips For Success 143
   Myths About Franchising 143

Business #31 145
Retail Arbitrage on eBay 145
   Ratings Based on Our Criteria 145
   Tips For Success 145
   Myths About Retail Arbitrage 146

Business #32 147
Create a Podcast 147
   Ratings Based on Our Criteria 148
   Tips For Success 148
   Frequently Asked Questions and Answers 149
   Myths About Podcasting 150

Business #33 151
Start a Deals Newsletter 151
   Ratings Based on Our Criteria 151
   Tips For Success 152
   Myths About Deals Newsletters 153

Business #34 154
Develop Wordpress Themes 154
   Ratings Based on Our Criteria 154
   Tips For Success 154
   Myths About Developing Wordpress Themes 155

Business #35 156
Dividend Investing 156
   Ratings Based on Our Criteria 156
   Tips For Success 157
   Myths About Dividend Investing 157

Business #36 159
Authority Sites 159
   Ratings Based on Our Criteria 160
   Tips For Success 160
   Myths About Creating An Authority Site 162

Business #37 163
Membership Sites 163
   Ratings Based on Our Criteria 163
   Tips For Success 164
   Myths About Membership Sites 164

Business #38 166
Putting Money into High-Yield Savings Accounts 166
   Ratings Based on Our Criteria 166
   Tips For Success 166

Business #39 168

    Rent Out Your Car 168
        Ratings Based on Our Criteria 168
        Tips For Success 169

Business #40 170
    Rent Out Your Clothes 170
        Ratings Based on Our Criteria 170
        Tips For Success 171

Business #41 172
    Rent Out Your Bike 172
        Ratings Based on Our Criteria 172
        Tips For Success 172

Business #42 174
    Rent Out Your Garage or Parking Spot 174
        Ratings Based on Our Criteria 174
        Tips For Success 174

Business #43 176
    Get Paid to Watch Videos and TV 176
        Ratings Based on Our Criteria 176
        Tips For Success 177

Business #44 178
    Vending Machines 178
        Ratings Based on Our Criteria 178
        Tips For Success 178
        Myths About Vending Business 179

Business #45 180
    Storage Rentals 180
        Ratings Based on Our Criteria 180
        Tips For Success 181

Business #46 182
    Licensing Music 182
        Ratings Based on Our Criteria 182
        Tips For Success 182

Business #47 184
    Network Marketing 184
        Ratings Based on Our Criteria 185
        Tips For Success 185
        Frequently Asked Questions and Answers 186

Business #48 189
    Cashback Reward Cards 189
        Ratings Based on Our Criteria 189
        Tips For Success 189

Business #49 191
    Cashback Sites 191
        Ratings Based on Our Criteria 191

    Tips For Success 191

Business #50 193
Refinance Your Mortgage 193
    Ratings Based on Our Criteria 193
    Tips For Success 194
    Frequently Asked Questions and Answers 194
    Myth Busters About Refinancing Your Mortgage 195

Introduction 198

Chapter 1 199
What Is Affiliate Marketing? 199
    History of Affiliate marketing 199
    The Affiliate marketing business model 200
    The Advertiser 200
    The consumers 201
    The Publisher 201

Chapter 1 Quiz 203

Chapter 2 205
Low Ticket vs. High Ticket Affiliate Marketing 205

Chapter 3 209
How To Become An Affiliate Marketer 209
    A website 209
    A profitable niche 209
    An organic source of traffic 209
    A membership to an affiliate marketing program 209
    How hard is the application process? 210
    My application has been approved, what now? 210

Chapter 3 Quiz 213

Chapter 4 215
The Top 20 Affiliate Marketing Programs 215
    1. Amazon Associates 215
    2. CJ.com 216
    3. Clickbank 216
    4. Rakuten Linkshare 216
    5. JVZoo 217
    6. Avantlink 217
    7. eBay 217
    8. Shareasale 217
    9. Avangate 217
    10. Affibank 217
    11. Maxbounty 218
    12. RevenueWire 218
    13. ReviMedia 218
    14. Flexoffers 218
    15. Commission Factory 218
    16. PeerFly 218

- 17. ClickFunnels 218
- 18. Tradedoubler 218
- 19. AffiliateWindow 218
- 20. BankAffiliates 218

Chapter 4 Quiz 219

Chapter 5 221
- **How To Choose An Affiliate Marketing Program** 221
  - Check the advertisers 221
  - Find the programs with the best commission rate 221
  - Based on the quality of backend services 221

Chapter 5 Quiz 222

Chapter 6 224
- **Writing Content For Affiliate Marketing** 224
  - Promote products you've used in the past 224
  - Presenting products you haven't used 224
  - What type of content should I create? 225
  - Putting the Tips into Action 225
  - Pick a topic you enjoy working on 227
  - Create specific types of content based on your marketing platform 227
  - Encourage followers to engage with your content 227
  - State a clear call-to-action to go to the affiliate website 227

Chapter 6 Quiz 229

Chapter 7 231
- **Using Social Media Platforms For Affiliate Marketing** 231
  - 1. Find the social media website or app where most of your target audience spend their time 231
  - 2. Identify what content to share in each network 231
  - 3. Find out how content is spread in the network 232
  - 4. Completely create your account and start sharing 233
  - 5. Facebook and LinkedIn groups 233

Chapter 7 Quiz 236

Chapter 8 238
- **Common Affiliate Marketing Mistakes** 238
  - 1. Thinking that a website is the only way to sell affiliate products 238
  - 2. Not building a community from day one 238
  - 3. Becoming too salesy by claiming exaggerated results 238
  - 4. Not working with a partner 239
  - 5. Shiny Object Syndrome 240
  - 6. Not delegating tasks 240
  - 7. Failing to track results 241

Chapter 8 Quiz 242

Chapter 9 244
- **Choosing the Right Niche** 244
  - Make a list of your hobbies, interests and passions 244
  - Arrange the topics you've chosen according to how much you enjoy talking about them 244

- Survey other people's interest about the subject ... 244
- Survey the competition ... 244
- Find the most commonly searched problems about this niche ... 245
- Find affiliate products that can solve the problems in these niches ... 245

Chapter 9 Quiz ... 246

Chapter 10 ... 248
Building your Email List ... 248
- Before your content ... 248
- In-content ... 248
- In pop-ups ... 249
- In the Sidebar ... 249
- AMP Pages and Facebook Instant Articles ... 249
- Other social networks ... 250
- Creating a Lead Capture/Squeeze page ... 250
- Limit the number of times you ask for visitors' emails ... 252
- Ask for emails in a natural way ... 252
- State your email campaign's unique value proposition in your email subscription forms ... 252
- Creating many types of lists ... 252
- Engaging with the customer ... 253
- Creating your autoresponders ... 253
- Choose your email marketing approach ... 254

Chapter 10 Quiz ... 256

Chapter 11 ... 259
Affiliate Marketing Strategies ... 259
- Track the movement of your users ... 259
- Judge each affiliate program based on their landing pages ... 260
- Factors that affect landing page conversion rate: ... 261
- Here are the qualities of the visitors that you should send to your affiliate marketing landing pages: ... 262

Chapter 11 Quiz ... 265

Chapter 12 ... 267
Tips to Become a Successful Affiliate Marketer ... 267
- Sell things and services that you are knowledgeable about ... 267
- Keep your online assets active ... 267
- Don't stop with one website ... 268
- Learn to cross sell related products ... 268
- Create a core team to grow your business ... 268
- Reinvest profits to growing your business ... 268
- Renegotiate the terms with the advertiser ... 269
- Don't just create websites, create brands ... 269

Chapter 12 Quiz ... 272

Chapter 13: ... 274
Proven Ways to Improve Website Traffic ... 274
- Guest posting ... 274
- Guesting on a Vlog ... 275
- Search Engine Optimization ... 276

  How to optimize content for search engines 276

  Marketing in forums and other online communities 279

  Using ads to get traffic 279

  Free versus paid traffic 280

  Paid campaigns enhance organic marketing efforts 281

  Using Ads to Get Traffic 281

  Tracking success and refining your campaigns 282

  Starting your first campaign 283

Chapter 13 Quiz 288

Conclusion 290

The End 292

Appendix A 293

  Solution to Chapter 1 Quiz 293

Appendix B 293

  Solution to Chapter 2 Quiz 293

Appendix C 294

  Solution to Chapter 3 Quiz 294

Appendix D 294

  Solution to Chapter 4 Quiz 294

Appendix E 295

  Solution to Chapter 5 Quiz 295

Appendix F 295

  Solution to Chapter 6 Quiz 295

Appendix G 296

  Solution to Chapter 7 Quiz 296

Appendix H 296

  Solution to Chapter 8 Quiz 296

Appendix I 297

  Solution to Chapter 9 Quiz 297

Appendix J 297

  Solution to Chapter 10 Quiz 297

Appendix K 298

  Solution to Chapter 11 Quiz 298

Appendix L 298

  Solution to Chapter 12 Quiz 298

Appendix M 299

  Solution to Chapter 13 Quiz 299

Passive Income Ideas

50

Ways to Make

Money Online Analyzed

By

Michael Ezeanaka

www.MichaelEzeanaka.com

Introduction

In this day and age, it has become much easier to generate passive income. The internet, in particular, has given birth to a plethora of opportunities that enable smart and business-minded people to earn significant profits with very limited work. The lure of generating passive income has never been stronger. The idea of earning an income while vacationing in the Virgin Islands is a truly attractive prospect. However, things are easier said than done. Just like any form of profit-oriented activity, you have to put in the time and the work before you can see a stream of passive income going your way.

A lot of people make the mistake of equating earning passive income with get-rich-quick schemes. I hope that you don't make the same mistake. This is why I've put together this guide about the most common ways on how to earn passive income. My intention is to help you decide if an opportunity is right for you or not. I also want to help you debunk the myths and misconceptions surrounding these income-generating methods. The information and analysis you will find in this book are based on facts and observable trends. I want to make sure that you are on the right direction when you finally decide to find a way to generate passive income.

I also highly recommend that you nurture the attributes of patience and determination when you pursue any of the methods discussed in this book. These are virtues you are going to need because most of the methods here won't deliver instant income. Most of the time, you have to build the business from the ground up. If you don't have patience, you will give up before you start reaping the rewards that you deserve. If you don't have determination, then one setback can easily break down your spirit. My suggestion is that you should look into your passive income journey with long-term goals.

Take your time. Don't rush things. If you don't achieve a goal, just sit back and try to understand what went wrong. What did you do? What didn't you do? Then do things all over again. Sooner or later, things will come into place. Once you start seeing the earnings roll in, just sit back once again and try to see how you can scale the earnings. This is what successful online entrepreneurs do. You should do the same.

Furthermore, all businesses are not equal. Some of the business opportunities covered in this book are by their very nature passive while others aren't – this is why a passivity grade is assigned to them to help you compare and contrast. However, every business can be made more passive by applying certain strategies. Where necessary, strategies that will help increase the passivity of the business are suggested.

Finally, please bare in mind **this guide is by no means a comprehensive analysis of 50 business opportunities.** As much as I would have loved to cover every minute detail of each business, it'll be difficult to achieve that without making this book unnecessarily long.

However, what you'll find herein is a **brief overview of 50 ways you can earn passive income, or at the very least, make money online.** The intention here is to help you quickly compare and contrast each business model, pick out the opportunities that interest you the most and then do further research on them. It's my sincere hope that what you'll discover in this book will bring you one step closer to achieving the financial freedom you deserve. Without further ado, lets get right into it!

What is Passive Income?

There are various definitions of passive income but the most common one is this: "It is income that you earn even if you are not actively trying to earn it." You are still earning it even if you are mowing your lawn or if you are on vacation in the Bahamas. In short, it's income that goes to your bank account whether you actively work for it or not. Rental income is one of the most common examples of passive income. You own a piece of land that a farmer rents for $1000 a month. Whether you do anything or not to the property, you will still receive the $1000 at the end of every month.

Passive income has been around since the dawn of civilization. Tributes that tribesmen bring to their chiefs can be considered as passive income by the nature of the tributes. These are products or goods that the chiefs themselves didn't work on. They simply receive them after every harvest cycle. With that said, the concept of passive income has been around for centuries.

However, it has evolved with the times. Economic movements have given birth to dozens of other ways on how to generate passive income. For example, the current technological revolution has created online economies that allow people to earn significant amounts of passive income. Anyone can start a website, sign up with Amazon, promote Amazon products, and earn commissions from every sale. These commissions are considered as passive income.

Why Is Passive Income Important?

Passive income is very important in the sense that it allows people to achieve some sort of financial freedom while getting the chance to indulge in the things that they are passionate about. For example, with an alternative source of income, you can spend more time doing something you love like going to the beach to surf, going to the mountains to hike or spending quality time with your loved ones. It enables to you to earn money without having to work day in and day out for it. Of course, the importance of passive income largely depends on where you are coming from and what your goals are in pursuing it.

But the bottom line here is that passive income offers you an opportunity to earn good money with less work. It is hard work at first but you slowly unburden yourself from the work as your business and passive income stream grows. That's the beauty of it. It gets easier and easier with the passage of time provided that you are doing things the right way and that you are scaling your business with the right strategies. The work you have done yesterday will continue to benefit you in the coming days, weeks, months, or even years. This is especially true if you are running a content-based business that's hosted online.

To cut the story short, passive income is important to those who are looking for a good source of alternative income that requires minimal work. It's important to those who want to supplement their income from their 9 to 5 jobs. It's important to those who want more time to pursue their passions. It's important to those who want to build businesses that have the potential of completely replacing their income from their ordinary jobs.

Finally, having a good passive income base will make you less dependent on your job. If for any reason you were to lose your job, you'll still have peace of mind knowing you have other ways of making money – ways you can easily scale up to replace the income from your job. This means, you'll not be at the mercy of the economy (i.e. economic downturn and subsequent job losses) or your boss. You'll be in control of your financial life.

Success Mindset

The two most important virtues that you need to achieve success in generating passive income are patience and determination. If you have both of these attributes, then you have the ideal mindset required to achieve success. Majority of those who fail in generating passive income do so because they give up too easily or they get discouraged with the slightest setback. Make no mistakes. The opportunities discussed in this book are by no means get rich quick schemes. If you don't have patience and determination, then it will be very difficult for you to create a great source of passive income.

In the context of passive income, patience means sticking to your guns for weeks, months, or even years. You have to always remember that it will take time before you get to see meaningful returns on your investments. For example, let's say that you built a blog which you monetized with advertisements and affiliate products. You should not expect your blog to generate income right out of the bat. It takes time for the blog to attract and grow readers. Sometimes, for the first months, you are going to earn nothing. If you don't have patience and determination, it's so easy to get discouraged and just give up.

Taking Responsibility for Your Success and Failures

In your passive income journey, you are going to go through a lot of ups and downs, failures and successes. You should own up to these failures because it's the only way to learn from your mistakes. It's easier to find solutions to problems if you accept the fact that you are responsible in fixing them. You see, one of the most common reasons why many aspiring online entrepreneurs fail is that they play the blame game when things don't go their way. They blame everyone but themselves. They blame the freelance writers they hired. They blame the social media marketers running their social media campaigns. They blame their staff. They actually spend more time finding someone to blame than finding a solution to the problem that caused the failure.

In a nutshell, success and failure come hand in hand. It's not uncommon for beginners to encounter more failures than successes. What really matters is how you deal with the failures. Are you going to let them discourage you? Or are you going to use them as lessons to be smarter the second time around? In my experience, successful and determined entrepreneurs follow the latter route. You should do the same.

Having this book by your side will give you tremendous leverage and a good head start because you'll know which business opportunity suits you best and which to avoid. However, if you wish to further cut down your learning curve and reduce the number of mistakes you'll make, we advise working with a mentor – someone who has achieved success in what it is you're trying to do.

Bear in mind, the best mentors tend to be those who are not too far ahead of you as they will be able to better understand the challenges you're currently going through since it wasn't too long ago they went through the same challenges themselves.

Adopting an Abundance Mindset

When we say you should adopt an abundance mindset, we are urging you to stay optimistic and focus all your attention on the good things and positive things that are happening in your passive income journey. Everything you do should be geared towards achieving the abundance you envisioned when you started your passive income journey. Having this mindset will keep your efforts glued to your most important goals.

Adopting an abundance mindset also involves dealing with setbacks and learning from them. In most cases, it's about turning your weaknesses into strengths. You failed to sell products in your first weeks? This happens to almost everyone so don't let it get to you too much. A smart entrepreneur would look back at what he did or what he didn't do and go from there with renewed passion knowing that he's not going to make the same mistakes again.

Mapping Out a Course of Action

Goal setting and planning are two of the most important things you should do before you embark on a journey to earn passive income. In goal setting, you identify both your short-term and long-term goals. There should also be a corresponding time periods for your goals. For example, where do you envision yourself after six months of pursuing your goals? After setting your goals, you then proceed to mapping out a plan on how you are going to achieve them. You can call it the "master plan" or the "blueprint". What's important is that it should contain the course of action you are going to implement in your attempt to get to your goals.

To recap things, you are going to need patience and determination if you want to last long as an entrepreneur. Being patient and determined also means owning up to your failures and successes. It's also your responsibility to learn from these failures and ensure that you don't go through them ever again. To help you deal with failures and mistakes, you should adopt the abundance mindset. This mindset helps you in making the most out of your failures. This mindset helps you in turning strengths into weaknesses. And last but not the least, always see to it that you are being guided by a map or course of action. Without setting your goals and creating a blueprint on how to reach them, you are going to be blind going in. So set those goals and write a plan of action before you do anything else.

50 Online Businesses Analyzed

Let's now get into the meat of the matter. Discussed in the upcoming pages are 50 of the best strategies on how to generate passive income. Like I mentioned before, the word "passive" is relative and some of the business opportunities analyzed below are more passive than the other. However, every business can be made more passive by applying certain strategies. Where applicable, these strategies will be discussed.

That being said, in the coming pages, you'll learn about 50 business opportunities, and how you can increase your chances of being successful with them. Most of these businesses require minimal monetary investment, which means working hard, and working smart is what you need to get things done. You should take the time to analyze and understand every strategy and opportunity. You should also consider testing out the strategies to see which ones will work well for you.

Without further ado, let's get on with the first one!

Inspiration #1

"If you can dream it, you can do it."

Walt Disney

Business #1

Amazon Kindle Direct Publishing

If you think you are a good writer or you simply want to make money as a publisher then kindle publishing is an opportunity you might want to explore. There are thousands of people out there who are making a lot of money from Kindle Publishing. If they can, then you can as well. What's great about Kindle Publishing is that you have the flexibility to choose what to write. You can write fiction or non-fiction and short stories or full novels. Some people even publish magazine-type articles on the platform. What Kindle Publishing does is connect you with your target readers. It's the perfect platform for people who want to independently publish their works.

Kindle allows you to publish both ebooks and paperbacks. What's great about the platform is that you have control over your rights for the book and you get to set your own list prices. Furthermore, you can make changes on your books any time you want. As far as earnings are concerned, you can receive up to 70% in royalty from your book sales. For example, if you priced your ebook at $2.99 per download, your royalties will be $2.093 per ebook sold (excluding download fees). That may not look like much but it quickly adds up once your sales start to pick up. The 70% royalty applies to numerous countries with huge Amazon markets like the United States, United Kingdom, India, Italy, Japan, Mexico, Canada, Germany, France, Spain, Brazil, and Australia.

Basically, here's how you publish your ebook or paperback on the Amazon Kindle Direct Publishing platform:

1. Write a book yourself or hire a ghost writer to write for you
2. Prepare your manuscript and cover. You can use Amazon's in-house tools and resources to complete this process.
3. See to it that your manuscript meets the quality and content guidelines as put forth by Amazon. If you have the budget for it, try seeking the help of a professional editor and proof reader on upwork.com, fiverr.com or any other suitable website.
4. Sign up with KDP. If you have an existing Amazon account, you can use it to sign up with KDP. If you don't have an account, you should create one. It will only take a few minutes of your time.
5. Make sure that your internet browser is updated. Sometimes, if your browser is out of date, you can't access some of the features and functionality within the Kindle Publishing platform.
6. After completing the sign-up process, go the section that says Bookshelf, click on the button that says "Create a New Title", then click on the "Kindle eBook" option.
7. In the new window, you will be required to input your information and details about your book. These include Kindle eBook Details, Kindle eBook Content, and Kindle eBook Pricing.
8. After completing the steps above, just click "Publish Your Kindle eBook" and you're done.
9. Voila! Your book is now published and ready to be read by people from all over the world.

Amazon Kindle Direct Publishing is a great source of passive income for the simple reason that once you published the book, there's very little work you have to do. You can focus most of your time on promoting and marketing the book. That in itself is a breeze if you have a marketing plan in place. In fact, you can also automate the marketing campaign so that you don't have to devote a lot of time on it. Some writers hire freelance content marketers and social media marketers to do the marketing for them.

Ratings Based on Our Criteria

A. Simplicity:

As long as your manuscript is up to par with Amazon's standards, there's very little barriers along the way. You can have your book published by Amazon in a few days.

9/10

B. Passivity:

Most of the hard work in Kindle publishing is over once you have finished your book. After submitting and publishing your book, the majority of the proceeds are passive in nature.

8/10

C. Scalability:

To scale your publishing business you can either write more books or create bundles using your existing books. The more books you have the more royalties you can earn from sales.

8/10

D. Competitiveness:

You have to understand that the book business is one of the most competitive fields out there. To put things into perspective, Amazon alone published dozens of books every single day.

2/10

Tips for Success

1. Do your research. There are a lot of questions that you need answers to before you sit down and write your book. What niches and topics are the most profitable? Do non-fiction books sell more than fiction books? How much should you price your book? These are just some of the important questions you need to research on.

2. Hire a professional book cover designer to create the cover for your book. A lot of the people browsing through Amazon's book section judge books by their covers. Everyone is guilty of this habit whether you like it or not. We often buy books for the simple reason that we liked the cover. In the same light, we don't buy books because of how ugly the covers are. So set aside a little bit of your budget to hire a good cover designer.

3. Offer a few chapters of your book for free. This is a very common strategy for first-time authors. If you are confident about the quality of your content, then you shouldn't worry too much about providing some chapters for free. This strategy allows potential readers to get a taste of what you're offering.

4. Send out free copies of your book to reviewers and bloggers in your niche. This is a great way to start your word-of-mouth marketing. Bloggers and digital influencers love getting free stuff and if they

enjoyed your book, there's the likelihood that they'll write a glowing review about it. However, never ask for a review in exchange for giving out free copies. This is against Amazons terms and conditions.

5. Create a blog around your book. There will be readers of your book who will like your book enough to want to learn more about you, what you do, or maybe other content you wrote that's related to the topics in the book. You can fulfill this need by writing a blog.

6. Create a Facebook page for your book. This is free and easy to do so there's absolutely no reason why you shouldn't do it. Treat your Facebook page as a portal where you get to connect with those who have read your book and those who might be interested in reading it.

7. Think about writing a series. Many of modern publishing's most successful writers made a name for themselves by writing book series. Just think of JK Rowling, Robert Ludlum, Clive Cussler, etc. These are authors who wrote numerous books featuring the same characters. It's a powerful strategy. You should try it and see where it goes.

8. Collaborate with other writers. As much as possible, you should only work with writers who are your equals or your betters. Always remember that you are collaborating with them so that you can use their clout and influence as leverage to promote your book.

9. Advertise your book. To make money, you have to spend money. A good place to start advertising your book is Google Adsense. Make sure to use relevant keywords in your ads so that the ads will appear in websites and blogs that are relevant to your book's content.

10. Run contests and giveaways. You can run these contests and giveaways on a variety of platforms (i.e. blog, website, Facebook page, Twitter, Instagram, etc.).

Frequently Asked Questions and Answers

1. Is it free to publish a book on Amazon Kindle?
    - Yes, publishing your book through Amazon Direct Kindle Publishing is absolutely free. This applies to both ebook and paperback versions of your book. You don't have to pay a penny to get your book published.

2. How long does it take for the book to be published and become available for sale?
    - After uploading your manuscript and all the necessary sections of the book, it usually takes between 24 and 48 hours for your book to officially appear on Amazon's listings.

3. What is the process in publishing a book on Amazon?
    - The process is quite simple. One, create an Amazon account. Two, log into Amazon Kindle Publishing. Three, add your address, personal information, bank information, and tax information. Four, upload the final manuscript for your book. And five, hit the publish button.

4. What do I do if I encounter a problem during the publication of my book?
   - The first thing you should do is contact Amazon support immediately. There's a specific customer support for writers using Amazon Direct Kindle Publishing so you should approach them first. You should also consider seeking help from other authors through Amazon's Author Central page. Those authors who have encountered the same problem as yours may be able to help you out.

5. How much should I price a book I publish on Amazon?
   - It's up to you. There's no floor or ceiling on how much you want customers to pay for your book. You can price it at 99 cents or $10.

6. How much money can I earn from my book?
   - It depends on several factors. Is it your first book? Do you already have an established following? How good is your book? What niche does it belong to? How much budget do you have for your marketing campaign? These are just some of the factors that will ultimately determine how much you are going to earn from your book.

7. How many books can I publish on Amazon Kindle?
   - You can publish as many books as you like as long as these adhere to Kindle's rules and standards.

8. How do I promote my book on Amazon Kindle?
   - There are a lot of ways. These include blogging, social media marketing, advertising, running contests, and giving away copies of your book to reviewers and digital influencers.

9. Will Amazon ever remove my book from its listings?
   - Yes, that is definitely a possibility. But you have nothing to worry about if your book hasn't broken any of the platform's rules and regulations.

10. Will my book be available to anyone from around the world?
    - Yes, if you choose to. As the author, you have the option to decide whether your book is going to be available worldwide or on a select locations/countries only.

Myth Busters About Kindle Direct Publishing

1. Self-publishing ebooks on Kindle is easy and instantly profitable. No, it's not. A huge percentage of self-publishers on Amazon make very little from their work.

2. You need an original idea. Not necessarily. You can use the works of others as inspiration.

3. You need a big launch party to sell your book. If your book is good enough and if you market it enough, people will come to you.

4. There are too many ebooks already. Yes, indeed, but that doesn't mean you can't add your own book to the pool.

5. You need an agent. Nope, there's a reason why it's called self-publishing. You do it without an agent.

6. Amazon will own your ebook if you publish it on Kindle. Not true. You still have all the rights to your book. You're only using Amazon as your selling platform.

7. You need at least 20 reviews to appear in Amazon's "Also Bought" feature. Not true. Books with less than 20 reviews also appear on "Also Bought" lists.

8. The more reviews your book gets, the higher it will appear in Amazon's search results. Not true. This can easily be disproven by doing a quick search on the site.

9. Reviews affect your book's sales rank. It has some effect but it's not substantial. The biggest factors in determining sales rank are purchased and number of downloads.

10. Kindle Select's 90-day exclusivity also applies to paperback versions of your book. Not true. The 90-day exclusivity only applies to ebooks.

Congratulations!

The second character of the password required to unlock the business scorecard is letter i.

Inspiration #2

"Opportunities don't happen. You create them"

Chris Grosser

Business #2

Amazon FBA (Fulfilled by Amazon)

Fulfilled by Amazon or FBA is an e-commerce program by the online retail giant. The program's business model is very similar to that of dropshipping. If you are familiar with dropshipping or if you have experience with it, you will find it easy to understand Amazon FBA's business model. This opportunity can be very lucrative if you can think of a product that has very little competition within the Amazon network. The whole process can be simplified in the following steps:

1. You apply for the Amazon FBA program.
2. If you are accepted, you ship your products to one of their distribution centers. The company refers to these distribution centers as fulfilment centers.
3. You list your products for sale in Amazon.
4. If someone buys your product, Amazon ships the product to the customer.

Looking at the business model of the program, it's easy to recognize obvious benefits. For one, Amazon handles the sales and shipping process. The company receives the orders, process them, and ship the products. They are literally running the business for you. Your main responsibility is to keep on sending more of your products to Amazon's fulfilment centers before these run out of stock.

Earlier, we've mentioned how the business model is very similar to dropshipping. This is because you can turn it into a real dropshipping business. You can enter into a contract with a manufacturer or a supplier who makes the products then ship these on your behalf to Amazon's fulfilment centers. In this setup, your role is to make sure that the supplier keeps making and shipping the products. You can also choose to have the supplier send the products to you so that you will be the one shipping the products to Amazon. This is a good idea if you want to make sure that the products you are selling are of the highest quality possible.

Ratings Based on Our Criteria

A. Simplicity:

Starting a business with Amazon FBA can be very complicated because there are a lot of hoops you have to go through. You have to apply with the program. You need to make sure that the products pass certain standards (e.g. packaging and safety requirements) etc. And you have to be communicating with your manufacturer/supplier, inspectors etc. to make sure products are manufactured to specification. If they happen to be in China, the language barrier and time zone difference could present challenges.

6/10

B. Passivity:

Managing an Amazon FBA business can take a lot of your time and resources. Some of your time will be spent communicating with your suppliers, optimizing your listings, running promotions/giveaways, Optimizing your Amazon sponsored ads etc. However, passivity can be improved by outsourcing some of these tasks to virtual assistants who will take care of them for you. Virtual assistants can be hired from fiverr.com or upwork.com.

6/10

C. Scalability:

It's easy to scale your Amazon FBA business. Once you are accepted into the program and you have successfully launched your first product and familiarized yourself with the process, scaling is as simple as adding more products to your inventory or expanding your product offerings (i.e. offering your customers complementary products as part of a bundle).

9/10

D. Competitiveness:

Expect a lot of other merchants selling similar products as you. You might even be getting your products from the same suppliers. Furthermore, it's not unusual to compete directly with suppliers from China.

4/10

Tips For Success

1. Do your research before you jump into the bandwagon. As I've mentioned earlier, competition within Amazon is fierce. So what you need to do is research for products that have good demand but little competition. A good market research software for this is Jungle Scout or Viral Launch

2. Watch and observe your most successful competitors. What are they doing? What tools are they using? What marketing strategies are they implementing? Learn about these and maybe apply them on your own business.

3. Encourage your customers to leave reviews. The more reviews you get on Amazon, the greater the social proof and likelihood of it selling. However, do not offer incentives in exchange for review as this is against Amazon's terms of service.

4. Optimize your product listings with the right keywords and descriptions. A good keyword research tool to consider is Merchant Words

5. Use high-quality photos of your products. Ugly and unprofessional product photos can easily turn off customers.

6. Only deal with reliable manufacturers and suppliers. If they screw up, then your business is equally screwed.

7. Always check with Amazon to ensure that your products are in stock. Running out of stock can negatively affect your product rankings and once lost its difficult to regain.

8. Personalize/brand your products to make them stand out from the others. This is important if you are getting your products from a supplier who is probably sending the same products to other merchants.

9. Offer discounts and incentives to those who are buying in bulk. This is a great way to build loyalty among your customers.

10. Always follow the rules, regulations, and standards as set forth by Amazon. Amazon can easily terminate your account if you break a rule or two.

Frequently Asked Questions and Answers

1. What are the requirements in joining Amazon FBA?
   - You are going to need the following: email address, standard mailing address, phone number, social security number, tax identification number, credit or debit card, bank account, and bank routing number.

2. What are the costs of using Amazon FBA?
   - When using FBA, you should expect to be paying for three specific types of fees: storage fees, fulfilment fees, and inventory placement fees. These are not fixed fees. They depend on the types of products you are sending them for storage. They will inform you about the amount of fees you are going to pay after finalizing your shipments.

3. How do I get products ready for Amazon FBA?
   - Every product you have must be individually packaged, properly labelled, and ready to be sold. You should also strictly follow the company's product stickering requirements.

4. Can I sell products overseas through Amazon FBA?
   - Yes, you absolutely can. Amazon is flexible when it comes to importing or exporting your products. However, you should keep in mind that selling your products overseas has additional fees, requirements, and other complications. Make sure that you take this into account and look into your financials to see if it's worth it to offer your products to overseas customers.

5. How do I ship my products to any of Amazon's fulfilment centers?
   - The full procedure is detailed in Amazon FBA's help section. You have to log into your Amazon FBA account, go to Manage Inventory and choose the Send and Replenish Inventory option. You have to completely and properly label your products before you ship them to Amazon's fulfilment centers. Improperly packaged products will cause a lot of problems which can be very costly on your part.

6. What kind of products can I sell through Amazon FBA?
   - Amazon FBA has a long list of restricted products so I highly suggest that you check it out. Here's the list of products that you can't sell on Amazon FBA as an independent seller:
     - Alcohol

- Warranties, service plans, contracts and guarantees
- Tobacco and tobacco-related products
- Throwable personal flotation devices
- Surveillance equipment
- Subscriptions and periodicals
- String lights
- Stolen property and lock picking devices
- Squishy toys
- Sex and sensuality products
- Recycled electronics
- Recalled products
- FBA prohibited products exceptions
- Postage meters and stamps
- Plants, seeds, and other plant products
- Pesticides
- Personal electronic mobility devices or PEMs
- Organic products
- Offensive and controversial materials
- Medical devices and accessories
- Lighting products
- Laser products
- Jewelry and precious gems
- Invisible ink pens
- Infant sleep positioners
- Infant car seats
- Human parts and burial artefacts
- Hazardous and dangerous items
- Gambling and lottery products
- Chilled and frozen foods
- Food and beverages
- Fire and smoke masks
- Fire and other safety products
- Fidget spinners
- Export controls
- Explosives, weapons, and related items
- Electronics
- Eclipse glasses and filters for solar viewing
- Drugs and drug paraphernalia
- Dietary supplements
- Currency, coins, cash equivalents, and gift cards
- Cosmetics and skin and hair care
- Batteries and chargers
- Automotive and powersports
- Art home décor
- Fine art
- Animals and animal products
- Amazon devices: Fair Use and Compatibility Guidelines
- Amazon Device Accessories

7. How safe are my products when I ship them to Amazon?
   - There is always the possibility that your products can get lost during transit and storage. However, these problems are rare. As to security, Amazon has a payment fraud protection system that protects you from fraudulent orders and transactions.

8. How much does it cost to sell on Amazon?
   - Amazon offers two types of plans. The Professional Selling Plan costs $39.99 a month plus per item selling fees. The Individual Selling Plan is for sellers who only sells 40 items or less a month. This plan doesn't have a monthly fee. Instead, you pay a $0.99 fee for every item you sell.

9. Who handles customer support on my Amazon FBA products?
   - Customer support is the responsibility of Amazon. This is one of the biggest advantages of the Amazon FBA program. Once you shipped your products to their fulfilment centers, the company will handle the rest. They will manage customer inquiries, refunds, and returns. It's worth mentioning here that Amazon's customer support is available 24 hours a day, seven days a week.

10. Where can I get products to sell on Amazon FBA?
    - There are several avenues that you can explore here. One, you can create your own products. Two, you can enter a deal with a supplier who provides you with products which you then label and package as your own. Three, you can explore retail arbitrage. That is you purchase products from other stores in bulk then sell them for a profit on Amazon. And four, you can consider private labelling or white labelling.

Myth Busters About Amazon FBA

1. That it's very hard to sell products on Amazon. Yes, the system seems complicated but it's actually easy once you get the hang of it.

2. That you can't be successful selling on Amazon because of the immense competition. Sure, the competition is tough but the market is also growing. In short, Amazon is still a very profitable side business.

3. That you can just list your product and it will start selling like hotcakes. If you are to achieve success on Amazon, you don't just list a product, you have to market it like crazy.

4. That you need your own website to sell on Amazon. Amazon itself serves as your online store. List your product and the company does the rest.

5. That you need to invest a lot of money into Amazon. You can start a business on Amazon with just a few hundred dollars. In short, it's not that expensive.

6. That inventory management is a pain in the head. Yes, it can be confusing at first but just like everything else, you will get used to it.

7. That you need to give a lot of discounts to attract customers. Offering discounts surely helps but you don't have to if you are confident about the demand for your products.

8. That Amazon doesn't care about you. The fact that the company welcomes independent sellers tells a very different story.

9. That Amazon is losing its influence. This myth is perpetrated by competitors who want to steal sellers from Amazon and bring them into their own platforms.

10. That you can get rich quick on Amazon. Don't entertain such an exaggerated idea. Of course, it's possible but you should be realistic with your goals.

Inspiration #3

"There are two types of people who will tell you that you cannot make a difference in this world: those who are afraid to try and those who are afraid you will succeed."

Ray Goforth

Business #3

Blogging

The basics of earning money from a blog are quite simple. You create a blog, publish valuable content in it, then monetize it using any of various monetization methods like affiliate marketing, direct advertising, third-party advertising, etc. If you write the content yourself, the income you earn can still be considered as partly passive. But if you want to truly turn a blog into a source of real passive income, what you should do is outsource the content-creation process to freelance writers. You are going to pay other people to write the content that you are going to publish in your blog. With that said, you are not the one actively performing the difficult work of creating content.

Finding freelance content creators is not that hard. There are dozens of job sites and classified ads sites out there where you can find good writers offering affordable rates. These sites include Upwork, Fiverr, Freelancer, Craigslist, and even LinkedIn. What you do is hire a qualified writer then send him a list of keywords that will be the topics of his articles. It's as simple as that. Have the articles written, hone them to perfection, and then publish them on your blog. Then rinse and repeat. The more quality content you put in your blog, the more visitors it will attract. More traffic means more passive income (only if the affiliate products you promote on your blog are relevant to your visitors)

Ratings Based on Our Criteria

A. **Simplicity:**

Starting a blog is rather easy. In fact you can create one in just a few minutes.

9/10

B. **Passivity:**

Even if you outsource most of your content-creation process, the earnings you make won't be 100% passive. You still have to perform tasks like reading and replying to comments, brainstorming for new ideas, and communicating with advertisers and partners.

7/10

C. **Scalability:**

Blogging is highly scalable in the sense that you can duplicate your success in a specific niche by applying the same tactics in another niche. In addition, the same blog that serves 100 people can also serve 100,000 people without any significant increase in your fixed costs.

7/10

D. **Competitiveness:**

The blogging sphere is very competitive in the sense that there are literally millions of blogs out there on just about every subject. Simplicity can be a double edge sword because the easier the business opportunity, the lower the barrier to entry.

2/10

Tips for Success

1. Focus your attention on a specific niche. It's much easier to attract a following online if you keep on writing articles that revolve around a specific topic. It encourages people to return to your blog because they know the type of content you publish.

2. Focus on quality, not quantity. One good article will earn you more money than ten bad articles.

3. Optimize your articles for search engines. This is a no-brainer when it comes to blogging and content marketing. If you want people to find your blog posts, you should optimize them with the right keywords.

4. Promote your blog on social media. For example, you should create a Twitter, Instagram and Facebook page that links directly to your blog.

5. Enable comments in your blog posts. Readers who want to say something should be allowed to chime in. This encourages interaction.

6. Make your blog as simple as possible. Readers hate cluttered websites. You should get rid of unnecessary widgets, buttons, etc.

7. Follow a posting schedule. This is very important if you want to build a legion of followers. Nothing turns off a reader more than a stagnant blog. You can follow a daily posting schedule, a three times a week posting schedule, or a weekly schedule. What's important is that you stick to it so that readers will know when to expect new content from you.

8. Turn reader comments into content. This is why it's good to turn on the comments in every blog post you make. Feedback by readers is a great source for ideas for upcoming posts.

9. Use images, videos, and infographics in your blog posts. Articles can become boring at times so make it a point to spice things up by adding other types of media into your content.

10. Make it easy for readers to share your blog posts. At the end of every article you post, there should be buttons there that allow readers to share the article on social media or through email. You can attract a lot of new readers from this strategy alone.

Frequently Asked Questions and Answers

1. How do I start a blog?
   - You have two options. If you have web development skills, you can build one from scratch. If not, you can start with a blogging platform like Wordpress and Blogger.

2. How much do I need to spend to create and build a blog?
   - It depends. Your main expenses would be composed of the amounts you pay for domain registration and hosting.

3. How often do I need to update my blog?
   - It depends on your target audience and your topic. If you are talking about current news and events, you probably need to update the blog every day.

4. How do I monetize a blog?
   - There are several monetization methods that you can explore. These include direct advertising, affiliate marketing (Amazon, ClickBank, and eBay), sponsored posts, and advertising programs (Adsense).

5. I'm not very tech-savvy. Can I still make money from a blog?
   - Of course, you can. There are a lot of simple tools and resources that you can use to start a blog even if you can't write a single line of code.

6. How do I drive traffic to my blog?
   - There are so many ways. These include social media marketing, search engine optimization, advertising, and content marketing.

7. What is a niche?
   - A niche is a specific topic or theme which becomes the focus of your blog. If your blog is about basketball news and updates, then you are in the "basketball niche".

8. Can I really make money from blogging?
   - Yes. Hundreds of thousands of bloggers are currently doing it. If they can, then you can as well.

9. Should I get my own domain name for my blog?
   - Although it's possible to make money from a free-hosted blog on Blogger or Wordpress, it's highly recommended that you register your own domain name. It makes you look more professional and readers are more likely to take you serious.

10. Should I learn search engine optimization?
    - Yes, it's absolutely necessary that you learn at least the basics of search engine optimization (SEO) and apply these on your blog. It's one of the most effective ways on how to attract more people to your blog. Alternatively, you can partner with someone who is very tech savvy.

Myth Busters About Blogging

1. If you build it, they will come. Nope, they won't. Building a blog is just one aspect of blogging. With thousands of blogs being created and published every single day, yours can easily be lost in the immense stream. So don't just build it, you should also market and promote it like your life depends on it.

2. You can easily make money blogging. Nope, you can't and you won't unless you are Stephen King or JK Rowling. Earning money from a blog requires hard work and patience. For most bloggers, it can take months or even years before you get a significant amount of income coming your way.

3. Blogging is just a fad. If blogging is just a fad, then it should be dead in the water by now. Blogging started getting traction more than a decade ago but it's still going strong. In fact, more and more people are starting blogs these days given the ease of building one.

4. If you can't write well, you can't have your own blog. Newsflash, freelance content creators exist. If you can't write, you can always hire an army of freelance writers to do the dirty work for you.

5. You have to post everyday if you want readers to keep coming back to your blog. No, you don't. In fact, posting everyday can overwhelm your readers.

6. You need to be tech-savvy and have coding skills to start blogging. Quite the contrary because anyone who knows how to click a mouse can start a blog.

7. There's not much to learn about blogging. If you tell yourself this, then you are setting yourself up for failure. The blogging space is evolving. There are new things to learn every single day.

8. Free themes are just as good as paid themes. In a certain way this is true but if you are serious about blogging, you really need to get a paid theme that is uniquely yours.

9. You need comments on your blog to be successful. Not true. Some of the most popular blogs out there have their comments section turned off.

10. Social media is useless for blogging. You are missing out on a lot of opportunities if you don't link your blog to your different social media platforms.

Inspiration #4

"Successful people do what unsuccessful people are not willing to do. Don't wish it were easier; wish you were better."

Jim Rohn

Business #4

Domain Flipping

There are three main categories of domain flipping. One, you build a website from scratch then offer it for sale with a healthy profit margin. Two, you purchase an already built website, put a mark-up on your purchasing price, then resell it without changing the website. And three, you buy a website, improve upon it, then sell it for profit. Domain flipping is basically the business of purchasing and selling websites. This can be a very lucrative source of passive income if you know how to spot premium domains that you can sell at huge profits. It's about creating websites and improving websites with the sole intention of selling them for profit.

Needless to say, to be successful in this arena, you should have knowledge and skills in web development, coding, and programming. You should be able to build professional-looking websites at great speed.

To look for the people who might be interested in buying websites you created, you should sign up with the top domain flipping websites. These are websites that were built specifically for buyers and sellers of domains and websites e.g. www.Flippa.com. Some of these domain flipping websites charge membership fees but most of them are free to use. So there's absolutely no reason why you shouldn't utilize them to your advantage. Just sign up, customize your profile, and then list the domains you are selling. In some instances, the domain flipping website will take a percentage cut from your sales. It's important that you take into account these percentage cuts when pricing your domains for sale.

To be successful in the domain flipping business, you have to be a trend watcher. What does this mean? It means you should be on the lookout for the hottest trends and developments in the web. For instance, there's a new dance craze called "ABC Dancing" that's taking the internet by storm. If you are a trend watcher, you will be among those who will first be aware of this new dance trend. Putting your domain flipper hat on, you then start registering domain names that might be in demand in the next day, weeks, or months. Such domain names can be abcdancing.com, abcdancing.net, abcdancinglessons.com, etc. In a nutshell, you have to be a forward thinker.

You should learn how to spot these trends then cash in on them before anyone else can. A good tool to help with researching trends is Google Trends

Ratings Based on Our Criteria

    A. **Simplicity:**

        Domain flipping is quite simple in the sense that there's very little work associated with it especially if you focus on purchasing and selling the domains. Of course it's a little bit more complicated if you build the websites yourself from scratch.

        8/10

    B. **Passivity:**

Building websites from scratch, buying and improving websites, and promoting websites for sale can take a lot of your time and resources. To improve passivity, you may want to document the process of trend research and domain purchase. You can then hire a virtual assistant who will handle these tasks for you. Alternatively, you can just outsource the research and promotion tasks and focus only on the buying and selling.

6/10

C. Scalability:

Domain flipping is one of the most scalable business models online. You can pretty much scale the business overnight as long as you have the funds to purchase sites. The more valuable digital assets you have (i.e. sites), the more you can potentially earn.

9/10

D. Competitiveness:

There are thousands of other domain flippers out there. It also happens that there are only a few marketplaces for websites that are up for sale. In short, the competition can be tough.

4/10

Tips for Success

1. Do not be afraid to take risks. Flipping domains is kind of a gamble. You should be more than willing to gamble with domains that you think are going to be profitable. For example, let's say you come across a domain for sale that looks promising but has a steep price. If your experience tells you that the domain might be profitable down the line, then go and purchase it.

2. Choose a niche that you are familiar with. If you are knowledgeable about the niche, then you know what kinds of terms and phrases are popular within the niche. Register these words and phrases as domains and sooner or later someone will be calling to buy the domains from you.

3. Visit domain auction sites and see what kinds of domains are in demand. For example, you can check out GoDaddy Auction and get an idea of the kinds of domains that are getting the highest prices.

4. Be mindful of the domain extensions that you are using. Pay attention to the three most common extensions (.com, .net, and, .org). For example, if the domain successfulbusiness.com is not available, maybe the domains successfulbusiness.net and successfulbusiness.org are still unregistered. You have to be creative in brainstorming for domain ideas.

5. Be on the lookout for expired domain names. These are websites that expired and remains unrenewed by their original registrants. These expired domains are valuable in the sense that they already have page ranks and backlinks.

6. Create high-quality content for a domain before you offer it for sale. Good content can double or even triple the value and asking price of a domain. If you are selling numerous domains, try hiring a freelance writer to create the content for them.

7. Stay up to date with regards to latest news, trends, and developments in your niche. Maybe there's a new word or phrase that becomes very popular in your niche. You can quickly register the word or phrase as a domain name. Again, this is a bit of a gamble but it can prove very profitable if the domain you registered eventually comes in demand.

8. Always be on the lookout for discounts and offers from the biggest domain registration companies like GoDaddy. You can save a lot of money this way. If a company offers a promo period where domains are available for $1 each, jump in and get as many promising domains as you can. Just imagine the profit you can make if you are able to sell the domains for $100 and up.

9. Create an account in the top domain registrars. The biggest domain registrars today are Namecheap, Bluehost, HostGator, GoDaddy, and Dreamhost. It would be a good idea to create an account with all of them so you can take advantage of their promos, discounts, coupons, and other offers. Creating an account with them is free so you have nothing to lose.

10. Treat your domain flipping efforts as a business. This means you should create a website which will serve as your business headquarters. This is where people can look at all the domains you have for sale.

Frequently Asked Questions and Answers

1. How does domain flipping work and how do I make money from it?
   - Domain flipping follows the buy and sell model. You buy websites then sell them for a profit. Or you can create websites from scratch then sell them to interested buyers.

2. Where can I buy and sell domains?
   - There are several domain flipping platforms that you can use. These include Flippa, Sedo, Afternic, Igloo, Cax, BrandBucket, HuntingMoon, SnapNames, Pool, GoDaddy Premium Listings, Bido, Undeveloped, and even eBay.

3. How do I start flipping domains?
   - First of all, make sure that you have everything you need to get started. You should sign up with an online marketplace like Flippa where you can buy and sell domains. After signing up, you are free to list the domains you want to sell as well as purchase the domains you are interested in acquiring.

4. Is domain flipping still profitable?
   - Yes, of course it's still profitable. There are thousands of individuals and businesses out there looking for a good domain name every single day. To be successful in domain flipping, you should have an eye for the latest trends and where they're going. For example, a new dance craze hits the dance

scene. If you are smart, you should immediately starting registering domains and building websites around the words and phrases that describe the craze.

5. How much should I price a domain I'm selling?
   - There are several factors that you need to consider when pricing a domain. How much did you pay for it? How much did you spend in building it if you created it yourself? Do you think the domain's value accrue over time? Is it just a domain or you've published lots of content on it? These are just some of the considerations you must take into account when putting a price tag on a domain.

6. How do I market and promote the domains I'm selling?
   - There are several marketing strategies that you can use like search engine optimization, social media marketing, and advertising.

7. How do I increase the value of the domains I'm selling?
   - You can significantly increase the asking price for a domain by simply creating content for it. Focus on a niche to build a steady flow of traffic towards the website. A steady traffic can double or even triple the value of the website.

8. Where and how do I buy a website that I can then offer for sale?
   - You can purchase websites from any domain flipping website like Flippa, Igloo, and Sedo.

9. I'm not a web developer. Can I still be a successful domain flipper?
   - Yes, you can. Web development is a skill you only need if you are going to build websites from scratch or if you improve the websites you buy. But if you are going to simply purchase and sell websites, you don't need to be a web developer or programmer.

10. How long should I hold on to an expired domain?
    - It depends on the influence and metrics of the domain. If it's a fairly good domain with decent traffic, you should probably sell it as soon as possible before it loses some of its value.

Myth Busters About Domain Flipping

1. There aren't any affordable .com domains out there. Not true. If you look hard enough, you will find premium .com domains with affordable price tags.

2. GoDaddy is the greatest domain registration company today. For sure, it is the most popular but that doesn't mean there aren't competitive alternatives. There are other companies like Namecheap who offer similar, if not better services.

3. All the profitable domains have already been taken. This is just not true on many levels. If you are creative enough, you can research and find good and profitable domains that are yet to be registered.

4. Registering numerous domain names at a time is unethical. Some web developers look at domain flippers as selfish and greedy entrepreneurs. No, they are not. It's just business. There's a market for domains so they are in the business of buying and selling them.

5. Domains with .com extensions rank higher than domains with less common extensions (i.e. co, org, net). The domain extension does play a role in a website's search rankings but it's only applicable in rare instances. The quality of the website's content still remains as the most important factor in determining a website's worth and search rankings.

6. You can master domain flipping in a few weeks' time. Domain flipping is not just about buying and selling domains and websites. You must have the background as well as the experience to spot what domains are profitable. This takes time to learn and master.

7. Domain flipping is easy money. Nothing is farther from the truth. Just to provide you some hard truth, majority of domain flippers don't make that much money from the business. Only a few domain flippers earn full-time from their efforts. This is not an attempt to discourage you. We just want you to be realistic about how much you are going to earn if you start flipping domains and websites.

8. Build the websites and domain buyers will start coming. Yes, there's some truth to this if you can build beautiful and great websites. However, the adage that if you build them, customers will start coming isn't exactly true. You still have to do a lot of marketing and promotion to attract potential domain buyers.

9. Domain flipping is not susceptible to fraud and hacking. This is not true. Just like any online business model, domain flipping has its own problems with regards to fraud and hacking. Hackers can hack into your accounts in domain flipping websites and steal the sites you've registered and created.

10. Inevitably, social profiles are bound to replace the domain names. A lot of people in the marketing and advertising industry are worried that the growing popularity of social media networks will force businesses to focus on their social media presence and stop building their own sites. This isn't happening at all.

Inspiration #5

"Success is walking fro failure to failure with no loss of enthusiasm."
Winston S. Churchill

Business #5

Shopify

If you want to build your own e-commerce store, Shopify is a platform you should seriously consider using. There's a reason why this platform is one of the biggest players in online commerce today. Hundreds of thousands of entrepreneurs and merchants use the platform to market and sell their products. Shopify is great for two things. It's great for starting an e-commerce store. And it's great for building a dropshipping business. The company offers several plans for those interested in using their services. These plans and their corresponding rates (as of July 2018) are as follows:

- Basic Shopify: $29 per month
- Standard Shopify: $79 per month
- Advanced Shopify: $299 per month
- Shopify Lite: $9 per month
- Shopify Plus: Flexible rate per month

If you are still not sure if Shopify is the appropriate platform for you, you can always test their free trial version. This trial version allows you access to Shopify's most basic features and functions for free for a period of fourteen (14) days. There are no strings attached. You can cancel and terminate your account any time you want. If you want to continue with the service, you will be given time to choose from the various plans (i.e. Basic Shopify, Standard Shopify, Shopify Lite, Advanced Shopify, and Shopify Plus).

Using Shopify to build an online business is quite easy and hassle-free. This is one of the most important selling points of the platform. It allows you to create a professional-looking e-commerce store even if you have very limited knowledge about web development, coding, and programming in general. The platform has a website builder wherein all you have to do is choose the template and customize it using pre-fabricated options, features, and functions. There are dozens of templates that you can use for free. Another great thing about these templates is that they have been designed specifically for certain niches and markets. For example, there are templates that have been designed for online stores selling shirts and other apparel.

If you don't have your own products to sell, no problem. You can always choose the dropshipping route. What you do is create your Shopify store and list products that you will be ordering from a manufacturer or supplier. You will not be keeping any product inventory. In fact, you won't even be the one shipping the products to your customers. If a customer orders a product from your Shopify store, your store orders the product from your supplier. The supplier then ships the product to your customer. Although the product came from your supplier, it looks like it came from you. This process can be 100% automated which means you earn money around the clock. It's nearly 100% passive income. You don't make the products and you are not the one shipping them. The cost of running the business is really cheap. Your major expenses will only be composed of your monthly dues from Shopify and any amount you spend on advertising and other marketing campaigns.

Ratings Based on Our Criteria

    A. Simplicity:

The greatest thing about Shopify is that anyone can use the platform to build professional-looking online stores. Even if you have zero coding or programming skills, creating a store using their website builder is a breeze.

9/10

    B. Passivity:

Your store can be fully automated especially if you are following the dropshipping model. Additionally, there are tons of apps that you can use to make it easier to run and manage the business.

8/10

    C. Scalability:

There's no limit to the number of Shopify stores that you can make. As long as you follow the rules and terms of agreement, there's no limit to how big you can grow your store. Of course, there's also the fact that you can list thousands of products in a single Shopify store.

9/10

    D. Competitiveness:

There's a lot of competition within the Shopify platform, that's for sure. But if you are confident about the quality of your products and the speed at which you deliver them, then you have very little to be worried about.

4/10

Tips For Success

1. Take advantage of the platform's free trial version to familiarize yourself with the features and functions. The trial version will run for a period of fourteen (14) days.

2. Customize your online store for branding reasons. Make it unique so that it will stand out from the competition. Never forget the possibility that there are other merchants on the platform selling the same products as you. If they have better websites than you, then customers will likely choose them over you.

3. Focus on product quality, not quantity. Many new merchants on Shopify often make the mistake of assuming that the more products they list on their e-commerce website, the more sales they can make. This is a terrible approach in building a business. Quality should always be your main focus.

4. Promote your Shopify store whenever and wherever you can. Don't solely rely on the platform to send you customers. You should exert efforts in driving high-quality and targeted traffic to your website.

5. Make sure that your store is supported on a wide variety of devices such as desktops, laptops, mobile phones, and tablets.

6. Make it as easy as possible for a customer to navigate through your website. Customers should be able to see how much a product costs with just a click or a tap.

7. Always perform analytics to see what's working and what's not working. Shopify has its own analytics program but if you are not satisfied with it, you can also use Google Analytics.

8. Set up a blog for your store. Your Shopify store normally comes with a built-in blog but this won't be enough. You should try building a separate blog in another domain and use it to drive organic traffic to your store.

9. Run giveaways. This is a great way to engage your existing customers and to raise awareness about your store and products.

10. Build an email list. You have no idea how much repeat customers you can get by simply sending updates to your email list.

Frequently Asked Questions and Answers

1. What is Shopify and how does it work?
   - It's an ecommerce platform and website builder that allows you to create your own online store.

2. What products can you sell on Shopify?
   - You can sell both physical products and digital products or a combination of both.

3. How much does Shopify cost?
   - Shopify collects a monthly fee from merchants and entrepreneurs depending on the type of plan they are on. Basic Shopify costs $29 a month. Standard Shopify costs $79 a month. And Advanced Shopify costs $299 a month. Other accounts like Shopify Lite and Shopify Plus cost $9 per month and $1000+ per month respectively.

4. Does Shopify have a free trial version?
   - Yes, you can test their free trial version that runs for fourteen days.

5. How many products can you sell on Shopify?
   - One of the biggest advantages of selling on Shopify is that there's no limit to the number of products you can list in your store.

6. How do you collect payments from customers?
   - The company offers you several payment options.

7. Can you collect payments via PayPal?

- Yes, you can set up your store so that it can accept payments from PayPal and other companies that offer the same services.

8. Can I build more than one stores on Shopify?
   - Many online entrepreneurs run several stores on the site so it's definitely possible.

9. Does Shopify have a blogging feature?
   - Yes, Shopify has a blogging feature which enables you to write and create content to engage and attract customers.

10. Can I use third-party apps on my Shopify store?
    - Yes. In fact, Shopify has its own app store where you can purchase apps for your online store. Many of the apps in the store are also free to use.

Myth Busters About Selling on Shopify

1. That you can get rich quick on Shopify. Don't believe those self-proclaimed gurus that claim you can be a millionaire overnight with Shopify. It simply isn't true. Nothing worthwhile happens overnight. There's always a learning process.

2. That Shopify is purely a dropshipping business. Yes, dropshipping is a large aspect of Shopify's business model but it's just half of what the company offers for entrepreneurs.

3. That Shopify stores have a lot of security loopholes. This may be true several years ago but not today. The company is now one of the most secure ecommerce platforms in existence.

4. That Shopify is very expensive. The company's most expensive plan costs only $299 a month. That's a bargain considering the tons of features and functions you get.

5. That there's too much competition in Shopify. It's true that there's competition but it's the healthy kind of competition. If you have a good product and you market it well (i.e. emphasizing your unique value proposition etc.), you have very little to be worried about.

6. That Shopify has poor customer support. Quite the contrary because Shopify happens to have one of the most efficient customer support system in the industry. They can be contacted via phone, email, and live chat.

7. That Shopify stores are difficult to manage. Not true. When you log into Shopify, you can go to your admin panel and manage or even customize your store from there.

8. That the number of products you can sell on the site are limited and controlled. The truth is Shopify allows you to upload as many product listings as you want.

9. That Shopify is losing steam and will close operations in a few years' time. Shopify's stats and metrics are actually growing at a quick pace. Revenue is growing and the products being sold through the platform are getting better.

10. That you need to be tech-savvy to build a store on Shopify. Shopify's website builder is simple enough to be understood by anyone who knows how to browse the internet.

Inspiration #6

"If you are not willing to risk the usual, you will have to settle for the ordinary."
Jim Rohn

Business #6

Freelancing as a Virtual Assistant

Hundreds of thousands of professionals from around the world make decent incomes as freelance virtual assistants. You can do the same if you have the determination to be successful in it. The job description for a virtual assistant is as varied as the number of virtual assistants out there. Think of yourself as someone's personal assistant or secretary but you perform your duties remotely and online. For example, a business owner can get you as a virtual assistant and your job is to read and reply to emails being sent to the business owner.

Or you can be a virtual assistant to a data analyst. Maybe you will be performing tasks like creating graphs or building presentations for sets of data. Or you can be a virtual assistant to a social media manager. Your tasks will include managing Facebook and Twitter pages for certain clients of the manager. The point here is that your tasks as a virtual assistant varies and depends on the specific industry that you're in. You can find virtual assistant job opportunities in websites like Odesk, Freelancer, and Craigslit.

As a virtual assistant, 100% of the tasks you perform are done remotely. You can work for months or even years for a boss without ever learning about what he or she looks like. There are no specific standard that govern what a virtual assistant does or doesn't do. As long as you are performing tasks remotely for a company or individual as an employee, then you can be considered as a virtual assistant. The term "virtual assistant" in itself defines what you do. You are an assistant but you work online.

Ratings Based on Our Criteria

A. Simplicity:

I wouldn't describe the responsibilities of a virtual assistant as simple. There's no clear definition of what tasks you are supposed to do so sometimes you are at the mercy of your boss or employer.

6/10

B. Passivity:

Being a virtual assistant can't be really considered as a passive source of income since you are directly working for a fixed pay. It becomes passive if you hire a team of virtual assistants who will work under your wing. That way, you are not personally exchanging your time for money.

5/10

C. Scalability:

It will be difficult to scale your earnings as a virtual assistant. There's a ceiling to how much clients you can take. However, it can be scalable if you have your own business wherein several virtual assistants work under you. You can scale the business by hiring more virtual assistants.

5/10

D. Competitiveness:

The industry where virtual assistants operate is very competitive. There are literally millions of virtual assistants out there, most of whom are from third-world countries in Asia like the Philippines, India, and Pakistan.

Tips on How to Be Successful as a Virtual Assistant

1. Assess your skills to make sure that you have what it takes to perform your tasks. Basically, if you have experience working as a secretary or assistant in an office setting, then that's a good starting point.

2. You must be savvy in using the internet and all the communication tools you need to work for a remote client. You have to be adept in using email, video conferencing sites, chat rooms, Skype, etc.

3. You must have the necessary and appropriate equipment. First of all, you must have a fast and reliable internet connection. Other hardware you should have includes a printer, a scanner, a camera, or any other device that your boss requires from you.

4. Develop a specialty. It's very difficult to find a job as a virtual assistant if you promote yourself as a jack of all trades. You have to offer a special kind of skill to get the attention of potential employers. For example, you can focus on being a social media specialist, an SEO expert, a travel organizer, etc.

5. Don't promise what you can't deliver. In their desperation to get a gig, some virtual assistants exaggerate their capabilities. This is a huge mistake that can return and ruin your reputation for good.

6. Do a lot of networking. Many companies and professionals hire virtual assistants using a referral system. This means they hire a person if he or she has been referred or recommended by someone they trust. Needless to say, if you have a lot of connections in the industry, you have a better chance of finding jobs.

7. Attend trainings. There are a lot of virtual assistant trainings that are done online. Many of these are also free which means there's absolutely no reason why you shouldn't join any of them from time to time. There are a lot of lessons that you can learn from these free trainings.

8. Always be respectful. Whether you are still applying for a position or you have already taken it, always be respectful to your boss. Online jobs are mostly unregulated so there's not much that you can do if an employee suddenly decides to terminate your position.

9. Create a schedule. This is very important if you are working for more than one employer. You have to make sure that your schedules don't overlap. Time management is a very important skill that every virtual assistant must have.

10. Keep in touch with former employers. They might hire you again or they might refer you to others looking for someone like you. Again, networking is necessary in the industry. The more connections you have, the better it will be for you as a virtual assistant.

Frequently Asked Questions and Answers

1. What kind of tasks do virtual assistants perform?
    - It depends on who he/she works for. Sample tasks include handling email, answering remote phone calls, making appointments, doing paperwork, researching information, planning meetings and events, making travel arrangements, handling reservations, writing articles, proofreading content, etc.

2. How much can I charge clients for my assistance work?
    - It depends on the pay structure of the deal you entered into. You can be paid by the hour, per task, or per month. Typically, you can charge between $10 to $20 per hour. However, you can charge a lot more if your skills are highly specialized and there aren't many virtual assistants with those skillsets in the market. This is another reason you might consider specializing instead of being a jack of all trade.

3. Where can I find virtual assistance jobs?
    - Start your search in job sites like Freelancer, Codeable, Upwork, Guru, and even Craigslist.

4. What are the minimum qualities that a virtual assistant must have?
    - Since most of your potential clients will be dealing with you in English, it's important that you have good verbal English skills, written English skills, and organization skills. And of course, you should be familiar with online communication tools like email, Skype etc.

5. What tools can I use to make my work as a virtual assistant easier?
    - You must be equipped with tools Skype, Dropbox, Acrobat Connect, Facebook Messenger, Google Apps, LogMeIn, Team Viewer, and other necessary tools and apps.

6. How do I get paid as a virtual assistant?
    - There are a variety of ways on how you can get paid. So far, the most popular method is through an online payment provider like Skrill, PayPal and Payoneer. However, you can also be paid through bank transfer and cheques.

7. Is it possible to work as a virtual assistant full-time?
    - Yes, of course. There are businesses and entrepreneurs out there who are looking for full-time virtual assistants.

8. How do I get started as a virtual assistant?

- The first step is to create your resume. Don't forget to highlight the information that makes you a good candidate for a virtual assistant position. You then sign up with job sites and look for VA listings. Apply and if they ask for your resume, send it to them.

9. How many clients can I have as a virtual assistant?
   - Most virtual assistants maintain more than one clients. This is why it is very important that you learn how to organize your tasks and manage your time. You have to master the art of scheduling your job responsibilities. Having more than one client will also help you diversify your income stream instead of relying solely on one.

10. How do I protect myself from clients who turn out to be scammers?
    - Scams are quite common in the industry. The best way to protect yourself is to do your research and ensure that the person or company hiring you is legit. Another strategy is to ask for a retainer fee. That is you get paid a portion of your salary in advance. Sites like upwork.com also have a review system whereby the both the client and the virtual assistants review each other after a project is completed. Clients that are legitimate tend to have good ratings and a long profile history.

Myth Busters About Working as a Virtual Assistant

1. That you only need a computer and an internet connection to become a virtual assistant. There's so much more to it than that.

2. Working as a virtual assistant is just for work-at-home moms. Not true. The responsibilities of a virtual assistant can be performed by anyone.

3. Virtual assistants are employees. This is a misnomer because virtual assistants are independent contractors and self-employed individuals. They work "with" their bosses, not "for" their bosses.

4. It's easy money. Nothing can be further from the truth. The tasks of a virtual assistant can be difficult and time-consuming.

5. Virtual assistants do not need training. False again. To be an effective virtual assistant, you need to be aware of the ins and outs of the business.

6. That the market is too crowded because there are millions of virtual assistants out there. There's no truth to the claim that the market is too crowded. In fact, a lot of companies sometimes find it hard to find an available virtual assistant.

7. Virtual assistants all come from India and Pakistan. This is nothing but a stereotype. There are thousands of virtual assistants working from western countries like the United States, Canada, and the United Kingdom.

8. That virtual assistants can steal business ideas and data. Yes, there's a possibility but it's rare. Besides, you should never let a virtual assistant have access to your most important and most sensitive data. When outsourcing tasks, only consider those that do not expose sensitive information e.g. bank details etc.

9. That virtual assistants only work part-time. Although most virtual assistants work part-time, there's a lot of them who work at it full-time.

10. That virtual assistants need some sort of certification. Not true at all. In fact, 90% or more of virtual assistants out there don't have any certification for the simple reason that it's not required by most clients.

Inspiration #7

"All progress takes place outside the comfort zone."
Michael John Bobak

Business #7

Affiliate Marketing

Affiliate marketing follows a really simple business model. You sign up with an affiliate company then promote their products or services. Every time you make a successful sale, you earn a commission. Commissions can range from a few cents to several thousand dollars depending on the commission percentage and selling price of the product. For example, let's say you promoted and sold a product worth $500 with a commission rate of 10%. With that commission percentage, your take from the sale would be a good $50. As you can see, affiliate marketing can be a very lucrative source of passive income if you are very smart about it (i.e. promoting high ticket items or items with backend commissions). Another good thing about affiliate marketing is that there's absolutely no limit to the number of affiliate products you can choose to promote and sell.

The first step in starting an affiliate marketing business is choosing the right platform. The good news is that there are dozens of companies you can choose from. The biggest and most influential of these affiliate marketing companies are Amazon, Clickbank, Rakuten, eBay, and Commission Junction. If you are new in the industry, it's highly recommended that you start with these companies because they already have the reputation and influence. Joining them is much less risky compared to joining new affiliate companies.

Affiliate marketing offers several important benefits to entrepreneurs. One, you don't need to have your own product or service. All you have to do is promote the products of other people and other companies. Two, you don't have to keep inventory or track orders and sales. The product owner or manufacturer handles all these. Again, your sole responsibility is to promote and market the products. Three, there is no cap on the amount of money you can earn. You can earn a few hundred dollars a month or several thousand dollars a day. It's not uncommon for some affiliates to earn as much as six figures in a single month. The point here is that how much you earn depends on how smart and how hard you work on your affiliate marketing business. If you're interested in learning more about this business model, then my book – <u>Affiliate Marketing: Learn How to Make $10,000+ Month On Autopilot</u> will interest you.

Ratings Based on Our Criteria

    A. Simplicity:

Affiliate marketing requires a good amount of work. You also have to be smart with your product selection, commission/pay structure etc. It may be easy to build a YouTube channel or a website monetized with affiliate products but it takes time to build an audience around it.

6/10

    B. Passivity:

Affiliate marketing remains as one of the best ways on how to generate passive income. If you have a website that's full of valuable evergreen content, it can keep on earning you money even if you don't work on it for weeks or even months.

8/10

C. **Scalability:**

It's really easy to scale an affiliate marketing business considering how cheap domain registration and hosting are these days. You can create a dozen affiliate websites that will cost you as low as $100 a month, monetize them with high ticket and relevant affiliate products, drive traffic to them and earn passively. That is truly a bargain.

9/10

D. **Competitiveness:**

This is one of the things you should seriously consider before trying your hands on affiliate marketing. The competition can be very tough especially if you are targeting a very popular niche like personal development or make money online. However, smart niche selection (high demand and low competition e.g. landscaping, gardening etc.) can help you minimize the amount of competition you face. However, if you're very skilled at driving traffic from sources like Facebook ads, YouTube etc. you can do tremendously well regardless of competition.

2/10

Tips on How to Be Successful in Affiliate Marketing

1. Focus your attention on products that are relevant to each other. This is very important if you are selling the products through a website or a blog. This strategy is often referred to as niche marketing.

2. Promote products that you are knowledgeable about. It's much easier to talk about or write content about products that you know.

3. Focus on providing value first, selling the product second. This means writing content that clearly explains to the customer the pros and cons of a product.

4. Don't be too aggressive with your sales pitches. Many affiliate marketers fail because their sales tactics are too intrusive.

5. Know your audience. This is why research is very important. You have to be fully aware about the needs and wants of your target customers.

6. Always be honest and transparent about your affiliate relationships. Don't forget to provide disclosures whenever you are paid directly by a sponsor to write about or recommend a product.

7. Try different affiliate programs and see what works well for you. There are dozens of affiliate programs out there. You don't have to use all of them but you should take the time to experiment.

8. Write timeless or evergreen content when promoting affiliate products. A piece of content can be considered as timeless and evergreen if it remains relevant and true for years to come.

9. Utilize calls to action. Don't be afraid to tell a reader to click here or subscribe there if you are confident about the product you are recommending.

10. Always comply with the rules, regulations, and terms of agreement as provided by the program you are using. Weeks or months of hard work can easily go down the drain if the program suddenly terminates your account because you've broken a rule or two.

Frequently Asked Questions and Answers

1. How do I make money from affiliate marketing?
   - The affiliate marketing business model is quite simple. You sign up with a company that has an affiliate program like Amazon. You promote their products. If you make a sale, you earn an affiliate commission.

2. How do I get started in affiliate marketing?
   - The first step is to learn everything you can about affiliate marketing and how it works. My book on Affiliate Marketing will help you with this. However, if you are confident that you have the proper knowledge to get started, you can sign up with a company that offers an affiliate program like Amazon, eBay, and Commission Junction.

3. How long until I start making money from affiliate marketing?
   - It depends. It can be a day, it can be weeks, it can be months, and it can even be years. It depends on a lot of factors.

4. How do I get paid as an affiliate?
   - It depends on the affiliate marketing company you joined. For example, Amazon pays its affiliates through any of the following options: direct bank deposit, gift certificate (GC), and check. Other affiliate companies pay their marketers via online payment platforms like PayPal, Payoneer, and even crypto-currencies such as Bitcoin.

5. What is a niche?
   - The term "niche" is something you will constantly encounter in affiliate marketing. In the simplest of terms, a niche is a specific topic or theme which serves as the focus of your marketing efforts. For example, let's say that you have an affiliate marketing website that sells soccer memorabilia. In this case, your niche is "soccer memorabilia".

6. Do I need a website to make money in affiliate marketing?
   - Not necessarily. There are affiliate marketers who are still able to generate a decent amount of affiliate income although they don't have a website or a blog (i.e. they could have a YouTube channel with an established audience. They could focus on doing product reviews and posting affiliate links in the video description section). However, getting your own website is very important. With a website, you can double or even triple your chances of making it as an affiliate marketer. It's all about

strategically increasing your footprint in the online world i.e. Facebook, YouTube, Instagram, Twitter, Your Website etc.

7. Which affiliate marketing company or program should I join?
   - There are literally hundreds of affiliate marketing companies and programs out there. It's advisable that if you are just starting out, you should go with the more established companies. These include Amazon, Terra Leads, Clickbank, Rakuten, Shareasale, eBay Partner Network, Commission Factory, Avangate, and Revenue Wire.

8. Do I need to pay taxes?
   - You will have to consult with an accountant because taxation of online earnings differ from one country to another. You need advice on how to declare your online earnings.

9. What kind of products can I promote through affiliate marketing?
   - You can promote pretty much anything as long as it's not illegal. You can promote both digital and physical products. There's no shortage of products that you can promote. Amazon alone has millions of products in its marketplace.

10. How do I succeed as an affiliate marketer?
    - Succeeding in affiliate marketing is a combination of promoting high-quality products, high-ticket products and strategically driving traffic to your affiliate offers.

Myth Busters About Affiliate Marketing

1. That affiliate marketing is a walk in the park. Many people fail in affiliate marketing because they expect it to be a cakewalk. The truth is it requires a lot of work.

2. That more traffic equals more affiliate income. Higher traffic definitely helps but it's just one part of the equation. The quality of the traffic is more important than its quantity and the quality is determined by how relevant the offers you promote are to the people you expose the offer to and whether they trust you. After all, people buy from people they know, like and trust.

3. That affiliate marketing is more about luck than skill. This is completely false. Affiliate marketing is just like any business. You must have the skills to run it and make it profitable.

4. That affiliate marketing is only for professionals with advanced business degrees. You don't need a degree to be successful in affiliate marketing. In fact, most affiliate marketers don't have business degrees.

5. That affiliate marketing is all about advertising. Affiliate marketing is more on creating valuable content that convinces people to purchase products.

6. That social media popularity can easily translate into affiliate marketing success. That's not always the case.

7. That affiliate marketing is a dead end. Affiliate marketing has been around for decades and continues to grow strong. There's absolutely no reason to think that it's a dead end.

8. That affiliate marketing is dependent on content posted on a website. Website content is just one aspect of affiliate marketing. You can also leverage YouTube and popular social media platforms like Facebook.

9. That it's too late to get engaged in affiliate marketing. It's never too late.

10. That you need a lot of money to get started. Nope, you can even start without spending a single penny. However, it'll take longer to gain scale your business.

Inspiration #8

"Don't let the fear of losing be greater than the excitement of winning."
Robert Kiyosaki

Business #8

Dropshipping

The business model for dropshipping is quite simple. You set up a business website where you list down products for sale. However, these products are actually not your products although you make it look like they are yours. You have made a deal with a product manufacturer or supplier that they will ship the products to the customers who buy from your website. That means you are not holding the inventory for the products. You just have them listed on your website. Below is a quick overview of how dropshipping works:

- You find a product manufacturer or supplier and enter into a deal with them. The deal should basically state that you will be dropshipping their products.
- You build a business website and create listings of the products.
- A customer visits your website and decides to purchase a product from you.
- Notified of the purchased item, you then make an order from your manufacturer or supplier.
- The manufacturer or supplier receives the order, processes it, puts it in a package, and ships it to the customer.
- The customer receives the package as if it came from you although it actually came directly from a supplier.

As you can see, there are obvious benefits to this business model. First of all, you don't need to have your own products to create a dropshipping business. You are merely going to promote products by other people and other companies. That means you don't have to go through product development, product testing, and product manufacturing. This also means you don't have to spend huge amounts of cash that are required in making products. In short, there is very little investment on your part. The manufacturer or supplier you entered into a contract with has done the hard work of making the product. You only need to promote it.

You also don't need to keep inventory. Your only worry lies on the orders that are made through your business website. You have to make sure that the orders are immediately forwarded to the supplier so that these can be processed and shipped as soon as possible. So the bottom line here is that your responsibilities as the owner of a dropshipping business are composed of the following simple things:

- List products on your website.
- Process orders then forward these to your supplier.
- Maintain the website.
- That's basically it.

Ratings Based on Our Criteria

A. Simplicity:

I would describe dropshipping as very simple because you can pretty much automate the whole thing. As long as your online store is set up, there's not much else that you do. The only challenge here is learning how to effectively drive traffic to your website/online store.

B. Passivity:

Always remember that in dropshipping, you don't own the products and you don't ship them as well. In addition, the money you make is nearly all profits. However, you still have to deal with customer support issues when they arise.

8/10

C. Scalability:

Scaling a dropshipping business is a matter of either adding more products to your inventory or creating another online store.

9/10

D. Competitiveness:

The dropshipping scene is not as saturated as other online markets only because not many people are aware of the business model. You should expect the industry to become more competitive in the coming years as more people try their luck in building businesses online.

5/10

Tips For Success

1. Sell products that you are actually interested in. Why? Because it will be much easier to nurture loyal and repeat customers if you're personally invested in the products you are selling.

2. Choose a niche that you are passionate about. It's easier to build a dropshipping business if you enjoy running and managing it. In addition, if you're passionate about your niche then chances are you'll understand your customer avatar better and this will be reflected in the quality of traffic you'll drive to your online store.

3. Look for light and durable products to sell. They are easier to sell and there's less risk of breakage etc. when shipping them overseas.

4. Don't just build a dropshipping business, build a brand. Make people feel like they are getting something special when they purchase a product from you.

5. High quality presentation of your merchandise is very important. Put yourself in the shoes of your potential customers. If you see ugly and unprofessional product photos, would you trust the merchant selling them?

6. Establish a good relationship with your supplier and manufacturer. This ensures that you'll more or less get the products whenever you need them. Burning bridges in the dropshipping industry can easily wipe out your operations.

7. See to it that your pricing policy is reasonable. The general rule is that you should not underprice nor overprice your products. Underpricing creates the impression that your product are low quality. Overpricing, on the other hand, can turn off customers.

8. Ensure availability for all of your products. Nothing disappoints a customer more than learning that the product he badly wants is out of stock.

9. Automate certain aspects of your business. There are so many apps that you can use to make it easier to run your dropshipping business. You should take advantage of these tools.

10. Offer exceptional customer service. A lot of things can go wrong in a dropshipping business. A supplier may not keep his end of the bargain. The package arrives late. There are bugs in the ordering and payment system. These are just a few of the common problems associated with dropshipping. Make sure that you deal with them as soon as possible to keep your customers happy.

Frequently Asked Questions and Answers

1. What kind of profit margin can I expect from dropshipping?
   - Your profit margin will depend greatly on the products that you are selling and the suppliers you are getting them from. Average profit margins are in the 5% to 10% range. However, for some low-priced items such as accessories, profit margins can go as high as 90%.

2. Do I need to buy the products before I sell them?
   - No, that's absolutely not necessary. That is the beauty of dropshipping. You only purchase the products from your supplier or manufacturer when a customer orders them. This means you can sell hundreds of products while your supplier scrambles to ship them to your customers.

3. Do I need a website to be successful in dropshipping?
   - Yes, you need to set up a website in the form of an online store. There should be a place where customers can browse through your products and purchase them if they want them. If you are not a web developer, there are online tools and apps that you can use to get an online store. For example, you can sign up with Shopify, an online service that allows you to create a complete dropshipping website in minutes.

4. Do I need a supplier?
   - Yes. You are in the dropshipping business which means you don't make the products yourself. This also means that you need a supplier or a manufacturer to provide you with the products you are going to sell.

5. How do I find a supplier?

- Google is your best friend here. There are dozens of marketplaces online where you can find suppliers for any product you fancy. Such marketplaces include SaleHoo, Dropship Direct, Whosesale Central, Inventory Source, Alibaba, AliExpress, Doba, Worldwide Brands, and Megagoods.

6. What kind of fees do dropshipping companies charge?
   - Aside from the cost of the products you are dropshipping, companies may also charge you pre-order fees and monthly fees. It's quite common for companies to charge pre-order fees to cover the costs involved in packaging and shipping an individual product. Companies may also charge you a monthly fee for the privilege of doing business with them.

7. What are the requirements in starting a dropshipping business?
   - The requirements differ based on the country where you are headquartered. In the United States, you need to incorporate your business with your state. You need to request for an EIN number from the IRS. You need to request for a sales and tax ID from your state.

8. Who takes care of customer service in a business that follows the dropshipping model?
   - The responsibility is on you as the retailer. You have to handle support issues, solve problems, and deal with any other issue that arises form customer complaints. Your supplier simply ships the products to your customers. That's their only responsibility.

9. How much money do I need to get started?
   - It depends on several factors. Some dropshipping businesses can be started with just $100 while some require more than $1000. It depends on the products you are selling, the costs of shipping your products, the tools you are using, etc.

10. How do I attract customers to my dropshipping store?
    - There are a lot of ways. You can do social media marketing, direct advertising, blogging, and search engine optimization among others.

Myth Busters About Dropshipping

1. That dropshipping only works for low-priced general products. It's not true. Dropshipping works for all kinds of products and price bands.

2. That you need to be tech-savvy and a coding expert to be engaged in dropshipping. This is not a requirement. You can easily outsource the design of your website to freelance web developers on upwork or fiverr who will handle that for you.

3. That you can make money overnight. Dispel this notion from your mind. Like any worthwhile business, it takes time to achieve notable success. This is not a get rich quick scheme.

4. That dropshipping only involves listing products in a website. That's not true. You still have to process and forward orders to your suppliers and handle customer service when necessary e.g. a customer returning a faulty product etc.

5. That dropshipping is very expensive and only a few people can afford it. This is not entirely true. Some dropshipping businesses can be started with just $100 while some require more than $1000. It depends on the products you are selling, the costs of shipping your products, the tools you are using, etc.

6. That dropshipping is a saturated niche and that it's too late to get into the industry. It's never too late. The demand for consumer products continue to grow and with the right product selection, you can carve out a profitable niche for yourself.

7. That dropshipping is a scam. If you don't do your due diligence i.e. research the suppliers you work with, their reputation, trade history etc. then you may be scammed.

8. That dropshipping is only about exporting low-quality products from China. This is entirely false as you can dropship quality products manufactured in Europe or USA for that matter.

9. That dropshipping is too confusing for ordinary entrepreneurs. It depends on the person. Yes, there's always a learning curve. However, there are ebooks, courses online and mentors you can work with to provide guidance when required.

10. That if your supplier runs out of stock, you are toast. This is not true. You can minimize the risk of this occurring by diversifying i.e. partnering with multiple suppliers

---

Inspiration #9

"If you really look closely, most overnight successes took a long time."
Steve Jobs

Business #9

Create Online Courses

There is an immense market for all sorts of online courses. It doesn't matter what kind of course it is, there's always a group of people out there who will find the course helpful and valuable. How to plant and raise roses. How to paint using ground coffee beans. How to create a mobile application. How to make money from your YouTube videos. How to write and independently publish a novel. How to draw anime. How to create your own wedding dress.

These are just a few examples of simple but valuable ideas for courses that can find a profitable audience online. If you are good at something, there's a good chance that you can earn passive income from it by creating an online course around it.

If you are knowledgeable or skilled about a certain topic, creating a course about it should be a breeze. Even better is the fact that there are online platforms which allow you to make these online courses with ease. Udemy comes to mind. This is basically a company whose core service is to help people make courses and connect them with their target audiences. Udemy is just one of several companies that offer this type of service. With that said, you should take the time to explore other platforms to find the ones that are most appropriate to your brand of courses. But if you are just staring out in the business of making and selling online courses, Udemy would be a good place to start. They offer you a variety of tools and resources that will make your life a lot easier.

If you don't want to make use of third-party service providers like Udemy, you can always sell your courses directly to your target customers. The best way to do this is to make your course downloadable so that a paying customer can access them within a few minutes. It will be more difficult to find customers this way because you have to be aggressive in your marketing efforts. But if you are confident in your marketing skills, then go for it. It's important that you create a website or a blog which will serve as your main marketing machine. It's where you direct people who might be interested in your course.

To promote your courses, you should combine a lot of online marketing strategies like search engine optimization, video marketing, content marketing, direct advertising, and social media marketing. The last one (social media marketing) can be very effective if you learn how to leverage advertising programs by social networking sites. For example, Facebook has its own advertising program. What's great about Facebook's advertising program is that you can customize your campaign so that your ad will only reach the types of people you want to reach. You can customize your target audience by geographical location, by gender, by age, and by their hobbies and interests. It's a very efficient way to find people who are genuinely interested in your online courses.

Ratings Based on Our Criteria

    A. Simplicity:

I wouldn't call the business model simple given the fact that building an online course from scratch can be quite complicated. It requires a lot of research and writing. However, sites like Udemy, Thinkific and Teachable have done a lot to simplify the process.

6/10

B. Passivity:

Once the hard work of creating the course is over, there's not much work left aside from promoting the course. Most of the profits from this point on are mostly passive in nature.

8/10

C. Scalability:

To scale, you just have to increase your marketing budget to reach more people or create another online course. Ultimately, it's like writing a book on top of another. The more courses you have circulating, the more passive income you make.

9/10

D. Competitiveness:

Competition depends on your niche. If you are offering a course in a very popular niche, then the competition can be very tough. This is why before you start creating a course, make sure that the market is not already saturated with courses similar to what you have in mind. However, if you're very good with Facebook advertising, YouTube advertising or marketing in general, then you have a considerable edge over your competitors.

4/10

Tips For Success

1. Choose the perfect course topic. This means that the topic should be something that you love and something that you are actually knowledgeable in. It's much easier to build a course if you know what you are talking about.

2. Perform some research to ensure that your course idea has high market demand. No matter how good your course is if nobody out there wants it, you're not going to make any money from it.

3. Create a compelling presentation of the learning outcomes or the kind of transformation people can expect after going through your course. What are they going to get from it? Where can they apply the things they learn from your courses?

4. Structure your course modules. The general rule in structuring a course is to start with the simplest lessons then slowly graduate to the more advanced lessons. The goal in every module is to prepare the learner for the next module.

5. Gather content for your course from reputable sources. If you are going to cite someone in your course, make sure that he's someone who is considered as an expert in the field.

6. Make it as easy as possible for the learner to access your course. It should be as easy as downloading a file or logging into a website.

7. Make your course as engaging as possible by combining all types of media (text, video, audio, infographics, etc.)

8. Promote your course in every platform possible. Promote it in your social media networks. Promote it through email marketing. Promote it in your blog. Promote it in your podcast. Just get your name out there.

9. Create a whole series of courses. This is a great way to nurture your customers and build a following. This business model is similar to writing a book series. You keep giving your customers something to look forward to.

10. Collaborate with other online course creators. You get to use each other as leverage to increase your customer base.

Frequently Asked Questions and Answers

1. What is an online course?
   - It's a course which is delivered to learners online. It can be in the form of a series of articles, video tutorials, presentations, or even live lessons.

2. Where can I sell an online course I created?
   - You can market the course directly to your target audience. You can use platforms like Udemy, Teachable, Thinkific, Skillshare, LearnWorlds, CourseCraft, etc.

3. What is Udemy?
   - This is just one of several online platforms where you can create and sell your online courses.

4. What kind of online course can I make?
   - You can make any course you want as long as you're knowledgeable about the topic being discussed and there's a market for it.

5. How do I promote my online courses?
   - Use a variety of proven online marketing techniques likes search engine optimization, social media marketing, email marketing and advertising.

6. What's the cost of creating a course?

- It depends on several factors. These factors include the platform that you are using, the tools you are using to create the course, and if you are hiring other people to help you in making the course. That being said, you can create a course on Thinkific for free (as of July 2018).

7. How much money can I earn from my courses?
   - Again, it depends on a lot of factors. But for inspiration, you should know that there are some course creators who earn up to six figures a month.

8. Do I have to be a coder to create a course?
   - Not necessarily. There are some courses that you can create without any coding skills. You can also hire someone to handle the technical aspects of creating the course. Online course platforms like Teachable and Thinkific have so simplified the process that anyone can create a course.

9. What tools do I need to create an online course?
   - It depends on the kind of course you are making. Is it a video course? Then you need video-editing tools and software like Screenflow, Camtasia etc.

10. How do I deliver my online courses to clients?
    - The best way is to provide them with a downlink link.

Myth Busters About Creating Online Courses

1. That you have to be an expert in something before you can make a course about it. You don't need to be an expert to create an online course. As long as you are know enough to teach other people who may be slightly below you in the learning curve you're within your rights to create a course. If anything, your audience will relate more to you and your course because you understand their pain points better having been there yourself not too long ago. Its one thing knowing something and another thing being able to teach it in a way people can understand.

2. That you have to choose a course that is currently trending. This is false. Trending or not, all you simply have to do is choose a topic that has proven demand and you have some experience with it.

3. That you shouldn't create a course around a topic if there are already existing courses about it. Again, this is not true. The fact other courses exist doesn't mean they do a good job addressing the issue. If you believe you have something to offer you should give it a go.

4. That the tech stuff is so difficult that only develops are able to perform them. Platforms like Udemy, Teachable and Thinkific have made the course creation process so easy anybody with enough motivation can do it.

5. That creating a course is very expensive. Once again, this is far from the truth given that you can create an online course with platforms like Thinkific for free.

6. That you are required to be in front of the camera and talk to people. Being in front of a camera is not strictly required. You can tailor the course to suit your teaching style – talking over a presentation slide, showing a video of yourself delivering the course etc.

7. That no one will buy your course because people can just Google it. This is not true as people purchase courses to achieve a given aim or transformation in as short a time as possible. Not everyone has the time to sieve through all the information on the internet to find the ones that are specifically tailored to them – that's the purpose of a course.

8. That you need thousands of people in your email list before you can launch a course. This is not entirely true. It's more about the quality of the email list rather then the quantity. If you have a good relationship with the people on your email list and they know you, like you and trust you then you're golden. You build relationship by giving value first then selling later.

9. That no one will purchase your course if you increase the price due to upgrades. There'll always be a small section of your customers who will be interested in purchasing your premium products as long as they offer something of equal value. It's advisable to have different price tiers/packages to cater to as many of your customers as possible.

10. That you need to create lots and lots of courses to be able to earn real income from teaching courses. This is not necessarily true. Yes, you may need a lot of courses to scale but earning a real income comes from creating valuable content and marketing them well. This will allow you to charge a premium price, which means you don't need to sell a lot to make a significant income.

Inspiration #10

"The way to get started is to quit talking and begin doing."
Walt Disney

Business #10

Build an Application

It's not uncommon to hear about apps that earn their creators thousands of dollars every month. Hell, there are even app creators who became millionaires through simple but helpful applications. If you have good coding and programming skills that can be translated to app development, or you know how to hire good freelance programmers that'll develop apps for you then this is an industry you should explore. The market for apps, especially mobile apps, is at an all-time high. With more and more people getting connected to the internet through their smartphones, the market for apps will only grow bigger and even more lucrative. For sure, the app development sector is unbelievably competitive but there are new opportunities that are always emerging.

You can build an app from scratch or you can build one using an open-source software. Each strategy has its own pros and cons so it's up to you to choose the method that will work best for you. Take advantage of the tools and resources that are available online to build and polish your app. And before you launch and offer your app for download, make sure that you have tested it several times. A single bug (i.e. malfunction) in the app can easily destroy all your hard work. It's difficult to get a second chance in the app development field. So make sure that you get it right the first time.

After creating and extensively testing your app, the next step is to market it to the world. Your first move should be to have your app listed in popular app stores. This will expose your app to thousands of potential customers. If your app is good enough, people will start talking about it and that's where word-of-mouth starts. If your app offers something of value, it should be able to market itself. However, this doesn't mean that you just sit back and let your app do all the self-promotion stuff. You are setting yourself up for failure if this is your attitude.

No matter how good you think your app is, you still have to spend tons of your time and resources in promoting and marketing it. Create a page for it on Facebook. Endlessly talk about it on Twitter or Instagram. Purchase ads for it in technology websites and blogs. Do some email marketing. The point here is that you should put yourself out there and do everything that you can to let people know about your new app.

Ratings Based on Our Criteria

A. **Simplicity:**

Hey, building an application is not easy. You must have the educational background as well as the technical experience to create one from scratch or, at the very least, know how to hire people with the necessary expertise to build one for you (which will probably cost you).

5/10

B. **Passivity:**

Once the app is up for grabs, pretty much most of the income you generate are passive in nature.

8/10

C. **Scalability:**

It can be hard to scale an app business if you are operating solo. But if you are working within a team wherein you have the capability to develop several apps at the same time, then scalability can easily be achieved.

7/10

D. **Competitiveness:**

The app business is very hot right now so the competition can be fierce. You are competing not just against individual developers but against app-building companies that are backed by millions of dollars in funding.

1/10

Tips For Success

1. Outline your app's purpose before you even get started with the coding process. This will save you a lot of time and money down the road. What is your app for? What kind of value will people get from it? When you have a clear answer to these questions, then that's the time you get started.

2. Clearly identify the potential market for your app. If there's no market then there's no money to be made. Try asking your friends and family if your idea of an app is something they might be interested in.

3. Keep it simple. Don't you notice that majority of the most successful apps out there are often the most simple ones? It's because people need simplicity not complexity.

4. Make your app compatible with as many operating systems as possible. If your app is only available in one operating system, then you are limiting your app's potential.

5. Test your app several times before you launch. A launch that's riddled with errors and bugs can quickly ruin all your hard work. So test your app over and over again until you are completely sure that it's working properly and smoothly.

6. Less is more. Many developers often make the mistake of assuming that an app becomes better as you add more features to it. Just identify the problem you are trying to solve and make it the focus of your app.

7. Make your app free. Obviously, this strategy is not for everyone but it's a strategy you should consider. Making your app free can double and even triple the attention that your app gets. You make money by offering in-app purchases, selling advertising space or offering a paid version of your app that has no ads. Be creative

8. Marketing is everything. You should come up with a plan on how you are going to promote your app.

9. Think like a user. During the entirety of the development process, always look at your app with the perspective of your potential user. If you don't like what you are creating, then your user will probably think the same.

10. Seek feedback from other experienced app developers. Ask them what they think of your app. Take their comments and use these to build an even better app.

Frequently Asked Questions and Answers

1. How much does it cost to build a mobile application?
    - It depends on the size and nature of the app. Some apps can cost $5000 and some can cost six figures.

2. How long does it take to develop a mobile app?
    - Again, it depends on the size and nature of the app. Some apps can be built in a few days and some can take months or even years.

3. How do I validate my app idea?
    - You have to perform extensive research to determine if there's going to be a market for your app. Do similar apps exist and are people paying for them or at the very least downloading them?

4. What is the best way to monetize an app?
    - Aside from selling the app on a per download basis, you can also offer in-app purchases. This is a great strategy especially for gaming apps.

5. Should I develop apps using Android or iOS?
    - If you are skilled in both, you should use both to widen your potential market.

6. How do I get more app downloads?
    - You have to promote and market it like crazy. Use every imaginable marketing platform like social media sits, forums, and app stores.

7. How do I market my app?
    - Sign up with as many app stores as you can and have your app listed in them. You should also promote your app in social media, blogs, YouTube and on your own website.

8. How many times do I have to test my app before launching it?
    - Keep testing it until you don't see any bugs or flaws in it.

9. Can I still have an app created even if I'm not a developer?
    - Yes, of course. This is where freelance app developers enter the picture. You come up with the app idea and the developer will execute it for you. You can hire freelancers from Upwork, Fiverr etc.

10. Is it a good idea to offer my app for free?
    - Yes, if it's a marketing strategy. You can offer free download and usage for a certain period of time. Or you can simply give away the app but monetize it through in-app purchases.

Myth Busters About Building and Making Money from Apps

1. That mobile apps are cheap. We have already established that it'll depends on the nature of the app you want to build.

2. That mobile apps are for smartphones only. This is not true. Normal phones still have mobile apps like Gmail, Google map etc.

3. That you can be an instant millionaire after developing an app. While this is possible, it's highly unlikely. Nothing worthwhile happens instantly, there's always a learning process.

4. That app development is a one-time thing. This is not true, as you need still need to listen to customer feedback, provide updates/upgrades to keep your customers happy and the app competitive.

5. That you need to be a developer to have a functioning app created. This is far from the truth. If you have no technical skills, you can hire freelancers to develop apps for you.

6. That developing native apps for each platform is impractical. It's practical if the have the necessary resources and technical know-how

7. That the release of an app ends its development. Not true. You still have to look at customer feedback/review and work on releasing updates/upgrades to keep your app competitive.

8. That mobile app development is just coding and nothing else. This is not true. A lot of marketing is required after the app is launched

9. That you can build a perfect app for all platforms in a single attempt. While this is possible, it's highly unlikely.

10. That your app can get thousands of users without any marketing. I think we both know by now this is not true. Regardless of how good the app is, you'll need to market it, get the word out and raise awareness. If your app happens to be very valuable, word of mouth marketing may eventually kick in which will save you a lot of marketing spend.

Inspiration #11

"The successful warrior is the average man, with laser-like focus."
Bruce Lee

Business #11

Online Consultancy

Are you an expert in something? Maybe you are a pro in Adobe Photoshop. Maybe you are skilled in creating Facebook pages that pop. Maybe you have years of experience in social media marketing. Maybe you are adept in business law and taxation. If you are skilled in something, you should consider offering your knowledge as an online consultant. What's great about this business model is that anyone from anywhere in the world can become your client. Maybe there's a business student in London who needs your business law expertise. Maybe there's a company CEO in Japan who wants you to teach him how to optimize his company's Facebook page. The point here is that if you're good at something, you can create an income source from it by simply offering advice to people.

Online consultancy is a very competitive niche so you should be smart which fields or industries you enter. Getting clients for your consultancy business is all about proving to your potential customers that you are who they're looking for. You have to show them that you got the goods. Aside from providing samples or testaments to your previous work, you also have to constantly work on your personal branding. You have to get your name out there. The best way to do that is to keep on providing exceptional services to your clients.

To get the word out about your services, you must have a website, a blog, and a social media presence. These are the platforms that you are going to use to promote yourself to your target audience. The more you use them, the more people will know about you and your consulting business.

Ratings Based on Our Criteria

A. Simplicity:

Online consultancy can be an easy and simple job if you are genuinely passionate about it. If you like helping people out, the job can be fun and enjoyable.

8/10

B. Passivity:

As an online consultant, you are usually paid by the hour or with a fixed monthly pay. This is not exactly the definition of passive income. However, you can make it passive by structuring the deal with your clients so that you can get a certain portion of their profits, company i.e. stock option or royalties in exchange for helping them improve their bottom line. Dan Kennedy is one person I know who has successfully implemented such a strategy.

5/10

C. Scalability:

It's hard to scale a gig like online consultancy for the simple reason that you have limited time and resources as a singular person. Of course, you can scale the business by starting a firm where you hire other consultants to work under you and charge a premium for clients to work directly with you.

6/10

D. **Competitiveness:**

The online consultancy arena is full of competitors especially if you operate within a saturated niche. For example, if you plan on becoming a social media consultant, be prepared because you will be competing with thousands of other social media consultants out there.

Tips For Success

1. Offer free consultations. This is a very powerful strategy if you are just starting out. Getting your first clients is one of the hardest parts of online consulting. Offering free consultations is a good way to get the ball rolling.

2. Leverage your existing network. Again, this is a powerful strategy if you are just starting out. Reach out to your friends and colleagues if they know of someone who might be in need of your consulting services.

3. Learn how to approach potential clients. Yes, this sounds rather intrusive but it works. If you are confident with what you are offering, then there's no reason why you should be afraid to directly approach potential clients.

4. Connect with influencers in your niche. The relationships you build with well-known names in your niche have a huge impact on your reputation and brand.

5. Leverage social networks that are tailored to professionals and business-minded people. The biggest of these networks is LinkedIn so make sure that you have an account there.

6. Try offering free webinars. A webinar is a seminar that's done online. It's basically a videoconference where you get to speak to dozens or even hundreds of people. This is another great way to get your name out there.

7. Focus on building relationships, not revenues. The thinking behind this is that if you build relationships first and sell later, the revenue will follow. To be successful in consulting, you must have an army of loyal and repeat clients.

8. Familiarize yourself with the competition. Are they offering something that you don't? Are they getting more clients than you? What are they doing to be so successful? Learn from them and implement what you learn in your own consultancy services.

9. Be active on social media platforms. Be on Facebook. Be on Twitter. Be on Instagram. Hundreds of your potential clients are active users of these sites.

10. Regularly get in touch with your clients. Call them if you have to. Ask them for updates about the projects that you helped them with. A quick call or a simple email message can do wonders in rekindling the business relationship you have with former clients.

Frequently Asked Questions and Answers

1. What do online consultants do?
   - They have similar responsibilities as offline consultants. It's just that everything is done remotely on the internet.

2. How do I become an online consultant?
   - Do you have a skill or expertise that you think people will pay you for? If your answer is yes, then you can become an online consultant.

3. Do I have to sign up with a consultancy agency?
   - It depends on your preferences. You can sign up with an agency or you can offer your services directly to clients.

4. How much can I earn as an online consultant?
   - It depends in your niche and the amount of time you spend on the job. You can earn a full-time income from online consultancy if you work hard for it. If you become exceptionally good at it and build a strong reputation, you can charge pretty much what you want. Think of people like Dan Kennedy!

5. Where do I find clients?
   - Browse job sites and classified ads sites. Take note of individual entrepreneurs or businesses looking for consultants.

6. How do I get paid?
   - Most online consultants are paid through an online payment service like PayPal and Payoneer.

7. Do I have to pay taxes?
   - It depends on the country you are located. If you are based in the United States, yes you definitely need to disclose your earnings and pay the corresponding taxes.

8. Is it necessary to create my own website?
   - It's not a requirement per se but it can help you a lot if you have your own website.

9. How do I charge my clients?
   - You decide how you want to get paid. You can charge per hour or per project.

10. How do I promote my online consulting services?

- Same as what you would do when marketing anything online. Blogging, social media marketing, SEO, advertising, etc.

Myth Busters About Online Consultancy

1. That you can earn a lot of money doing very little work. You can ONLY when you have established yourself, clients know your reputation for delivering results and you have a notable brand.

2. That you should have a business degree before you can do online consulting. This is not a requirement. As long as you have experience with something and you can leverage that experience to help others you can be a consultant.

3. That online consulting is only for experts in their fields. It depends on your definition of on expert. As long as you have a personal experience and knowledge about something, you can be a consultant. You don't need a fancy degree or certificate to qualify. If you can get results for your clients you're golden.

4. That it's very easy to find jobs as an online consultant. It's not (at least at the very beginning when you're still trying to establish yourself). You have to put yourself out there. Get on social media platforms, business sites like LinkedIn etc. Market yourself.

5. That you don't have to pay taxes because most of your responsibilities are performed online. This is not true. Depending on the country where you operate, you may have to declare your earnings. We advise speaking to your accountant to better understand what your options are.

6. That online consulting is full of scammers. Every business opportunity has its fair share of scammers. You have to do your due diligence to ensure people you hire to help you are actually capable of doing what they say they're going to do. Look to reviews, personal reference, free consultation to gauge their skill level/knowledge etc.

7. That online consulting is a saturated field and that it's too late to join the industry. The online consulting industry continues to grow strongly and there's plenty of opportunity for success as long as you market yourself correctly.

8. That online consulting is only for work-at-home moms. This is not true. Anybody who has experience with something and can help others with that knowledge can become a consultant

9. That you can't make a full-time income from online consulting alone. That's not true at all. On the contrary, you can make a full time living as a consultant. If there's a demand for what you offer and you market yourself well, you can thrive in this industry. Look to people like Dan Kennedy for inspiration!

10. That entrepreneurs and businesses aren't in need of consultants because they can just Google solutions for their problems. That's far from the truth. Serious business people value their time. They most likely

won't waste it searching the web for answers. Besides, with a consultant, they get answers that are specifically tailored to their situation and, in some cases, ongoing support from someone who understands their business.

Inspiration #12

"There are no secrets to success. It is the result of preparation, hard work, and learning from failure."
Colin Powell

Business #12

Online Surveys

I'm going to be brutally honest with you here and tell you right now that you can earn good money from online surveys but don't expect such amounts to be consistent. You should only treat online surveys as a complimentary source of income. There are days wherein there's a good amount of surveys. But there are also days wherein there are zero surveys to accomplish. Of course, this depends on the survey company but this is always the trend within the online surveys niche.

How you make money from online surveys is pretty simple. You sign up with a survey company, log into their surveys dashboard to see if there are any surveys available, accomplish them, and get paid for your efforts. Some surveys can be worth a few cents. Some can be worth three figures. These surveys are usually questionnaires about products, services, and trends. A lot of these are done by companies for market research purposes.

There are dozens of survey companies out there that you can join. These include Swagbucks, Toluna, MySurvey, YouGov, Panel Opinion, Survey Bods, Hiving, Prolific Academic, Global test Market, PanelBase, Pinecone ResearchOpinion Outpost, and so much more. How you get paid depends on the survey company. Some pay in cash via PayPal, some pay through bank transfer, and some pay through rewards in the form of coupons, gift cards, and discounts on certain products and services.

To earn a nice amount of money from online surveys, you need to constantly check your dashboards to see if there are surveys available. You should also be constantly checking your email because many survey companies inform their members of new surveys through email.

Ratings Based on Our Criteria

    A. **Simplicity:**

    Making money from online surveys is very simple. Most of the questions are answerable by a yes or a no. Furthermore, majority of the surveys are in multiple choice formats.

8/10

    B. **Passivity:**

    Technically speaking, money you earn from online surveys are far away from being passive. If you complete a survey, you get paid for it. And it stops there. You don't earn additional income from surveys that you've already completed. Unless you have bots or virtual assistants hired to answer surveys on your behalf there's little you can do to make this passive. That being said, you can focus some of your time in referring friends. Many survey companies have their own referral programs. This means you get a cut from the earnings of those people you referred to the website. All in all, this is more a make money online option rather than a passive income opportunity.

2/10

C. Scalability:

The number of surveys you are given are controlled by the survey companies. Even if you want to scale your earnings, there's very little thing that you can do. You just complete what's given to you. That being said, you can scale to a certain extent by working with more survey companies to ensure there's always a steady stream of surveys to complete.

5/10

D. Competitiveness:

To be honest, the online survey industry has already reached a saturation point. There are too many people willing to complete surveys but there's not enough surveys to go round.

1/10

Tips For Success

1. Sign up with as many paid survey sites as possible. As I've mentioned above, survey companies don't always have surveys available. So if the available survey in one company runs out, you can always log into the other companies if there are surveys available.

2. Make sure that the survey company is legit before you sign up. There are a lot of fake websites out there that present themselves as survey sites but they're actually not survey sites.

3. Fill out your profile completely. You see, a lot of the surveys that will be available to you are dependent on the information that you have entered into your profile.

4. Be smart and honest when answering screening questions. Sometimes, before you gain access to a survey, you are required to answer screening questions. You should answer the questions as truthfully as possible.

5. Don't rush through the surveys. Keep in mind that some surveys won't pay you if your answers are riddled with inconsistencies.

6. Regularly check your email inbox for updates on the latest surveys. If you are using Gmail, you should create a folder where all your survey emails will be redirected to.

7. Take the survey as soon as you are notified of it. Once you receive a survey, complete it immediately before someone else does.

8. Focus some of your time in referring friends. Many survey companies have their own referral programs. This means you get a cut from the earnings of those people you referred to the website.

9. Get a PayPal account. This is very important because most survey sites pay their members through PayPal. Getting an account is super easy because all you need is an email address.

10. Don't be picky about the surveys you complete. Again, most of these surveys are limited. If you don't accept a survey immediately, someone else will.

Frequently Asked Questions and Answers

1. What is an internet survey?
    - These are surveys mostly conducted by brands for market research or product testing.

2. How does online surveys work?
    - Brands usually hire survey companies to conduct the surveys. The company then outsources the completion of the surveys to online contractors.

3. How do I earn money from online surveys?
    - You simply sign up with a survey company and complete the surveys that are presented to you.

4. How much can I earn from a survey?
    - It depends on the scope and nature of the survey. Some surveys pay a few pennies. Some can pay up to $100.

5. What are the best survey companies out there?
    - Some of the most popular survey sites today include Swagbucks, Toluna, MySurvey, YouGov, Panel Opinion, and Hiving.

6. How do I know if a survey site is legit?
    - Consider how long the site has been around. Fake survey sites don't survive that long. Also read as many reviews as you can about the site.

7. What are the requirements in joining a survey site?
    - The requirements vary from one company to another.

8. How do I get paid for completed surveys?
    - Most of the time, you will be paid in cash usually through PayPal. Other times, you will be compensated through rewards, coupons, discounts, etc.

9. Can I earn a full time income answering surveys?
    - It's possible but it's extremely rare. You should only treat it as source of side income.

10. Can I join several survey sites simultaneously?
    - Yes, of course. They are independent from each other so you can join and answer surveys from all of them.

Myth Busters About Online Surveys

1. That online surveys always ask dozens of questions at a time. It's not always the case. Some do but not all.

2. That majority of online surveys are scams. Sure, some of them are scams but not the majority. You just need to do your due diligence. Read reviews regarding the surveys, check forums for other people's experiences when completing the surveys etc. Fake sites don't tend to stick around for long.

3. That online surveys are only meant to steal your information and identity. That's not the case. More often than not, online survey companies run these surveys to better understand how consumers use their products and the features they desire etc. This research information allows them to come up with better products.

4. That brands are wasting their time and money in sponsoring surveys. Like I mentioned in 3 above, this is not always a waste of time. It has its use case when executed properly.

5. That paid survey sites only hire experienced participants. That's not the case. Anybody can participate in these surveys (you probably need to be above the age of 18)

6. That you can easily cheat the system. While this is possible, it's getting harder to pull it off as online survey companies are getting smarter. Inconsistent answers may get you disqualified and you won't get paid.

7. That paid surveys are an overnight get-rich-quick scheme. On the contrary, its difficult to make a full time living doing this, much less getting rich quickly!

8. That you can get rich by participating in just one paid survey site. This is definitely not feasible.

9. That you can simply guess the answers in order to finish them faster and answer more surveys. Like I said before, too many inconsistencies in your answers can get you disqualified.

10. That you can make thousands of dollars a month answering a few surveys each week. While this is possible, it's rare. You need to complete a LOT of surveys to possibly make thousand per month

---
Inspiration #13

"Success seems to be connected with action. Successful people keep moving. They make mistakes, but they don't quit."

Conrad Hilton

Business #13

Online Auctions

Online auctions operate exactly like what you'd expect. You list a product in an auction site, set an auction period, set the minimum bid, and then click launch. Customers will bid on your product listing until the auction period ends. Whoever bid the highest after the auction period expired will get your product. This can be a lucrative online business if you are able to target a niche and build an army of loyal customers.

Online auctions require a little bit of work because you need to regularly check which of your auctions have expired and which auctions are still running. Products that didn't get any bids have to be manually relisted. So yes, running an auction business can be time-consuming. But it's worth it if you have products that are easy to sell.

Ratings Based on Our Criteria

    A. Simplicity:

The business model of online auction sites is quite simple. Just sign up, list a product, and let potential buyers bid on it.

8/10

    B. Passivity:

You are directly selling products to customers so most of your income isn't passive. Of course, to make it more passive, you can document your processes and hire virtual assistants to help you perform these tasks e.g. listing your items, monitoring bids, relisting unsold items after auction period ends etc.

5/10

    C. Scalability:

To scale the business, you simply add more products in your inventory.

8/10

    D. Competitiveness:

Online auctions are very competitive. Be ready to match other sellers when it comes to prices and quality of products.

2/10

Tips For Success

1. Price your items by reviewing similar products in the auction site that you are using.

2. As much as possible, try to offer free shipping. You can double or even triple your customer base with this strategy.

3. Learn of the best time in posting your listings. Some products tend to sell better when they are listed within a particular time of the day.

4. Always treat your customers properly. Selling in auctions also involves making your customers happy so they'll buy from you again in the future.

5. Treat the whole operation like a business. Even if you are not doing it full time.

6. If possible, avoid putting reserve prices on your products. Auction customers tend to look for great discounts on items. If they feel there's a limit to the bidding process, it may discourage them from participating.

7. Make use of high quality images of your products. It'll make you look more professional and your listings will attract more bids.

8. Cross-promote your product listings. If your listings are closely related then this could be a very profitable strategy to implement.

9. Offer a return policy. This removes a lot customer fear and barrier to purchase and you can subsequently attract several loyal customers.

10. Ask your customers to provide feedback or reviews.

Frequently Asked Questions and Answers

1. What is an online auction?
   - An online auction occurs when you list a product for sale and enable customers to bid on it.

2. What are the best auction sites today?
   - eBay is without a doubt the largest online auction site today but there are smaller alternatives like Listia, Ubid, Webstore, eCrater, and Bonanza.

3. What kind of products can I sell in auction sites?
   - Before you list a product in an auction site, make sure to thoroughly read the terms and agreements and look for the section where the prohibited products are listed.

4. How do I collect payments from successful bidders?
   - Auction sites make use of various payment methods. However, the most common methods are through credit card and PayPal.

5. How do I cross-promote by product listings?

- In the description box for a product listing or in the recommendation box, you should feature and highlight your other product listings.

6. Is free shipping a good idea?
    - It's a great strategy because it attracts more customers. However, make sure that you aren't at the losing end when you offer free shipping for your products.

7. How should I price my products?
    - There are several factors you should consider. These include the cost of the product, the shipping fees, and the charges collected by the auction site.

8. What is a reserve price in an online auction?
    - A reserve price is a hidden minimum price that a seller is willing to accept for a product.

9. Where can I get products to sell in auction sites?
    - Selling in auction sites is basically a form of retail arbitrage. That is you purchase products from retailers like Target or Walmart and other sources then resell them in an auction site lie eBay.

10. How do I promote my product listings in auction sites?
    - Use standard online marketing methods like search engine optimization, social media marketing, advertising, etc.

Myth Busters About Selling in Auction Sites

1. That you can't sell products at a fair market value. The word "fair" is subjective. When you list a very valuable product it'll attract a lot of bids and consequently the sale price or "fair price" will be very high. The reverse is the case for poor quality products.

2. That selling products using an auction site can be very expensive and inflate the prices of products. It is not unusual for auction sites to take a cut of the revenue made from selling your product. However, it need not be expensive. You can mark-up your product to account for this additional fee.

3. That auctions only attract buyers who are looking for a bargain. This may be true at times. However, it's not always the case. You get the occasional customers who appreciate the value of what you're offering and are willing to bid accordingly

4. That it's very difficult to find good deals in auction sites. If you look hard enough you'll always find good deals.

5. That auction sites are rigged by both the sellers and owners of the site. This is not true. Rigging or Shill bidding is against most website owners terms of service e.g. Ebays would ban you if you're caught in violation of their TOS. That being said, some sellers do engage in shill bidding.

6. That online auctions serve as a last resort for both buyers and sellers. There are other sites where buyers and sellers can transact e.g. Amazon

7. That most of the products being sold in auction sites are either pre-owned or of lower quality. This is not true. You can purchase brand new items from ebay.

8. That auction sites are swindling sellers and buyers with hidden costs and fees. Some are but not all of them. Do your due diligence and understand which features are free and which aren't. Research the auction sites, check their reviews on other independent sites, read forum comments and see what sellers are saying about the auction site. Are they mostly positive or negative etc.

9. That you can't make real money selling in auction sites. You can if you know what you're doing with regards to pricing, finding products at a great discount so you have enough margin for profit when you resell, great list photos and optimized sales pages highlighting the product features/benefits etc.

10. That auction sites are taking most of the profits you make from your sales. They don't take the majority of your money. However, it's not uncommon for auction sites to take about 10-15% of your revenue in fees.

Inspiration #14

"If you really want to do something, you'll find a way. If you don't, you'll find an excuse."

Jim Rohn

Business #14

Cryptocurrency

If you haven't heard about cryptocurrencies, then you have probably been living under a rock for the last decade or so. Just kidding. Cryptocurrencies have taken the online economy by storm. Just a few years ago Bitcoin, the very first digital currency, was introduced to the world. Today, a single Bitcoin is worth more than $6000. Bitcoin was a huge success that other digital currencies like Litecoin and Ethereum were able to rise in value and influence. Now, you can generate a nice income by trading and investing in digital coins.

There are three main ways on how you can make money from cryptocurrencies. One, buy and trade them. There are several cryptocurrency exchanges out there that can facilitate such transactions. Two, you accept cryptocurrencies as payment for specific products and services. And three, you mine your own cryptocurrencies. If you are new in the industry, I suggest that you follow option 1 or 2 or both. Option 3 is just too difficult and/or expensive to pull off these days.

Ratings Based on Our Criteria

A. Simplicity:

Trying to make money from cryptocurrencies if far from being simple. You need to spend time educating yourself on the latest revolution and the intricacies of how they work.

4/10

B. Passivity:

You can make passive income from your Cryptocurrency by lending it to people who will pay you interest on them. There are B2B lending platforms that specialize in helping you lend your Bitcoin e.g. Bitbond, BTCPOP, KIVA etc.

7/10

C. Scalability:

To scale up your earnings, you have to purchase more coins and repeat the steps discussed above.

6/10

D. Competitiveness:

The cryptocurrency industry is already competitive. Expect it to get even more competitive in the coming years as more people warm up to it.

3/10

Tips For Success

1. Learn everything you can about the industry before you jump into the bandwagon.
2. Do your research and determine the differences between popular cryptocurrencies like Bitcoin, Litecoin, and Ethereum.
3. Trade only amounts you can afford to lose and only when you have a clear strategy.
4. For each trade, you must set a clear target level for taking profit and more importantly, a stop-loss level for decreasing losses.

5. Always consider the risks and don't be greedy. Look for the smaller profits that can accumulate into bigger profits down the road.
6. Be aware of the fees that are associated with multiple trade actions.
7. Don't go looking for crashed coins expecting them to rise in value again.
8. Don't put all of your eggs in one basket. Invest in at least two cryptocurrencies.
9. Only use cryptocurrency exchanges that have proven themselves to be secure and reliable.
10. Use an exchange, not a broker. You'll save a lot of money and time this way.

Frequently Asked Questions and Answers

1. What is a cryptocurrency?
   - It's a virtual exchange medium that utilizes cryptography to secure transactions and control the creation of the currencies.

2. Why use cryptocurrency?
   - Cryptocurrencies are well-known for their anonymity and security.

3. How many types of cryptocurrencies are out there today?
   - Estimates show that there are over 900 cryptocurrencies today, most of which are obscure and operate under extreme secrecy.

4. What are the biggest cryptocurrencies that I should invest on?
   - The most widely used digital currencies today are Bitcoin, Ethereum, Litecoin, Zcash, Dash, Ripple, and Monero.

5. How difficult is it to obtain a digital coin?
   - It depends on several factors. But there are basically three ways on how to get one. Purchase it, accept it as payment for goods or services, or mine it.

6. What is cryptocurrency mining?
   - This is a process in which transactions for various forms of cryptocurrency are verified and added to the blockchain digital ledger.

7. What is a cryptocurrency wallet?
   - This is a secure digital wallet used to store, send, and receive digital currency like Bitcoin.

8. When is the right time to sell a digital coin?
   - There's no universally accepted "best time" to sell your cryptocurrency. Suffice it to say, this will depend on your investment strategy i.e. are you investing for the long term or are you a short term trader looking to profit off of temporary fluctuations in cryptocurrency prices. Be that as it may, you may want to consider selling your coin when its value is 25% more than that of when you purchased it.

9. How risky is cryptocurrency trading?
   - Just think of the risks associated with the stock market. The cryptocurrency market is subjected to similar fluctuations and risks.

10. Can I transfer cryptocurrencies across countries?
    - Yes, that's the beauty of digital currencies. They are decentralized.

Myth Busters about Trading Cryptocurrencies

1. That cryptocurrencies are being used by criminals to avoid the law and taxes. With Bitcoin, every single transaction is public, which is not exactly ideal if you are looking to engage in illegal activities.

2. That it's easy to buy and sell digital coins. It's one thing buying and selling digital coins and another thing doing it profitably. To do the later, education is very important.

3. That cryptocurrencies have no real value at all because they aren't backed by anything. The intrinsic value of Bitcoin partly lies in the ability to mine it. It's infrastructure is intentionally set up to reward miners: if more miners attempt to create Bitcoin then it automatically becomes more difficult to profit from the process. Likewise, if fewer miners make the attempt, then it becomes easier to make money this way. A Bitcoin's intrinsic value, therefore, is in the representation of the effort it takes to mine it.

4. That cryptocurrencies always prioritize anonymity.

5. That it's illegal to trade and deal in cryptocurrencies. The legal status of Bitcoin varies substantially from country to country and is still undefined or changing in many of them. Whereas the majority of countries do not make the usage of Bitcoin itself illegal, its status as money varies, with differing regulatory implications.

6. That cryptocurrencies are mere fads that will soon go away. According to investor James Altucher, cryptocurrencies like Bitcoin are here to stay. Mainstream banks will accept Bitcoin, and will start offering storage and software access. They will also create cryptocurrency derivatives – as the CME is about to start doing. Despite the optimism, there will be a massive wipeout, and 95 percent of the alt-coins out there will go away – just like the dot-com bust.

7. That cryptocurrencies are only for tech-savvy hackers. Anyone can invest in cryptocurency if they're willing to educate themselves or, at the very least, partner with people who know what they're doing

8. That bitcoins are associated and connected to organized crime. This is not entirely true. Criminals understand that Bitcoin's blockchain technology can work against them. This is because the digital ledger meticulously records which addresses send and receive transactions, including the exact time and amount – great data to use as evidence.

9. That cryptocurrencies can't be used to purchase real goods and services. This is not true. As cryptocurrencies continue to go mainstream, more and more businesses are accepting it as a means of payment for real goods and services.

10. That cryptocurrencies are all the same. This is not true. Ethereum is backed by a blockchain, much like Bitcoin, but the technology is slightly different and aimed at a specific use case: smart contracts.

Congratulations!

The fourth character of the password required to unlock the business scorecard is letter c.

Inspiration #15

"I cannot give you the formula for success, but I can give you the formula for failure--It is: Try to please everybody."

Herbert Bayard Swope

Business #15

Commodities Trading

Commodities trading can be an effective way to diversify your portfolio. It doesn't matter if you are in it for the short term or for the long haul. Always keep in mind that a commodity market is a market that trades in primary economic sectors rather than manufactured products. Tradable commodities include metals, energy, livestock and meat, and other agricultural products. Commodities trading has a lot of similarities with stock trading. The biggest difference lies in the assets that are being traded. Commodity trading focuses on buying and trading commodities like gold and other precious metals instead of company shares as in stock trading.

However, you should take note that there's a process you need to follow to become a commodities trader. This process varies per country. For example, in the United States, in order to become a licensed commodity trader, you need to register and get licensed by the National Futures Association or NFA. It's advisable that you get in touch with the proper agencies on how you should proceed.

Ratings Based on Our Criteria

A. Simplicity:

To be a successful commodities trader, you need to be ahead of the curve and smart (i.e. have the ability to see the big picture, make sense of macro and micro economic events, policies, regulations etc. and, more importantly, understand how the market will react to them and how to position yourself to profit from such market moves)

6/10

B. Passivity:

Just like in the stock market, a lot of the income you make from commodities trading are passive income. You analyze the situation, establish your position, set your stop loss and wait.

7/10

C. Scalability:

To scale the business, you have to invest in more commodities and/or trade on margin. Note that trading on margin can be very risky but it'll give you more leverage (especially if you know what you're doing).

7/10

D. Competitiveness:

The commodities market is very competitive. You have to compete against both small businessmen and huge corporations (investment banks etc.).

3/10

Tips For Success

1. Seek the help of an expert or a financial consultant before you jump on the bandwagon.

2. Adopt a definite investing plan.
3. Don't trade in too many markets. Chances are your investment strategy will work exceptionally well in either bull or bear markets but not both. Understand when to take action and when to sit on the fence.
4. Don't trade in a market that is too thin i.e. not enough liquidity. These tend to be highly volatile and if you do not have the emotional maturity to tolerate such fluctuations, you may not follow through with your investment strategy.
5. Always start with your own investment and financial goals. Make sure you know how a financial product helps you advance towards your goals.
6. Don't chase a hot tip. When you make an investment, its important you know the reasons for doing it
7. Sell the losers and let the winners ride
8. Never ever overtrade because you might lose all of your capital.
9. Unless you know what you're doing, never add to a losing position because if the position continues to go against you, your account will suffer huge losses especially if you are trading on margin.
10. Focus on the future. The tough part about investing is that we are trying to make informed decisions based on things that have yet to happen. It's important to keep in mind that even though we use past data as an indication of things to come, its what happens in the future that matters most.

Frequently Asked Questions and Answers

1. What does it mean to trade in commodities?
    - To trade commodities involves watching the commodity market and then taking positions based on forecasted trends or arbitrage opportunities.

2. What are the most common commodities being traded?
    - The most commonly traded commodities are crude oil, natural gas, heating oil, sugar, gold, corn, wheat, soybeans, copper, and cotton.

3. How do commodities markets work?
    - The commodities market works just like most markets. It's a physical or virtual marketplace where one can purchase, sell, or trade various commodities.

4. How do I invest in the commodity market?
    - You can do it by investing in commodity-related stocks or you can trade the commodities yourself.

5. How much money does a commodity trader make?
    - It depends on your experience. Traders with less than three years of experience usually have an average base salary of $100,000 to $150,000.

6. How do I get licensed as a commodities trader?
    - It depends on your location and country. Get in touch with the proper agency for further advice.

7. Can I trade commodities online?

- Yes, many online trading platforms allow you to do so.

8. Where can I trade commodities online?
    - Some of the more reputable online trading platforms today include TD Ameritrade, TradeStation, Generic Trade, MB, and Lightspeed.

9. Is it safe to trade commodities online?
    - It's safe as long as you only deal with reliable brokers, companies, and trading platforms.

10. How huge are the risks in trading commodities?
    - Commodities trading is often riskier than stock trading. Always keep that in mind.

Myth Busters about Trading Commodities

1. That commodities trading is for speculators only. Speculators are an important link in the market. However, they work only because someone on the other side of the trade is hedging their risk. These market participants could be hedgers, arbitrageurs etc. They help in efficient price discovery and price-risk management.

2. That understanding the commodities is too difficult for ordinary people. All commodities are globally traded and the demand supply dynamics are widely known and available to the public. So, understanding commodities trading is not complex as long as you're willing to learn.

3. That there is no assurance on quality of commodities delivered. Most exchanges have quality control measures in place to ensure that commodities delivered to their warehouses meet high quality standards.

4. That commodity markets are too volatile. Commodities are no more volatile than stocks if the leverage is removed. Unlike stocks, which can move up to 20 percent in a single session, metal and energy contracts can rise or fall up to 6% in a single day.

5. That commodity markets and exchanges provide fire for inflation.

6. That it's too difficult to earn money through commodities trading. This happens only when market participants do not trade with discipline and fall victim to greed and fear.

7. That commodity trading is only for high net-worth investors and large traders. This is not true. Like any other derivatives market, anybody can trade by paying a small percentage of the total value of the contract.

8. That the delivery of commodities is compulsory. There is compulsory delivery in commodities such as gold. However, an investor cannot take delivery of crude oil and metals, as trade in these two commodities are cash settled.

9. That prices in the commodities market are too easy to manipulate and rig. Most commodities that are traded are produced and consumed across the globe. As such, any person or group of persons cannot easily manipulate prices.

10. That you need a lot of money to get started trading commodities. This is not true as you can wield tremendous leverage trading on margin with little capital.

Inspiration #16

"If you dream it, you can do it."
Walt Disney

Business #16

Make YouTube Videos

YouTube can be a great source of passive income if you have a unique voice and unique content that gets a following on the video-sharing website. Money you earn from your YouTube content is passive income because the videos will keep on earning as long as they are up on the site. There are three major ways on how you can monetize your YouTube videos. One, you sign up with Google Adsense. Two, you directly promote a product or a service on your videos. And three, you promote products in the descriptions of your videos. You can use all three monetization strategies if you want.

Setting up a YouTube channel is free and easy. But if you want to turn it into a source of passive income, you have to approach it like a business. This means you need to do your research and decide on the kind of topics and material that you are going to cover in your channel. You also need to decide what genre your channel will be in. Will you be doing commentary videos, unboxing videos, comedy skits, science videos, tutorials, etc.?

You also need to build your audience first before you monetize your videos. This is going to take some time so you should have long-term goals. Don't expect people to be flocking to your channel after several videos. Sometimes, it takes dozens of good videos to finally get their attention.

Ratings Based on Our Criteria

A. Simplicity:

Shooting and editing videos require a lot of time and a lot of work. This is especially true if you are not that skilled when it comes to video editing. It gets easier with time but maintaining the quality of your videos still requires effort. That being said, the editing process can be outsourced to freelancers who are good at them. This will free up time for you to do what you do best – record quality videos!

6/10

B. Passivity:

If you have an archive of videos, you can earn a good amount of passive income from them. What's especially good about this business model is that videos you filmed and uploaded months or years ago will continue to earn you passive income as long as the ads stay active.

9/10

C. Scalability:

You can scale your passive earnings from your videos by creating not only higher-quality content but also more videos. The math is simple. If you double your output without compromising the quality, you can potentially double your earnings. Furthermore, the world is your oyster as there's no limit to how many people can view your videos and how much you can earn.

9/10

D. Competitiveness:

Competition depends on your niche but whatever niche you are in there are probably dozens of other YouTubers talking about the same topics as you.

Tips For Success

1. Focus on a niche. If you are going to look into the most successful channels on YouTube, most of them are focusing on a specific niche. If you are going to talk about movies, then 99% of your content should be about movies.

2. Make your titles, tags, and descriptions clear and direct to the point. This is one way of getting your videos found within the platform. With the right titles and tags, your video will appear as a recommended video alongside other videos that have the same or similar themes and topics as yours.

3. Use analytics to understand how viewers interact with your videos. YouTube has its own in-built analytics tool that you can use. There you can see where your viewers are coming from, how they are commenting, and which sections of your channel are getting the most attention. Essentially, you figure out what works best and double down on it.

4. Share links to your content in other platforms like Facebook, Twitter, Instagram, and Pinterest. The more you share your videos, the more views you get.

5. Post teasers of your YouTube videos in other video-sharing websites like Vimeo and Facebook. For example, you can cut a 1-minute video from the full video and post it on Facebook. People who enjoyed the video will want more so they end up watching the full video in your YouTube channel.

6. Create an eye-catching thumbnail for your videos. This is a powerful technique because a lot of viewers often pre-judge a video's content by looking at the thumbnail. Eye-catching thumbnails translate to more views for your videos.

7. Collaborate with other YouTube creators in your niche. For example, if you are doing movie reviews, you can collaborate with another movie reviewer to create a double feature review. You leverage each other's influence to build your subscriber list.

8. Try doing live videos on YouTube. The platform has a livestream feature which is a good way to build relationships with your most avid viewers.

9. Develop video series. This is similar to creating a book series. You nurture interest in your content by creating a series wherein your viewers can't help but look forward to the next installment.

10. Commit to a schedule when posting videos. This way, your viewers will know when the next video will be uploaded. If weeks go by without a new video, people will starts unsubscribing.

Frequently Asked Questions and Answers

1. How exactly do I monetize a YouTube video?
   - There are several ways but the three most common monetization methods are as follows. One, you sign up with Google Adsense and activate it in your videos. Two, you promote affiliate products in the description box of your videos. And three, attract brands and businesses that might be willing to sponsor your videos.

2. What is Google Adsense?
   - At least 70% of the people earning money from their YouTube videos earn it through Google Adsense. Google owns both Adsense and YouTube. Adsense delivers the ads that are shown inside and alongside your videos on YouTube. To make money from Adsense, you have to submit an application first. Once you are approved, you connect your Adsense account with your YouTube account. You then activate ads in your videos. That's it.

3. What is vlogging?
   - The term is a shortened version of the phrase "video blogging". The term became very popular with the rise of video bloggers using YouTube. Instead of writing down your content in the case of blogging, you create a video log.

4. How do I sell merchandise like affiliate products on YouTube?
   - There are two major ways on how you can do this. One, you simply talk about a product in one of your videos either in the form of a review or as a recommended product in relation to the topic of the video. You then place in the video's description box a link to where viewers can purchase the product. Two, you can place a link back to your own store in the description of every video you make.

5. How do I get more subscribers on YouTube?
   - Your success as a YouTube content creator or vlogger is often measured by how much subscribers you have. With that said, you should spend a considerable amount of your time and resources in attracting new subscribers. The quality of your content is still your most important tool in getting subscribers. Aside from creating great content, you should also make use of well-known strategies like instructing viewers to subscribe at the end of every video, running contests, and buying ads within YouTube.

6. How do I get my videos to be added in the recommendation bar in YouTube?
   - If you watch a video on YouTube, you can see a list of recommended videos on the right side of your screen. This is a feature that you can exploit to get more views for your own videos. So how do you do it? Well, it's just a matter of using the right titles, tags, and descriptions for your videos. Let's say you have a video about hiking in Alaska. You should make use of clear titles and tags like "hiking",

"Alaska", "mountain climbing", "trekking", "adventure", or "nature" if you want your video to be recommended in the side bar of videos that contain the same themes and topics.

7. Why am I getting a copyright strike on my videos?
   - This is a question that a lot of newbies ask because they are unfamiliar with YouTube's content policies. Generally speaking, you can't use licensed and copyrighted materials in your videos. If you do, you will likely receive a copyright strike. If you get numerous strikes, YouTube can easily and suddenly terminate your account. With that said, avoid using video clips, images, and music that you don't own or don't have any right of using.

8. What is the YouTube Partner Program?
   - This is the advertising program by Google that allows vloggers and content creators in YouTube to earn money from their videos. It enables creators to have ads served on their videos. Before you can be in the program, you have to apply first through your account in the Creator Studio.

9. What are the requirements of the YouTube Partner Program?
   - In early 2018, YouTube has changed the requirements for eligibility in the YouTube Partner Program. For your channel to be eligible, you should have at least 1,000 subscribers and 4,000 hours of watch time within the past twelve (12) months. YouTube explained that these new rules serve as protection against spammers, impersonators, content thieves, and other bad actors who are ruining YouTube's ecosystem.

10. If I get a strike on a video, is there a way to fix it and make the video monetizable again?
    - Yes, you can always appeal if you receive a strike for a video you uploaded. However, your video wouldn't be reinstated if it's clear that you violated any of YouTube's policies and rules. Your appeal can only be reviewed if none of your content made use of licensed and copyrighted materials.

Myth Busters About Making Money on YouTube

1. That you don't need expertise to attract a following. You don't need to be an expert per se. However, you need to be knowledgeable about something – something you can share with the world, have your own opinion on and add your own unique spin on things.

2. That you can earn hundreds of dollars in your first month. Consistently coming up with quality content and growing a following takes time. This is by no means a get rich quick scheme!

3. That monetizing your videos is easy. Not necessarily, you still need to come up with quality content that'll attract and keep viewers subscribed. You also need to comply with YouTube's terms and conditions

4. That attracting sponsors for your videos is easy. It's only easy if you have a strong bargaining chip i.e. a good following and quality content on your YouTube channel. When you have these in place, businesses will be eager to partner with you.

5. That success in other social media sites like Facebook and Instagram can translate to instant success in YouTube. That's not always the case. Some of these platforms appeal to different demographics and people there consume information in a different way.

6. That product review videos are a thing of the past. On the contrary, these are still going strong. People are always looking to learn more about items they're considering purchasing and most prefer to consume this information via video instead of articles.

7. That unboxing videos are no longer popular. Like product review videos above, these are still popular.

8. That more views equal to more revenue. This isn't always the case.

9. That you can upload a video and watch the revenue roll in. It takes time and consistency to build a following. Once that is in place, you'll begin to see your income grow.

10. That YouTube will shut down sponsored videos in the future. This is doubtful as YouTube, much like Facebook, rely on revenue from ads. Unless they figure out a more profitable way to monetize their platform, sponsored videos aren't going anywhere.

Secret Bonus Offer

Congratulations on getting this far! You are a very motivated person and, seeing as not a lot of people actually bother to read a book once they purchase it (much less read more than 200 pages), you are definitely one in a million! Here's my small reward to you. Go to www.MichaelEzeanaka.com. Navigate to Free Stuff > Ebooks/Audiobooks > Getting Started Online. The password to download the Getting Started Online guide is passive (all lower case letters)

Finally, please kindly leave a review for this book letting me know what you loved about it and which business model in particular resonated with you the most.

Inspiration #17

"A successful man is one who can lay a firm foundation with the bricks that other throw at him."

David Brinkley

Business #17

Social Media Influencer

What is a social media influencer? Think of the Kardashian sisters. Whether you like them or not, they are the very epitome of social media influencers. They have millions of followers in social networking sites like Facebook, Instagram, Twitter, and Snapchat. To be a social media influencer, you must have a sizable following in social media. It doesn't have to be as big as the Kardashians but it should be enough to get the attention of businesses and brands. Your following should be enough to the point that businesses and brands approach you to promote or review a certain product or service.

As a social media influencer, your main source of income will be from businesses and brands that get you to promote and talk about a product. But that's not the only monetization model that you can use. If you have thousands of followers, you can always direct them to another digital asset like a blog where you promote and sell products and services. That's how other social media influencers monetize their following. You can follow the same business model.

For example, let's say that you run a Facebook page with thousands of followers. In the page, you talk about and review beauty products. To earn passive income from your influence, you can tie up a blog with your Facebook page. In the blog, you have more content about the beauty products that you have featured on your Facebook page. Your avid followers and fans will visit your blog with the right promotion. In the blog, you can earn money by promoting affiliate products or by displaying advertisements that are relevant to beauty and makeup.

Ratings Based on Our Criteria

A. Simplicity:

Being a social media influencer takes a lot of time and work. You have to spend time running and managing your social media profiles every single day. If you slow down, you run the risk of losing some of your influence. Like most other business models, this can be simplified by outsourcing the management of these social media accounts to virtual assistants.

8/10

B. Passivity:

This business model is not entirely passive. As I mentioned above, it takes a lot of time and work. Yes, some of your earnings are passive in nature (e.g. earnings from affiliate products, podcasts, webinars, retainer fee from being a brand ambassador etc.) but others earning avenues aren't (e.g. hosting events, doing store appearances, product reviews etc.). How passive this is for you will depend on which avenue you leverage the most and how successful you are at outsourcing those tasks that aren't so important e.g. managing your social media account, editing your videos etc.

7/10

C. Scalability:

The only way to scale your earnings in this business is to increase your influence. That means you have to attract more likes, more followers, more subscribers, and more loyal fans. Networking and collaborating with other influencers can also help you achieve this.

6/10

D. **Competitiveness:**

It can be difficult to maintain your influence on a social media platform given the fact that there are probably thousands of other people trying to get to where you are.

3/10

Tips For Success

1. Find your focus. In order to transform yourself into an influencer, you must be a master in a specific topic or niche. In short, please don't cast your net too wide.

2. Subscribe to other platforms blogs so that you are in the loop when changes are implemented. For example, what if Instagram introduces a new feature? If you are not in the loop, it will probably be too late before you start using the new feature.

3. Set alerts for topics and keywords in your niche. As a social media influencer, your followers expect you to be updated about the latest happenings in your niche. You can use Google Alerts to track the latest developments in your niche.

4. Write a blog and tie it up with your social media accounts. If you are popular in Instagram, that doesn't mean it's unnecessary for you to start a blog. In fact, you can direct more potential followers to your Instagram account through your blog.

5. Get on LinkedIn. Many people dismiss LinkedIn but it can be a very powerful tool to connect you with the right people at the right time. It's a great place to find business partners and collaborators.

6. Engage with your fans and followers whenever you can. Try to reply to as many comments and messages as you can. A single reply can make the difference between a disgruntled fan and a lifelong fan.

7. Always keep it real. It's getting easier to spot bullshit on the internet so don't ever think of lying to or misleading your followers. One lie can ruin everything that you've worked for.

8. Collaborate with other social media influencers. Popular online celebrities do this all the time and after every collaboration, there's always a significant boost in their subscribers and fans.

9. Have a sense of humor. Funny sells. That's a fact. Again, if you look into the most popular social media influencers online, majority of them are popular because they are funny. If you can make a person laugh, that person can be easily converted into an avid fan.

10. Run contests and giveaways. This is a tried and tested method of getting a boost in attention. Not only is this a powerful way of engaging with your established fans, it's also a powerful way to attract new fans.

Frequently Asked Questions and Answers
1. What is a social media influencer?
   - A social media influencer is someone who has a following on a social media platform.

2. What is influencer marketing?
   - This is the practice of hiring online influencers to promote products and services to their followers and fans.

3. How do social media influencers make money?
   - There are several ways. They can be paid by sponsors. They can earn money from their own blogs and websites. Sometimes, fans can even pay them directly e.g. via Patreon.

4. What's the difference between an influencer and a brand ambassador?
   - The two are very similar. The biggest differences lie in the kind of work they do and how they are compensated.

5. How do I qualify as a social media influencer?
   - There are no written rules on what separates an influencer from the rest. All you need is a good following online. You are an influencer if there are people following you and your every move.

6. Which social media sites are the best platforms for social media influencers?
   - So far, the most popular influencers are concentrated in just a few platforms which include Facebook, Instagram, YouTube, and Twitter.

7. How do I reach out to brands who might want to partner with me as an influencer?
   - Just directly contact them and present your sales pitch. Show them why your following is good for their business. You can either contact the directly via their website, email or LinkedIn.

8. How much should you charge for your services as an influencer?
   - It depends on various metrics and factors. How many people are following you? How lucrative is your niche? What's your main demographic? Etc.

9. Can you make a full-time income from being a social media influencer alone?
   - It's definitely possible.

10. How do I get paid as a social media influencer?

- You can choose to be paid in cash or with rewards. It depends on your deals with brands and sponsors.

Myth Busters about Being a Social Media Influencer

1. That it's easy to become a social media influencer. Nothing worthwhile is easy at first. It takes time to build your own following

2. That influencer marketing is only for beautiful and attractive people. That's not true. Anyone can become an influencer. As long as you have something to offer be it your knowledge, your lifestyle etc.

3. That you can monetize any social media platform. That may not always be the case. Some are much harder (if at all possible) to monetize e.g. YouTube vs Twitter.

4. That if you have a huge following, brands and sponsors will start reaching out to you. While this can happen, it's not always the case. You still need to reach out to them. Let them know who you are and what you can offer them.

5. That you don't need to spend money to become a social media influencer. You will need to spend money creating content, running ads to your website, YouTube and Facebook page etc.

6. That working with social media personalities is unprofessional. There's nothing unprofessional about working with social media influencers. They are a trusted voice and they help create content, build brand awareness, generate sales etc. Partnering up with them is a no brainer.

7. That the effectiveness of influencer marketing can't be tracked and measured.

8. That influencers will only work with brands if they are compensated in cash. There are other creative ways influencers may want to be compensated e.g. Invitation to events, exclusive access to brand updates and products, all-expenses-paid trips etc.

9. That an influencer's total reach and social follower numbers are more important than audience engagement and relevance. Engagement and relevance are more important. Otherwise, you'll lose a lot of subscribers who feel your content isn't consistent enough or relevant to them.

10. That short-form social content yields the same value as long-form content. It's not that clear cut as this can be platform specific e.g. people on Instagram or Facebook don't expect to consume hour-long videos. However, on YouTube they won't mind.

Inspiration #18

"Many of life's failures are people who did not realize how close they were to success when they gave up."
Thomas Edison

Business #18

Photography – Royalty from Photographs

If you have photography skills, you can earn from your photographs by listing them in stock photography sites. In the simplest of terms, stock photography sites are e-commerce platforms where you can upload high-resolution copies of your photos and have people use them for a fee. For example, let's say that a nature magazine like National Geographic wants to use a wilderness photo you uploaded in a stock photography website. For a fee, the magazine can use your photograph one time (or several times) depending on the terms of agreement. You earn a royalty from the transaction.

You still own the photograph so other magazines, newspapers, online media outlets, businesses, and individuals can use it. You earn a royalty every time a customer downloads and uses your photo. There are numerous stock photography websites out there that you can use. These include Fotolia, Overstock, and ShutterStock. Try signing up with these stock companies and test out their services. Some stock companies are good for certain types of photographs so you should take the time to experiment with them.

Ratings Based on Our Criteria

A. Simplicity:

Earning passive income from stock photographs is simple in the sense that the barriers to entry are low. All you have to do is sign up with stock photography companies and upload your best photos.

9/10

B. Passivity:

As long as a photo of yours is uploaded in a stock photography website, it has the potential to earn you royalties in perpetuity. It doesn't get anymore passive than that!

10/10

C. Scalability:

To scale your earnings from stock photography, you simply increase the quality and number of photos you upload.

9/10

D. Competitiveness:

Unfortunately, given the low barrier to entry, the competition in stock photography is really tough. Pretty much anyone with a camera can become a photographer. Even with just a smartphone, you can take high-quality photos and upload them in stock photography sites.

3/10

Tips For Success

1. License and copyright your photos before you upload them in stock photography websites and agencies. Theft is very rampant in the photography industry. You can't make money from your photos if someone steals it and claims it as his or her own.

2. Focus your attention and efforts on the most reputable stock photography sites. These are Shutterstock, Dreamstime, Fotolia, iStockphoto, and Freedigitalphotos. These have the biggest clientele and marketplace so you have a much better chance of getting sales from them.

3. Create a portfolio of your best photos. You can show off this portfolio in your website, blog, Facebook page, or Instagram page.

4. Submit only your best and most interesting photos. Always keep in mind that if you upload a photo, there's probably hundreds of photos that are similar to it. So make sure that your photo is unique before you hit on the upload button.

5. Keep it simple. Stock photography is not high art. Most of the people and companies looking for photos in stock photography sites are looking for something clear and simple.

6. Don't over-retouch your photos. It's so much easier to spot retouched photos these days. There are even programs and apps that can easily identify retouched photos from the un-retouched ones.

7. Look for a niche and master it. There are hundreds of thousands of professional photographers out there trying to make their mark in stock photography. Needless to say, the competition is very tough. You can make your life easier by finding a niche with less competition and dominating that niche.

8. Make use of descriptive titles and tags when naming and describing your photos. Search engine optimization is very important in helping your photos get found online. Think of yourself as a customer. If you are looking for a particular stock photo, what are the words and phrases that you are going to use to search for it?

9. Learn how to negotiate. This is very important if you are directly communicating with companies or people who want to purchase some of your stock photos. Don't undersell or oversell your work.

10. Invest in high-quality photography gear. If you have better gear, you will be able to shoot better-looking photos. It's as simple as that.

Frequently Asked Questions and Answers

1. What are stock photographs?
   - These are licensed and copyrighted photos that clients can use for a one-time fee.

2. Do I still own the rights to my photographs?
   - Yes, the photographs are still yours. Clients are merely paying you a fee for the chance to them.

3. What are the top stock photography sites?
   - These would be Shutterstock, Fotolia, Dreamstine, Getty Images, and iStock Photo.

4. What are the requirements in uploading photos to these sites?
   - It varies per site so you should read their Terms of Agreement well before joining.

5. Are my photos safe when I upload them in stock sites?
   - There is always the possibility that some people will steal them and use them without your permission.

6. How much can I earn listing my photos in stock sites?
   - It depends on the stock photo agency and their corresponding rates.

7. What kind of photos sell best in stock sites?
   - Go for images that have commercial appeal. These are the kinds of images that are usually used in advertising and in the media.

8. Can I submit my photos to more than one stock site?
   - Yes, you absolutely can. Remember that you own the rights to your photos.

9. What about exclusivity?
   - An exclusivity deal is when you agree to upload your photos in just one stock site. There are obvious benefits to this some of which are earning a higher royalty, higher upload limit, higher ranking in search engines, showcasing your work on the websites homepage etc. However, there are disadvantages too, like the fact you cannot sell it anywhere else (and in many cases not even on your own website), higher selling price of your image (even if your image cannot be purchased anywhere else, will a customer be happy to pay more for it? If its top quality, probably yes. But that's a big if)

10. Do I need a model release for photos that feature recognizable people?
    - Yes. All photos containing recognizable faces require a model release.

Myth Busters about Stock Photography

1. That you don't need stock photography because you can just Google for images. Unless you're willing to entertain potential legal issues, you'll do well to steer clear of images from Google that aren't labeled for reuse.

2. That stock photography is available to everyone so everyone ends up with similar images. If you spend time brainstorming concepts and reviewing your model choices, medium and color schemes, it's highly unlikely you'll have the exact same image as someone else.

3. That stock photography is too stocky and cheesy. If you follow current trend, you'll have a better understanding of the type of images that are in high demand and one thing is for sure – they're far from stocky.

4. That stock photography is very expensive. This is not always the case. Depositphotos has a flexible plan where images will cost about $1 each.

5. That stock photos are all the same and that they rarely change.

6. That majority of stock images are done by amateurs.

7. That stock images don't always look professional. This is simply not true. The majority of photographers tend to be professional

8. That stock photography lacks authenticity. This is not always the case. That being said, Stock photography is always evolving. The majority of photographers understand this movement and are edging closer to more authentic photography

9. That stock images are homogenous. No they're not. If you're not finding the images you want, it's a matter of being more specific and creative with keywords.

10. That stock images are blatant knock-offs.

Inspiration #19

"Don't be distracted by criticism. Remember--the only taste of success some people get is to take a bite out of you."

Zig Ziglar

Business #19

Real Estate - REITS

Investing in real estate is one of the purest ways of generating passive income especially if you plan on accumulating property that you then improve and rent out. Rental income is a common example of passive income. What's great about real estate is that you have numerous options on how to invest in it. You can purchase a property, build a structure upon it, and then rent it out.

To take the hassle out of real estate investing and make it even more passive, you can invest in what is referred to as real estate investment trusts or REITs. Basically, a REIT is a firm that owns, operates, and finances a range of income-producing real estate properties. Examples of properties that a REIT may own and operate include office buildings, apartments, warehouses, hospitals, shopping centers, hotels, motels, and even timberlands.

To invest in REITs, you should look for a REIT whose stocks are publicly traded. Get in touch with a reliable broker who will purchase the shares for you. You can also purchase shares from a non-traded REIT through another broker who deals with offerings by non-traded REITs.

Ratings Based on Our Criteria

A. Simplicity:

Investing in real estate especially in real estate investment trusts can be very complicated. You need to educate yourself to understand how to analyze REITS and make investment decisions. Working with a mentor can fast track this learning process.

5/10

B. Passivity:

What's great about real estate investments is that the vast majority of the earnings you make are passive.

9/10

C. Scalability:

To scale your earnings, you just have to invest in more real estate properties.

7/10

D. Competitiveness:

Real estate is one of the most competitive industries out there.

3/10

Tips For Success

1. Work closely with your accountant to understand the tax implications of REIT investing and how to take advantage of them.

2. Know the different types of REITS. While there are some diversified REITS, most specialize in a single property type. Common REIT specialties include: retail, healthcare, industrial, residential, hotel etc.

3. Know the right metrics to use when evaluating REITS. The first metric you need to learn is funds from operation or FFO, which is the REITS version of "earnings". This metric adds back in property depreciation and makes a few other adjustments to accurately show a REITS income and, therefore, its ability to pay dividends. There are other important metrics you can learn such as debt coverage, net asset value, intrinsic value etc.

4. Understand the risks involved. Interest-rate risk is a big one, as higher interest rates tend to create downward pressure on REIT stock prices.

5. Keep and maintain a good credit report. This comes in handy for a lot of your future investments and will save you a lot of money.

6. Don't over-leverage yourself. You can be very successful for a long time and still go broke if every rental property is mortgaged to the hilt. Find the right balance and a few longer-than-expected vacancies or dips in your cash flow won't be the end of your career.

7. Look for rental properties in emerging neighbourhood. An emerging neighbourhood is a section in a town or city that's attracting moneyed and influential people.

8. Diversify your investments. Investing across a large geographical area will also further diversify your investments and protect your portfolio against the volatility of local markets.

9. Do not overload your portfolio to chase REIT yields.

10. Stick with publicly traded REITs. Non-traded REITs are still good but you have better chances achieving success with their publicly traded counterparts. It's also more appealing in the sense that the market for publically traded REITS are more liquid and offers you quick and easy exit when you need to go to cash.

Frequently Asked Questions and Answers

1. What is an REIT?
   - This is a company that mainly owns income-generating real estate and distributes its earnings to shareholders.

2. What types of REITs are there?
   - REITs are often placed into two categories: equity REITs and mortgage REITs.

3. What kinds of properties do REITs own and operate?

- These include storage facilities, data centers, timberlands, shopping malls, hotels, office buildings, apartment buildings, warehouses, cell towers, family homes, health care facilities, and shopping centers.

4. Can anyone invest in REITs?
   - More or less. Individual investors of all kind are welcome to purchase shares. However, depending on the country, you probably need to be above a certain age to qualify

5. What are the benefits of investing in REITs?
   - They provide high dividends plus the potential for capital appreciation.

6. How much do REITs pay to shareholders?
   - It depends but you must keep note that REITs are mandated by law to pay 90% of their yearly earnings to shareholders.

7. Are returns from REITs taxable?
   - Usually, REITs that distribute 90% of their earnings to shareholders are exempt from paying income taxes. However, we advise you consult your accountant to verify this applies to your specific situation.

8. How do I get started investing in REITs?
   - Get in touch with a broker or a financial consultant. They will guide you along the way.

9. Why should I have REITs in my portfolio?
   - Because it's a great way to diversify your investments and gain exposure to real estate without doing the less appealing tasks like fixing up houses, toilets etc. It has a very high potential to be passive.

10. Are all distributions made by a REIT derived from the REIT's earnings?
    - No. Sometimes, the REIT distributes part of its capital to shareholders.

Myth Busters about Real Estate and REITS

1. All tenants are bad. This is not true. If you learn to carefully review rental applications, check references and previous landlords, verify employment and carefully screen tenants you will end up with good tenants most of the time.

2. That land is unlimited. On the contrary, land is a limited resource and thus very valuable. Even more so is land in a good location.

3. All contractors are thieves. Again, this is not true. The truth is that there are some great reputable contractors who would love to help you rehab some houses. However, they need to be qualified before

they can work on your houses. Make sure they are licensed and insured, have great referrals and be sure to document everything with an iron-clad contract.

4. That the taxman always wants his cut. You always want to pay your tax but you don't have to overpay. This is why its very important you work closely with your accountant and/or lawyer.

5. That it's hard to buy and sell REITs. Knowing when to buy and sell isn't very hard especially when you've educated yourself, you understand the industry and any effect the state of the economy can have on it.

6. That owning a REIT is hard work. It need not be. Doing the initial research to decide on which REITS to invest in can be hard work. However, once that initial hard work is done and you're earning it becomes very passive.

7. That landlords collect monthly income while REIT investors don't. Not all landlords collect monthly income. Some do on a yearly basis.

8. That REITs are restricted to factories, malls, and offices. That's not true. They can also own storage facilities, health care facilities, to name a few.

9. The least expensive estate agent is the best value. The agent to select is always the one with the best experience, local market connections, exceptional negotiating skills and a strong pool of buyers. Those don't tend to come cheap.

10. That only people with business degrees and extensive real estate experience can invest in REITs. Anyone who is willing to learn and understand how the process works can become a successful real estate investor. A degree is not compulsory

---
Inspiration #20

"The secret to success is to do the common things uncommonly well."
John D. Rockefeller Jr.

Business #20

Become a Business Silent Partner

First of all, what is a business silent partner? A silent partner is usually an individual whose involvement in the business is limited to providing capital. He is seldom involved in the management and day-to-day operations of the business. As a partner in the business, the silent partner shares in the income. For example, let's say that a friend of yours is opening a coffee shop. He needs additional capital so he invites you to become a silent partner.

You agree and provide the additional capital with the agreement that you are going to share in the profits. Of course, this is just the tip of the iceberg. The deal between you and your friend can include other factors that may pertain to operations and management. But the bottom line is that your involvement in the business is often limited to providing capital.

Ratings Based on Our Criteria

A. Simplicity:

Becoming a silent partner is quite simple especially if you know and trust the business owner.

7/10

B. Passivity:

Once you recover the capital you infused in the business, every dollar that goes your way is pretty much passive income, as you're not actively exchanging your time for the money.

8/10

C. Scalability:

To scale your earnings, you have to either increase the size/ownership percentage of your current investments or invest in more businesses as a silent partner.

6/10

D. Competitiveness:

If your terms are favorable, there's little or no competition unless there are other people trying to become silent partners with the business owner.

6/10

Tips For Success

1. Only enter into business partnerships with people you trust.
2. Only invest in businesses that you think will be profitable. Don't invest in a business just because you know the owner.
3. Make sure that you understand each other's commitments and responsibilities.
4. Make sure that all the technical aspects of the deal and contract are documented and put into paper.
5. Decide on your percentage share of the profits.

6. Decide if you are going to get a fixed or a flexible percentage share in the profits.
7. Make a provision in the contract that you have the right to request or look into the financial sheets of the business.
8. Stay in touch with the business owner whenever you can.
9. Have the contract checked by your lawyer before you sign it.
10. Keep a separate record of all the contributions you've invested into the business.

Frequently Asked Questions and Answers

1. What is a silent partner?
    - A silent partner is an individual who invests in a business by providing capital but isn't involved in the operation and management of the business.

2. How does a silent partner benefit from the business?
    - He gets a percentage share in the profits of the business.

3. Can a silent partner have a say in the operation and management of the business?
    - The silent partner is rarely involved in these activities but if it's stipulated in the contract that he can get involved, then he has the right to be involved.

4. How much is the percentage share of the silent partner?
    - It depends on what was stipulated in the contract but the share is usually decided upon based on the silent partner's capital contribution.

5. Can a silent partner exit from the business?
    - Yes, as long as it's stipulated in the contract that he has exit options.

6. Does the silent partner also share in the losses?
    - Yes, he shares losses in the same way that he shares in the profits.

7. What are the limitations of being a silent partner?
    - You have very little involvement in the operation and management of the business.

8. Can a silent partner invest more capital in the business after his initial investment?
    - Yes, if it's stipulated in the contract that he can do so.

9. Will the silent partner receive a salary on top of his shares in the profits?
    - It's very rare for silent partners to receive salaries. They usually only share in the profits.

10. Can I be a silent partner in numerous businesses?
    - Yes, there's no law prohibiting you from investing in as many businesses as you can.

Myth Busters about Silent Partners in Business

1. That you need a lot of money to invest in a business as a silent partner. How much you need to invest will depend on the value of the business.

2. That you can't invest as silent partner in several businesses. Such restrictions usually don't exist unless there's a stipulation in a previous partnership contract that demands exclusivity.

3. That being a silent partner is a waste of one's time. On the contrary, partnering with someone can save you a lot of time if you have the money to invest but not the time to get bogged down with the day-to-day operation of a business.

4. That you will lose a lot of money investing as a silent partner. It can go both ways. You can win big as well as lose big. Carefully analyzing the proposal and the business owner's management skills will help reduce the risk of failure and maximize the proportion of your investments that turn out to be profitable.

5. That it's always better to start your own business than invest as a silent partner. This depends on your situation. Like I said earlier, if you have the money to invest but not the time to be hands-on with the business, then this option will most likely suit you.

6. That silent partners have zero say in the operation and management of the business. How much say you have in the management of the business will depend on what's stipulated in the contract between you and the business owner.

7. That silent partners can be easily kicked out of the partnership by the main owner of the business. Again, this depends on the terms of agreement as stipulated in the contract. Make sure to have your lawyer look through the fine print to make sure there're no surprises.

8. That you can't increase your shares in the profits if you're a silent partner. What you can and cannot do will depend on what's stipulated in the contract you signed with the business owner.

9. That you can't renegotiate the stipulations in the original contract. You can if it says so in the contract.

10. That you can't make good money as a silent partner. Your ability to make money will depend on your ability to spot good investment opportunities and your judgment when it comes to partnering with the right people.

Inspiration #21

"I failed my way to success."
Thomas Edison

Business #21

Rent Out Unused Space with AirBnb

If there's unused space in your home or apartment, you can earn extra passive income from it by listing the space on Airbnb. Signing up with Airbnb will take just a few minutes of your time. You have full control on how much you rent out your unused space.

Airbnb offers their services in 191 countries and nearly 90,000 cities. Chances are it's available in your location. However, you should keep in mind that Airbnb gets a cut from the transactions you process through their online marketplace. The company charges a 3% fee that covers the cost of processing the transactions.

Ratings Based on Our Criteria

A. **Simplicity:**

It's quite simple. List your unused space on Airbnb and wait for anyone to rent it.

9/10

B. **Passivity:**

Most of the income you earn from your unused space are passive income.

8/10

C. **Scalability:**

To scale your earnings, you need to find more spaces and properties to rent out.

5/10

D. **Competitiveness:**

It can be very competitive if you live in an urban area that's teeming with tourists and outsiders.

3/10

Tips For Success

1. Prepare the space and make it as comfortable as possible.
2. Provide as many amenities as possible.
3. Take high-quality photos when creating your listing on Airbnb.
4. Encourage your guests to leave reviews and comments.
5. Offer an individualized experience. Talk and interact with your guests.
6. Offer a reasonable price. Don't underprice or overprice your space.
7. Be quick in responding to questions and comments.
8. Make your listing as descriptive and detailed as possible.
9. Be very honest when making your listings. Don't say there's Wi-Fi if there's not.
10. Assure your guests of security. You may be able to command a higher rent if your guests know that when they stay in your space, they'll be safe and that their belongings won't be stolen or anything.

Frequently Asked Questions and Answers

1. How much does Airbnb take from you?
   - Airbnb takes a 3% fee from your transactions.

2. How does payment work on Airbnb?
   - Depends on the payment method. You can either get paid via credit cards, PayPal, Alipay, Postepay, etc.

3. How much money can I earn from Airbnb?
   - If you make $4000 a month from an apartment, your take-home pay is usually half after taking into account the Airbnb fees, utilities and other expenses.

4. How much does it cost to list a space for rent on Airbnb?
   - Creating a listing is free. You only get charged a fee when someone books your space.

5. Is it necessary to ask for a deposit from guests?
   - Most hosts require a security deposit but it's not mandatory.

6. How do I deal with guests who cancel their reservations?
   - You should create a cancellation policy for your listed spaces.

7. Can I list multiple spaces with different hosting policies?
   - Yes you can as long as you are following Airbnb's own listing policies and regulations.

8. What's a cleaning fee?
   - This is a fee that the host collects to help cover incidents incurred during a stay such as broken items, damaged furniture, or unreturned keys.

9. Can you be an Airbnb host even if you are a renter yourself?
   - It's possible but you have to talk to your landlord first to make sure that they are okay with it.

10. What are the responsibilities of an Airbnb host?
    - Deliver the services that you promised in the listing you made on Airbnb.

Myth Busters about Renting Out Space in Airbnb

1. That if you list it, guests will start coming. That's not always the case, you still need to optimize your listings with use quality pictures, earn good reviews, offer competitive rates and promote your listings.

2. That it's very expensive to list a space in Airbnb. Listing is free. You're only charged when your space is booked.

3. That you can earn more from your space if you advertise it yourself and not list it on Airbnb. Taking charge of the advertising or hiring an agent to help you find a client will probably cost you more as opposed to leveraging the Airbnb platform, their global reputation and established database of clients looking to rent etc. all for a small service fee.

4. That it's not secure to transact with strangers on Airbnb. Payments are made on Airbnb via a secure payment system.

5. That the cost of running an Airbnb space is more than the earnings you make from your efforts. That's not the case. Airbnb charges hosts a 3% fee that covers the cost of processing payments

6. That Airbnb has hidden fees you don't know about. In most cases, guests are made aware of all fees, including service charges and taxes, prior to confirming their decision to book a listing.

7. That Airbnb is selling your personal information to other companies. Airbnb may collect your personal information in order to help improve customer service, personalize user experience, to process payment etc. However, its highly unlikely they'll sell that information to other companies without your express permission. That would be against the law.

8. That you can't create multiple listings on Airbnb. If you want to list multiple rooms in your house, you can create a separate listing for each space you have available. Each room will have its own calendar and listing page that should accurately reflect the number of beds and amenities available.

9. That it's illegal to rent out your apartment if you are renting it yourself. The legality of this will depend on the agreement you have with the owner of the house.

10. That the Airbnb service fee is non-refundable. According to information on the Airbnb website, the service fee is refundable up to 3 times per year if you cancel within 48 hours of booking the reservation (as of July 2018)

Inspiration #22

"The only place where success comes before work is in the dictionary."

Vidal Sassoon

Business #22

Invest in a Lending Club

The business model for Lending Club is quite straightforward. There are borrowers who are looking for unsecured loans through the site. As an investor and a lender, you can browse through these loan listings and find those that you would like to lend to. Needless to say, you make money from interest returns.

Investing in Lending Club is a great way to earn passive income if you have cash that you can lend. Interest rates range from 6% to 26% depending on the credit grades assigned to the borrowers requesting for a personal loan. What's great about Lending Club's business model is that you have the freedom to choose the loans you want to invest in.

Ratings Based on Our Criteria

A. Simplicity:

Investing in loan listings in a Lending Club is simple. Just sign up as an investor and start browsing through the loan requests.

8/10

B. Passivity:

Almost 100% of the interest you earn are passive income.

9/10

C. Scalability:

To scale, you simply have to invest in more loan requests.

8/10

D. Competitiveness:

There are thousands of other investors in Lending Club so competition can be tough which can potentially drive down interest rates.

4/10

Tips For Success

1. Since loans are unsecured, defaults are bound to happen so you may want to diversify your account across multiple notes.

2. Keep your account fully invested. As your loans get repaid, your cash reserve will begin to build up. This idle cash earns no interest so you have to keep reinvesting or your overall return will decrease. The easiest way to stay fully invested is to activate Lending Club's Automated Investing tool.

3. Strategically increase the risk in your portfolio. The more risk you take the more return you earn on your invested dollar. However, you will need to choose the level of risk that is appropriate for your risk tolerance. In a bad economy, the unemployment rate goes up, so more borrowers than normal default on their loans. If you're good at tracking the state of the economy, it might be a good idea to take more risk when the economy is doing well and reduce your exposure when key performance indicators (from Bloomberg, Reuters etc.) show that the economy might be struggling.

4. Filter for loans with no previous inquiries.

5. Invest through an IRA. Taxes can have a detrimental effect on peer-to-peer investments. Investing through an IRA (which is essentially a tax free account), will allow you to save more money.

6. Don't be greedy and expose yourself to too much unnecessary risk.

7. Always endeavor to learn from your previous investments (good or bad) in order to understand what strategy is working for you and do more of it or learn from mistakes and avoid them in the future.

8. Take the time to research about a borrower before you grant him/her a loan.

9. Take the borrowers job security into account. When selecting notes to invest in, don't just look at how much money someone makes. Take a look at what the person does for a living and how long they've been doing it. Government employees with a decade of experience are much less likely to experience a bout of unemployment.

10. Pay attention to the reasons for borrowing, as this can often be predictive of default rates. Is the borrower looking to get a loan to cover vacation, weddings, medical costs or home improvements? On average, loans to cover home improvements have an average default rate of 3.5% while those for educational expenses have an average default rate of 5%.

Frequently Asked Questions and Answers

1. How does Lending Club work?
   - Borrowers create loan listings and requests on the site. As an investor, you get to choose which of these loan applications you want to invest in.

2. How do you make money from Lending Club?
   - You earn money through interest in your investments.

3. How do I choose which notes to buy?
   - Consider information like loan grade, purpose, term, debt to income ratio, and credit score.

4. How do I get returns on my capital and interest?

- Whenever monthly payments by borrowers are received and then disbursed by the company.

5. Can I reinvest or withdraw my capital and interest earnings?
    - Yes, any time you want to.

6. How do I withdraw my money?
    - You can withdraw available cash to your bank account any time you like.

7. What if a borrower misses a payment?
    - Lending Club deal with delinquencies. You don't have to do anything.

8. How do I improve returns on my investments?
    - Follow an investing plan to increase your returns while minimizing the risks.

9. Are my earnings taxable?
    - Yes, they are taxable as regular income.

10. Are my investments insured?
    - Your account cash balance is covered by FDIC insurance up to the limits put forth by the FDIC.

Myth Busters about Investing in Lending Club

1. That because the loans are unsecured, there's more risks than returns. You can significantly reduce your risks by diversifying and analyzing notes closely before investing.

2. That investing is only for millionaires. On the contrary, being a millionaire isn't necessary. You can invest as little as $25. All that's required is that you know what you're doing. Seek to educate yourself, work with mentors who are successful peer-to-peer investors, learn from their mistakes and your mistakes.

3. That it's safer to invest $1000 than invest $10,000. Regardless of how much you invest you can lose it all if you invest carelessly (without any education, due diligence etc.)

4. That it's illegal or it's within the confines of a grey market. Peer-to-peer lending platforms are not illegal

5. That the company doesn't have a clear business model. The company has a clear business model which you can find on their website

6. That the company doesn't care about its lenders. The company has been around since 2007. It definitely wouldn't survive that long if it didn't care about its lenders. Part of their commitment is to deliver world class experience to borrowers and investors alike

7. That the returns are too low compared to the risks involved. The more risk you take the more return you can potentially get on your money. Invest strategically (i.e. doing your due diligence, screening notes carefully prior to investing, diversifying your portfolio etc.) and you can potentially get the good returns while not risking too much.

8. That you are always better off investing your money somewhere else. That's not always the case. Sometimes, you can find better ROI opportunities on peer-to-peer platforms than other places.

9. That online loan applications are confusing and too complicated. Lending Club has made significant progress with regards to simplifying this process.

10. That borrowers need high credit scores to be approved. Credit scores are not the only criteria when it comes to making lending decisions. Other factors like job security can play a major role.

Inspiration #23

"Keep on going, and the chances are that you will stumble on something, perhaps when you are least expecting it. I never heard of anyone ever stumbling on something sitting down."

Charles F. Kettering

Business #23

Get Cash Back Rewards on Credit Cards

Using a cashback rewards credit card is a nice way to get back a percentage of your purchases. If you do a lot of your shopping online or if you use your credit card often, you should consider making use of one that offers cashback rewards. A cashback is basically a rebate of a percentage of the purchases you make on the card. There are three main types of cashback reward cards. These are category bonus cashback cards, tiered rewards cashback cards, and simple cashback cards.

Ratings Based on Our Criteria

A. Simplicity:

Simply use your cashback reward credit card when you do your shopping.

8/10

B. Passivity:

The rebates you receive from your credit cards can be considered as passive income.

8/10

C. Scalability:

To get more rebates, you need to use your cards more often.

5/10

D. Competitiveness:

There's little or no competition here.

9/10

Tips For Success

1. Align rewards with your interests and goals. For example, if travelling is your thing, you should get a rewards card for airline miles.

2. Make sure that the products and services you are purchasing are covered by your rewards card. Keep in mind that there are always exemptions.

3. Pay attention to the annual fees because cards with the highest rewards often collect the highest annual fees.

4. Skip cards with excess restrictions. An excess restriction means you can no longer earn rewards when you reach a certain amount of purchases.

5. Look for sign-up bonuses. A sign-up bonus can be akin to free money.

6. Use multiple cards if possible. More rewards cards means you have access to more products and services that have cashbacks.

7. Take advantage of bonus offers if these are offered by your credit card provider.

8. Make your purchases through online shopping malls because these often have partnerships with credit card providers.

9. Make the most of bill pay options. Use your credit card to pay for your bills if you get rebates on your payments.

10. Keep your spending in check. Getting more rebates doesn't always mean you are saving or earning money.

Frequently Asked Questions and Answers

1. What is a cashback rewards credit card?
   - This is a credit card that offers rebates on your purchases.

2. Which credit cards have the highest cashback rewards?
   - These would be Discover, Wells Fargo Cash Wise, Citi Double Cash, Chase Freedom, and Capital One Quicksilver One.

3. How does a cashback work?
   - Every time you use the card, you earn a percentage of your purchase in the form of a cashback.

4. Can I keep several cashback cards at the same time?
   - Yes, you can.

5. What stores can I get a cashback?
   - These would include Staples, Rite-Aid, Walgreens, Whole Foods, and Best Buy.

6. Is there such a thing as a 100% cashback?
   - Yes, sometimes credit card companies would offer 100% cashback for certain items and transactions.

7. When do I receive a cashback?
   - Usually during the point of sale or when your points accumulate over time until you get to claim your rewards.

8. Do cashback credit cards come with annual fees?
   - Yes, most of them collect annual dues.

9. Are there any excess restrictions?
   - Some cards stop offering cashbacks when you reach their maximum limitation.

10. How about minimum purchases?
    - Some credit cards also apply their rewards system only when you reach the minimum amount of purchases.

Myth Busters about Using Cashback Credit Cards

1. That credit card rewards are easy to redeem. They can be if you make an effort to always pay attention to the fine print. You need to make sure you fully understand the conditions under which the rewards apply.

2. That pursuing rewards will ruin your credit score. It need not be. When done correctly, the impact on your credit score is minimal.

3. That you are actually paying for those miles. You partially pay for some of the miles since you have to spend to qualify. However, you don't pay for the complete mile.

4. That credit card rewards make travel free. This is true only when used properly. Some people are so good at the credit card game they're able to finance around-the-globe travels almost entirely on points alone.

5. That credit card rewards are not worth the effort. How useful the rewards are to you will depend on your lifestyle. Using cash or debit cards to pay when you could be earning reward points with a credit card means throwing money away – money that adds up over the long haul.

6. That applying for a reward credit card will hurt your credit score. It's true that inquiries stemming from a credit card application can have a negative effect on your credit scores, but in most cases the effect is minimal, and any effect they do have is temporary.

7. That cancelling your credit cards will improve your credit score. Having a good credit score depends on many factors, one of which is the age of your credit history. Cancelling old credit cards can reduce the age of your credit history – negatively impacting your credit score.

8. That earning points and miles is a waste of time. It depends on the person's situation. This type of reward is especially useful for those people who travel a lot.

9. That you can't just apply for a credit card to get the sign-up bonus. You can do this. However, bare in mind this can significantly affect your credit score. Everything you do with credit cards, from applying to closing them, impacts your credit rating. A hard inquiry will be placed on your reports soon after you applied, which would shave a few points from your score.

10. That you can carry a balance and still earn rewards. More often than not, these rewards are conditional on you not carrying a balance. Moreover, paying interest on a credit balance can negate the effect of the reward.

Inspiration #24

"Your time is limited, so don't waste it living someone else's life."
Steve Jobs

Business #24

Create a Comparison Website

If you regularly purchase products online, I'm sure that you've come across a comparison website. A comparison website is sometimes called a comparison shopping engine, shopbot, comparison shopping agent, or price analysis tool. The main function of a comparison website is to offer online shoppers the ability to compare products based on price, reviews, features, and other criteria. What a comparison website usually does is collect and aggregate data from various online shopping sites then present the information in the form of a comparison table.

How does a comparison website make money? Most comparison websites earn through affiliate marketing. If an online shopper clicks on a product link on the comparison website, he gets redirected to Amazon or eBay or any online shopping portal. If the shopper ends up buying the product, the comparison website earns an affiliate commission. As you can see, this business model can be lucrative if your comparison website gets a lot of traffic.

You can create the comparison website yourself. Or you can hire a web developer to do it for you if you don't have the necessary coding and programming skills. Affiliate marketing isn't the only way to make money from a comparison website. You can also earn through advertising and sponsored listings.

Ratings Based on Our Criteria

A. Simplicity:

Creating and maintaining a comparison website can be hard especially if you are not that technically savvy.

5/10

B. Passivity:

Majority of the income you earn from a comparison website is passive income. However, it may require a lot of time commitment since you need to regularly update your comparisons of products – unless you use software to automate this.

7/10

C. Scalability:

To scale your earnings, you need to double the number of entries in your website or you create another one.

7/10

D. Competitiveness:

There are a lot of general comparison websites so competition can be tough. However, you can avoid much of this by going into a specific niche.

4/10

Tips For Success

1. Do your research first before you jump into the fray.
2. You can hire a professional web developer from upwork.com or fiverr.com if you are not a developer yourself.
3. Consider focusing on a specific niche. Most of the competition are general comparison websites.
4. Sign up with as many affiliate programs as you can.
5. Hire freelance writers to regularly create content for your comparison website.
6. Make your website mobile-friendly.
7. Promote your website on major social media platforms.
8. Run contests and promos on social media platforms to attract visitors.
9. Optimize your website for search engines.
10. Set aside a budget for advertising campaigns.

Frequently Asked Questions and Answers

1. What is a comparison website?
    - This is a website that collects and compares products from various online shopping stores.

2. How do comparison websites earn money?
    - Mostly through affiliate marketing.

3. What is affiliate marketing?
    - This is an online marketing model which involves promoting products by other companies and earning commissions from your sales and referrals.

4. Is it difficult to operate and maintain a comparison website?
    - Yes, it can take a lot of your time because you need to regularly update your comparisons of products.

5. How much does it cost to build a comparison website?
    - It depends on factors like the size of the website and if you are hiring a team of developers.

6. Where can I find products to compare in my website?
    - Make use of popular online shopping portals like Amazon, eBay, Walmart, Target, etc.

7. Do I need software to run a comparison website?
    - Yes, you do. You can have the software created by a freelancer or you can purchase software being sold in the market.

8. How much money can I earn from a comparison website?
    - It depends on the size, scope, and popularity of your website. Some comparison websites earn up to six figures a month.

9. Aside from affiliate marketing, are there other ways to monetize a comparison website?
   - Yes, you can use advertising and sponsorships.

10. How do I promote my comparison website?
    - Get active with social media marketing, search engine optimization, and advertising.

Myth Busters about Building a Comparison Website

1. That it's easy to build a comparison website. If you're tech savvy yes. If not, it can be a challenge unless you happen to know a good web developer – but this will cost you.

2. That building a comparison website is not worth it because of the competition. Most business opportunities have competition. You should go in with the mindset to be better than the competition.

3. That you can't create a comparison website if you're not a developer or coder. You can always outsource this to someone who can develop the site for you.

4. That it's very expensive to create a comparison website. How expensive it is will depend on may factors like the complexity of the site, whether you're using a site builder like wix, godaddy, weebly or hiring a web developer, cost of maintenance etc.

5. That it's very difficult to monetize a comparison website. Like I mentioned earlier, you can easily monetize your comparison site with sponsored listings and affiliate products.

6. That affiliate marketing is the only way to monetize a comparison website. You can also use sponsored listings, selling advertising space for banner, display and text ads, inviting third-party suppliers to pay a subscription fee in order to feature on your site etc.

7. That a comparison website is useless because consumers can just compare the products themselves. This can be very time consuming. Comparison sites, by their very nature, are there to make things easier.

8. That you don't need software and apps for a comparison website. You need software to automate some of the processes. Failure to do this erodes the passivity of this business model.

9. That comparison websites don't offer updated and accurate information about products. Sometimes, sites that are updated manually may be guilty of this. However, comparison sites that have been set up to update automatically provide more accurate and reliable information.

10. That comparison websites are manipulating price lists to make money off their visitors. This would be illegal. While we cannot speak for every price comparison site out there, the majority of them make money via the avenues we discussed earlier e.g. affiliate marketing, sponsored listing etc.

Inspiration #25

"Paying attention to simple little things that most men neglect makes a few men rich."
Henry Ford

Business #25

Create a Software Program

If you have skills in programming and coding, you can create your own software program which you then sell to interested buyers. There are numerous ways on how you can monetize your skill as a software programmer. You can offer your services as a freelancer. You can create the program then sell it per download or offer it with a subscription business model. There's a huge market for practical software programs out there. Your clients can be individual entrepreneurs, companies, government agencies, non-profit organizations, educational institutions, gaming companies, and even medical institutions.

The trick to finding a good idea for a profitable software is to look for practical problems out there that are in need of a solution. For example, let's say that you have a hard time organizing the PDF files in your computer. What if you can create a piece of software that allows you to separate them into several categories with just a click of a button? What if you can create a software that enables you to easily access a PDF file by merely entering a keyword into a search bar? In a nutshell, find simple problems that a lot of people have, and try to solve it with a software.

Ratings Based on Our Criteria

    A. **Simplicity:**

        I wouldn't call software programming simple. It's a time-consuming endeavor.

        4/10

    B. **Passivity:**

        Once your software is finished and launched, most of the income you earn from it is passive.

        7/10

    C. **Scalability:**

        To scale the business, you have to create more programs or make your existing programs available on a lot more platforms and to more people.

        7/10

    D. **Competitiveness:**

        The software industry is very competitive. You are up against both freelance programmers and programmers working for million-dollar companies.

        3/10

Tips For Success

1. Work on projects that you are passionate about and have proven demand
2. The software industry evolves at a very fast pace. To stay ahead, you need to continue learning and upgrading your skill set.

3. Connect, network and learn from other programmers.
4. Try to learn as many programming relevant languages as you can. This will help you diversify your options incase one programming language is no longer in high demand
5. Write clean code that you can reuse over and over again and other people will understand.
6. Focus on projects that have commercial value for businesses.
7. Focus on functionality and practicality.
8. Collaborate with other programmers.
9. Do not market yourself with just one specialization.
10. Understand and be updated about current technology trends.

Frequently Asked Questions and Answers
1. What does a software developer do?
    - Their responsibilities include reviewing current systems, maintaining systems, testing software, improving software, and creating software specifications.

2. Who hires software developers?
    - As a software developer, you can work independently as a freelancer or you can work for design and technology firms.

3. Which types of coding languages should you know?
    - The most common programming languages include C++, Java, Visual Basic, PHP/MySQL, HTML, CSS, and Ruby on Rails.

4. How to increase your chances of getting hired?
    - Get as much experience as you can to improve your portfolio.

5. Where can I find jobs for software developers?
    - There are numerous online job sites that you can use such as Freelancer, Odesk, Fiverr, Upwork and Craigslist.

6. How much does a freelance software developer earns?
    - It depends. A large number of freelancers earn up to six figures a year.

7. How competitive is the demand for software developers?
    - It can be tough so you need to get a lot of experience so you can show a better portfolio and resume.

8. How do I market myself as a software developer?
    - Follow basic online marketing strategies like search engine optimization, social media marketing, content marketing, advertising, etc.

9. Do I need to create an online portfolio?

- Yes, you have to.

10. Should I have my own website?
    - Yes, a website is a great place for you to talk about your skills and experiences as a software developer.

Myth Busters about Software Development

1. That software development comes with a hefty price tag. You can develop software for a relatively low price. How much you spend will depend on the complexity of the software and/or who you hire to develop it.

2. That software development has a fixed cost and a strict timeframe. There's rarely a fixed cost when it comes to software development. Unexpected things happen and adjustments need to be made. However, since this is rare, your ability to consistently stay on budget and meet a set timeframe will enable you to command a premium price as a developer or software company.

3. That when the software is released, the project is over. You need to take on customer feedback, continually test the software to fix bugs and release updates.

4. That outsourcing solves everything. It doesn't. You still need to make sure you outsource to capable people

5. That outsourcing means compromising quality. There are very talented software developers out there looking for work. The key to developing quality software using freelancers is finding these people.

6. That software development is a predictable process. It is anything but predictable. Problems do occur during the development stage and good entrepreneurs adapt accordingly.

7. That adding more people to the project will speed things up. Quantity doesn't necessarily equate to quality. If you're going to hire more people, you need to make sure they're capable and everyone in the team is well informed with regards to what other people in the team are doing. Effective collaboration is key.

8. That software development is all about coding. It's not. At the end of the day, if you're unable to market the software you develop, you can't sell it.

9. That there is a silver bullet software development methodology. There isn't

10. That adding extra features at any point of the project isn't a big deal. Adding extra features require thorough regression and positive testing to ensure they work as intended. This can have a tremendous effect on the team's ability to meet its deadlines. It's probably better to add features at the beginning of

the development when there's still a lot of time to adjust to setbacks than to add features closer to the deadline.

Inspiration #26

"Formal education will make you a living; self education will make you a fortune."

Jim Rohn

Business #26

Buy and Rent Out Expensive Equipment

Many people are often in need of expensive equipment that they are only going to use once or twice e.g. construction equipment, luxury cars for wedding etc. So buying the equipment is often out of the question. They would rather rent than purchase. This is where you enter the picture by creating an equipment rental business. The business model is simple. You purchase expensive equipment and put them up for rent. You can do this both offline and online.

The biggest drawback of starting an equipment rental business is that you are going to need a large capital. A single piece of equipment can cost you a few thousand dollars. Imagine if you get a dozen or so of them. And of course, with a large capital, it's going to take you some time to recover the costs of purchasing the equipment. That said, if you want to be in the equipment rental business, make sure that you are in it for the long haul.

Ratings Based on Our Criteria

A. **Simplicity:**

The business model is simple but running the business can be hard and time-consuming. Besides the formalities of starting any business, a rental business has extra insurance liabilities. Your entire business depends on non-employees interacting with your equipment.

6/10

B. **Passivity:**

For the first months or years, you will be earning back the costs of the equipment. Once that is completed, your earnings become passive income.

7/10

C. **Scalability:**

To scale the business, you need to purchase more equipment to rent out.

6/10

D. **Competitiveness:**

This is fairly location dependent. Situate your business in a place that has little or no equipment rental businesses to compete with and you'll do well. Otherwise, it'll be a struggle. Furthermore, you can minimize competition by niching down i.e. focusing on specific or unpopular equipments that still have proven demand.

5/10

Tips For Success

1. Study your market. Before you get started, make sure you know what your customers are looking for. What kind of equipment are they looking for – budget or high-end? How much are they willing to pay? Do they need more than rentals i.e. any add-on services?
2. Don't buy more, buy smarter. Avoid idle inventory at all cost – it only takes up space and money that you could use to grow your business.
3. Find the best deal for your equipment. Can you buy used equipments?
4. Get your paperwork in order. Make sure you have the right insurance.
5. Stake your claim online. It's vital that you have an online presence.
6. Create partnerships. What other products or services are your customers looking for? Contact the companies that offer these services and ask them if they would be interested in a referral partnership
7. Find the right tools for your business. Accounting software, communication tool kit etc.
8. Treat your equipment right. Spot and fix potential problems before your customers do.
9. Treat your customers well. Create a hassle-free experience
10. Create a waterproof agreement. Make sure you and your customers are on the same page

Frequently Asked Questions and Answers

1. How do I get started in the equipment rental business?
    - First of all you need to decide on which kind of equipment you are going to rent out. Get your business plan in place and register it with the proper government agency.

2. How much capital do I need?
    - It depends on the equipment you are going to rent out. Capital can be as low as $30,000 and can be as high as $1 million.

3. How do I collect payments?
    - Payments are usually done in cash, credit card, or check.

4. How much should I charge for the equipment?
    - It depends on the equipment and for how long the customer is going to use it.

5. What if a customer doesn't return an equipment?
    - You should set up policies, regulations, and penalties about overdue and unreturned equipment.

6. How do I promote the business?
    - If it's a local business, try putting out advertisements in the local paper or radio. You can also try promoting your business online especially on social media.

7. How about taxes?
    - Since you are a registered business, you need to pay your taxes.

8. Do I need a partner in the business?
    - Starting an equipment rental business can be costly. You should consider getting partners to help in providing the needed capital.

9. How about insurance?
    - It's important that you insure all of your business equipment as a buffer against disasters.

10. How do I deal with equipment damaged by clients?
    - You need to come up with rules, regulations, and penalties that cover damaged equipment.

Myth Busters about Renting Out Equipment

1. That it's easy to start an equipment rental business. That will depend on your level of expertise going into this business. If you're a complete novice, you'll need to, among other things, conduct adequate research and proper niche selection.

2. That you don't have to buy insurance for your equipment. You absolutely need to if you want to protect yourself from potentially catastrophic losses.

3. That you can only cater to a local clientele. This depends on the nature of the equipment you're renting. While something light and portable could lend itself to a larger market, something big and heavy may not.

4. That it will take years before you start earning profits from the rentals. Your breakeven point will depend on a lot of factors such as how much you invested in purchasing the equipment, how much rent you charge for it, how much you're paying in insurance premium and equipment maintenance etc. Get the balance right and you may breakeven a lot quicker.

5. That it's a waste of time to try and promote the business online. Chances are a lot of your clients will have social media accounts and will spend some time there. Being able to put your offer in front of them will give you an edge over your competitors.

6. That a rental business is not worth the huge capital you need to get started. This depends on how well you've researched the market before going in. Is there demand for the equipment you're looking to purchase? Have you conducted a survey to determine what your ideal customers are willing to pay in rent? Will this rent amount be enough to make you profitable in the long haul? Like any business, if you fail to prepare, you prepare to fail.

7. That the equipment will break down before they even recur their costs. This can be avoided with proper and regular maintenance

8. That you can only rent over a long-term basis. On the contrary, rental terms are very flexible. You can arrange for the terms that suit your situation.

9. That the risks are too high. The inherent risk can be managed if you have the right knowledge. You need to understand what your customers want, the equipment that are in demand, where to locate your business and how to properly insure your equipment.

10. That the equipment rental market is saturated and thus too competitive. With the right location, good customer research and proper niche selection, you can avoid unnecessary competition.

Inspiration #27

"Stopping advertising to save money is like stopping your watch to save time."

Henry Ford

Business #27

Buy an Existing Online Business

Why start a business from scratch when you can just buy one that's already been established? This is the concept behind the idea of scouring the internet for businesses that are up for sale. These are usually online businesses whose owners simply don't have the time in operating and managing them. These can be in the form of authority websites, forums, affiliate sites, membership websites, subscription-based websites, Amazon FBA businesses, and so on and so forth. To find these businesses for sale, you need to search for listings in online marketplaces like Flippa.

Ratings Based on Our Criteria

A. **Simplicity:**

It's definitely much simpler than starting a business from scratch. Online marketplaces like Flippa.com have made it relatively easy to filter out the businesses that match your interest and make a fairly informed purchase decision based on their key performance indicators.

8/10

B. **Passivity:**

Passivity of your earnings will depend on the nature of the business you purchase.

6/10

C. **Scalability:**

To scale the business, you need to buy more businesses or expand your operations.

6/10

D. **Competitiveness:**

The competition for established businesses that are for sale can be tough. You can have a lot of people bidding to have their hands on the same business you're interested in.

4/10

Tips For Success

1. Only buy a business with a good track record.
2. Try to request for a copy of the previous financial statements of the business.
3. Is it an evergreen business? To be an evergreen business, it has to be profitable all year round as opposed to something seasonal.
4. Check out the products and services of the business if they're updated and still saleable.
5. Ask if the business has ever been flagged for illegal or unethical practices. What's the owner's reason for selling?
6. Check and read reviews by former customers of the business.
7. Check all the legal documents associated with the business before you sign the deal.

8. Make sure that the business doesn't have any outstanding debts or payables before you take it over.
9. Only buy businesses in niches and industries that you are familiar with. Or at least consult first with someone knowledgeable about the business.
10. Make improving and growing the business your main objectives.

Myths About Buying An Existing Business

1. That you could never afford it. You'll be surprised that many businesses could be affordable if you're willing to downsize, reel in incredulous spending, and make smart personal and business decisions.

2. That it's too much of a risk. You can minimize the risk by doing your due diligence, hiring the services of professionals (accountants, lawyers etc.) to look over the financials presented by the seller and the agreement fine print to make sure all is in order.

3. That it's too much work. You aren't the first person to purchase a pre-existing business or franchise – many tools for streamlining the process exist.

4. That you don't need to worry about the seller after the sale. Thought must be given to whether a buyer expects a seller to refrain from working in the industry, and to be sure the seller agrees to these terms. Don't just rely on the seller's assurance that they'll retire after the sale. Get that in writing if it's important that they don't end up being your competitor after the sale

---
Inspiration #28

"We are what we repeatedly do. Excellence then is not an act but a habit."

Aristotle

Business #28

License Out Your Smart Ideas and Earn Royalties

Let's say you have a great idea for a gadget which you think has the potential of finding a market. You did your research, you determined that it's an original idea, and you're determined to make money out of it. However, you don't have the money nor the resources to create the gadget and bring it to market yourself. This is where you should consider licensing your idea. In licensing your idea, you are basically renting out your intellectual property.

When you license your idea, there's another player in the transaction called the "licensee". The licensee is the company who has the ability to manufacture your product and bring it to market. They have the money, the tools, the manpower, and the resources that you don't have. They manufacture and distribute your product with the intention of generating profits for all parties involved. The licensee puts a markup on the cost of manufacturing and distributing the product. This is how they earn from the deal. You on the other hand earn royalties from sales of the product.

How do royalty payments work? Your royalty payment is a percentage of the product's wholesale cost. Let's say that the licensee spent $1 to manufacture the product then sold it to the retailer for $3. The retailer then sold the product to a customer for $6. Your royalty will be based on the wholesale cost of $3. If your royalty percentage is 5%, then you earn a royalty of 15 cents for every product sold.

Ratings Based on Our Criteria

A. **Simplicity:**

The business model is easy to understand and follow. As long as you can find a licensee to rent out your ideas, you're good to go.

8/10

B. **Passivity:**

Royalties are purely passive income.

10/10

C. **Scalability:**

To scale, you must come up with more ideas that you license out.

6/10

D. **Competitiveness:**

If your idea is original and/or legally protected, you may face little or no competition. However, bare in mind you might compete with other substitute ideas that are similar but not exactly the same as yours.

5/10

Tips For Success

1. Do extensive research about your idea to make sure that it's truly original. Problems can arise down the road if other people start claiming that the idea is theirs.

2. Find a licensee that fits your product category. If you have an idea for a kitchen gadget, don't bring it to a licensee that specializes in car parts.

3. You should consider working with a licensing agent. A licensing agent is a professional who specializes in connecting idea originators with a proper licensee.

4. Polish your sales pitch before you contact a potential licensee. Make sure that your proposal is flawless before you pick up the phone to set up an appointment.

5. Call the licensee first and talk to someone who deals with sales pitches and product proposals. Don't just barge into the company's headquarters.

6. Come up with a presentation that completely covers all aspects of your product idea. Present sketches of the product, descriptions of the features, the materials they will be made of, etc.

7. Try making a rough prototype of your idea. Studies show that idea proposals with prototypes have higher approvals compared to proposals without a prototype.

8. Follow up with the company after making your pitch. Gather the courage to call them and inquire if they are still interested. Being persistent helps.

9. Create a backup plan. What if the licensee you visit isn't interested in your idea? You should have a list of other potential licensees that you can approach.

10. Negotiate for a higher royalty percentage. If you are confident about the marketability of your idea and you have proof of it e.g. pre-orders, idea goes viral on social media etc., you should request for a higher royalty rate. Sometimes, you just have to ask then fight for it.

Myths About Licensing Your Ideas

1. That licensing is complicated. Although some licensing agreements are complex, the process itself is not complicated. At its most basic level, it requires you to prove your intellectual property works, and then finding a partner to license it.

2. Licensing is a legal process. That's only a small but important part of it. The essence of licensing is really a marketing and sales process. The more you know about marketing, the better your chance of succeeding.

3. Licensing partners are hard to find. Finding the right partner takes time but its not necessarily hard – especially if you know where to look.

Inspiration #29

"What the mind of man can conceive and believe, it can achieve."

Napoleon Hill

Business #29

Invent Something, Have It Patented, and Earn Royalties

In order to profit from your invention, you have to go through the process of patenting it. Whether it's a product, a method, or a device, you need to patent it as soon as possible. Once your patent application has been approved, you will have exclusive property rights over the invention. This prevents competitors from making and selling the product. Patents normally last for twenty (20) years starting from the date you applied for the patent.

After getting the patent, you now have two choices on how to profit from it. You can either sell it or you can license it so that you get to earn recurring royalties. I highly suggest that you choose licensing it because you can profit from your invention for years or even decades. For a better understanding on how you earn royalties by licensing an invention, please refer to entry #28 above (License Out Your Smart Ideas and Earn Royalties). Selling your patent is not advisable because you only profit from your invention once. But if you license it, you earn money from every unit of your invention that gets sold in the market.

Your royalty percentage depends on several factors. Such factors include the following: the novelty of the product, the quality of the patent protection, and the profitability of the product. If you think that you invention passes these factors with flying colors, then you should negotiate for a higher-than-average royalty percentage rate.

Note: For the ratings and tips for this method, please refer to the ratings and tips in the preceding chapter about licensing your smart ideas. The ratings and tips there are basically the same and applicable for this method. Inventing and patenting something boils down to whether you sell it or license it out.

Inspiration #3

"Failure defeat losers, failure inspires winners"

Robert T. Kiyosaki

Business #30

Franchise a Business

If you currently run a business which you think can be easily replicated, then franchising it is something you should consider. What makes a business franchisable? One, it should have a product or service that can be offered anywhere and for any demographic. Two, the operation of the business should be simple enough that it can be easily replicated. And three, the business must be profitable. Because what's the point in franchising a business that's losing money.

The process of franchising your business is a long and arduous one. With that said, I highly recommend that you seek the help of a franchise consultant. A single error in your application papers can cost you dearly. Errors would be minimized if there's a franchise consultant guiding your every move. Last but not the least, you should let your lawyer go over your franchising documents to ensure that everything is right and is in accordance to the law.

Franchising is a powerful strategy on how to grow your business fast. Not only that, you get to utilize the capital of your franchisees instead of putting up your own money. If the process goes well, you and your franchisees share in the earnings.

Ratings Based on Our Criteria

A. Simplicity:

As I said above, the process of franchising a business can be very complicated. There are many hoops that you have to go through.

4/10

B. Passivity:

The cash inflow from franchisees is mostly passive income.

8/10

C. Scalability:

Franchising is quite frankly one of the best ways to scale a business.

9/10

D. Competitiveness:

The franchising industry is teeming with businesses that are looking for franchisees. Expect a lot of competition along the way.

3/10

Tips For Success

1. Create a document that precisely describes how your business works and how it makes money. Your potential franchisees need the exact details and guidelines on how to get their own business running.

2. Hire an attorney. Getting advice from a professional is crucial during the franchising process. Even the smallest mistake can completely put a stop to the process.

3. Be extremely selective when choosing franchisees for your business. It's easy to find people with capital but are they capable of running the business on their own. Your franchise business is at stake here. One bad franchisee can ruin everything.

4. Take a look at the location of the new business before you award a franchise. Logistics is something that you should seriously consider especially if you are just starting to expand into franchising.

5. Always be supportive of your franchisees. The success of your franchisees is also your success. Regularly have some face time with them. Call them often to see how they are doing or if they need help with the business.

6. Build a brand. If you look at the most successful business franchises out there, you will see that they share something in common. All of them are maintaining their own unique brand. They have their own culture, beliefs, and attitudes toward their customers.

7. Get a franchise consultant. This is a person who specializes in helping entrepreneurs go through the franchising process. A franchise consultant knows the ins and outs of the industry.

8. Have a unique and exciting concept. It would be difficult to attract franchisees if your business doesn't offer something that's different from other franchises.

9. Set aside a budget for continuous product and service research and development. You have to keep on improving your products and services if you want to stay sustainable and competitive.

10. Be specific in setting restrictions for your franchisees. You have to make sure that every single one of your franchisees are operating within the bounds of the brand you are trying to build. It's necessary to set up specific instructions and restrictions on hiring, training, and other business practices.

Myths About Franchising

1. It's impossible to fail with a franchise. Every business has the potential to fail. Despite the fact you have a set business system to follow, you still have to implement it correctly. In addition, these systems aren't perfect. Identifying where you can make improvements will ensure the franchise grows stronger.

2. The franchise needs to be something I'm passionate about. This is not always the case. If you love playing tennis and think a franchise in this area is a good idea – think again!

3. Buying a fast-growing franchise is a good idea. You need to think about what it's going to be like running one of these franchises and whether you'll enjoy doing it. Furthermore, a franchise that may be experiencing rapid growth may equally slow down rapidly, and by the time you've invested, it could be too late.

4. A franchise is just a business in a box. You can't just expect to buy a franchise and watch it grow overnight without doing anything. You still need to apply your business skills, have a good understanding of the industry and be dedicated to effectively marketing the business.

Inspiration #31

"Expect the best. Prepare for the worst. Capitalize on what comes."

Zig Ziglar

Business #31

Retail Arbitrage on eBay

Before anything else, we need to clearly define what retail arbitrage means. In retail arbitrage, you simply buy a product from a retail store then resell it at a higher price for a profit. For example, you purchase a piece of clothing from a retail store like Target or Walmart for $10 then list it for sale on eBay for $15. If someone buys it, then you have a $5 profit. Just rinse and repeat.

Retail arbitrage on eBay simply involves purchasing products from various sources (sometimes at a great discount) then listing them for sale on eBay. You can get your products not just from retail stores. You can even purchase products from other eBay sellers then list them for sale on the site. It's basically a process of buying and selling products. To make the most out of retail arbitrage, you need to focus on a niche. Working within a specific niche makes it easier for you to attract repeat customers. They know what types of products you are selling so they are more inclined to visit your store and listings.

Ratings Based on Our Criteria

A. Simplicity:

The business model is really simple. Buy products from retail stores then list them for sale at a profit on eBay.

9/10

B. Passivity:

You are directly selling products the way traditional stores do. So the income you earn is mostly direct income.

5/10

C. Scalability:

You can easily scale the business by adding more products in your eBay store.

8/10

D. Competitiveness:

Competition depends on your niche. For example, there are too many people selling books on eBay. So you might consider targeting a less competitive niche.

4/10

Tips For Success

1. Focus on selling high-quality products. Keep in mind that eBay has its own review and rating system.
2. Understand the costs of selling on eBay before you jump in.
3. Start the bids in the lower margins to attract bargain hunters.
4. Take high-quality photos of the items you are selling.

5. Timing is everything so you should schedule your listings.
6. Make your product descriptions as clear and informative as possible.
7. Promote PayPal as your primary payment option. Many online shoppers are wary about paying through their credit cards.
8. Promote your eBay store in social media (i.e. Facebook, Twitter, and Instagram).
9. Cross-promote your products within eBay.
10. Have a return policy. This is great in building your brand and in nurturing loyal customers.

Myths About Retail Arbitrage

1. That retail arbitrage is too competitive. Every profitable business has a certain degree of competition. To minimize that, you simply need to niche down and provide quality products that will compel customers to be loyal to your brand and become repeat customers.

2. That scaling a retail arbitrage business is difficult. If you leverage the power of social media, you can bring your offers in front of your ideal customers at a cheap price. This will allow you to sell a lot more products without having to increase the number of products you sell. Of course another way to scale would be to add more to your product line.

Inspiration #32

"A goal is a dream with a deadline."

Napoleon Hill

Business #32

Create a Podcast

If you like talking to people, creating a podcast might be something that will fit perfectly into your alley. But what is a podcast? Generally speaking, it is an online version of a radio show or program. But there are a lot of significant differences between a podcast and a radio program. One, a podcast is usually self-produced which means you have to invest in your own gear from microphones, headphones, recorders, and other necessary equipment. You can record your podcast in the comforts of your home or office.

Another great feature of a podcast is that you have the ability to reach anyone in the world. Your potential audience is basically limitless. A sushi waiter in Japan and a millionaire in New York have as much the same chance to listen to you and whatever it is you are talking about in your podcast. This gives you incredible leverage. The biggest podcasters out there today can command millions of listeners per episode. For instance, Joe Rogan of the Joe Rogan Experience podcast says that his podcast gets more than 10 million downloads every episode. That's huge. We are not saying here that you should target the same figures. We are just pointing out the fact that podcasting can be lucrative if you have can build an interesting podcast.

However, the biggest advantage of creating a podcast is that you have the flexibility to talk about anything you want. Unlike in a traditional radio show wherein you have to follow the script provided by a producer or by the station itself, podcasting gives you the freedom to talk about any topic in any way you want. If you are an independent podcaster, you have full control over your podcast.

Starting a podcast is not too difficult. If you have the necessary equipment, you can start right away. The first step you should take is to sign up with an online podcasting platform. There are several companies that offer such a platform. Some are free and some have monthly subscription fees. Needless to say, the paid podcasting platforms offer better services with more features and functions. But if you don't have the budget, you can always start with the free alternatives. In fact, some successful podcasters suggest that you start with the free platforms to test the waters and gain some experience. With this strategy, you get to learn how podcasting works and how you can promote your podcast. You can learn about the ins and outs of the industry this way.

How do you make money from podcasting? There are several monetization methods that you can explore. Some podcasting platforms pay their podcasters based on various metrics. It could be per download or per listen (CPM). You can forego using a podcasting company and record and upload your podcast on your own website or blog. You earn passive income through this method by allowing ads to run on your website. These advertisements can be third-party ads from an ad program like Google Adsense or advertisements from an affiliate marketing company.

You can also earn good income from your podcast by promoting products and services in the podcast itself. For this to work, you must have a decent number of regular listeners so that businesses and brands will be willing to become sponsors. How podcast sponsorship works is quite simple. A company or brand basically pays you to mention or promote their products or services in your podcast. This can be in a per episode basis or the company can sponsor your whole program.

Ratings Based on Our Criteria

    A. Simplicity:

Podcasting is really simple if you consider how easy it is to start one. All you need are the necessary equipment and a distribution platform.

8/10

    B. Passivity:

Most of the money you earn from podcasting will be from sponsors that you directly plug about in your podcast. Initially, some of the income you earn will not be passive in nature since you're exchanging your time for it. However, residual earnings that continue to accrue from episodes you created in the past will be passive.

5/10

    C. Scalability:

There is no other way to scale a podcast than to increase your viewership and acquire more sponsors. Of course, you can consider starting a completely different podcast on top of the current one but this is not advisable at all. It will just divide your time and resources.

5/10

    D. Competitiveness:

There's very little competition in the podcasting arena. It seems that many people are not yet sold on the power of podcasting to attract an audience and create influence online.

5/10

Tips For Success

1. Find your voice and stick to it. Having a unique voice is very important in podcasting. You must have a unique style in talking about your topic to separate yourself from other podcasters. Offer a different way of tackling the topics in your niche.

2. Address questions from your listeners in your podcast. This is a powerful technique in encouraging your listeners to connect and interact with you. Reading and answering questions by your audience live in your podcast creates the impression that you care about them and their thoughts.

3. Do not saturate your podcast with ads and sponsorships. It is understandable that you make some money from your podcast but there should be a good balance between your content and the things you are promoting. If you plug a product or service every several minutes, your listeners will get turned off.

4. Invest in high-quality recording equipment. Low-quality sound will make your listeners think that you do not seem to be serious about your podcast. With that said, you should get good equipment to ensure

that you deliver the best possible sound in your podcast. Having high-quality sound also means listeners can download or even repurpose your audio files without them losing their quality.

5. Create a schedule and stick to it. You have to follow a schedule so that your listeners will know when to tune in. This also allows your listeners to set aside time to listen to your podcast.

6. Find a niche and stick to it. If you look into the most popular podcasts today, you will quickly realize that most of them have niche topics. It's much easier to grow a loyal following if you stick to a specific niche. If it's a general podcast wherein you talk about topics from numerous sources and disciplines, listeners will just come and go. For example, there's very little incentive for a soccer fan to be listening to the next episode if he knows that you won't be talking about soccer.

7. Don't alienate your listeners. As much as possible, stay away from creating controversy. Yes, controversy can easily attract a nice number of new listeners but if it's the type of controversy that can alienate a lot of your listeners, it won't benefit you in the long run.

8. Collaborate with other podcasters. Look for other podcasters who are in the same niche as yours then ask them if they would be willing to collaborate with you for certain episodes. This is a great way to leverage each other's audience. It is a win-win situation for you and the other podcaster.

9. Promote your podcast in social media. Use popular social networking sites like Facebook, Twitter, YouTube, and Instagram. What you do is upload bits or excerpts from your podcast to these social networking sites to give people a taste of what you are offering in your podcast.

10. Reach out to potential sponsors. In this business, you should have the confidence to directly approach brands and ask them if they would be interested in sponsoring your podcast. If you have great content and a good following, brands would be more than happy to talk to you about sponsorships.

Frequently Asked Questions and Answers

1. How much money can I make from a podcast?
   - There are a lot of factors that determine how much you should be earning from your podcast. The biggest factor is of course the monetization model you are using and the average number of listeners you attract per episode. The industry average is that you should be earning between $25 and $50 for 1,000 listeners. This is just a rough estimate.

2. What equipment do I need to start a podcast?
   - Basically, you need the following gadgets: microphone, headphone, pop filter, boom, recording and editing software, ID3 Editor, and a camera.

3. Do podcasts use a lot of data?

- As a rule of thumb, majority of podcasts use approximately 1MB per minute. So a 40-minute podcast will consume around 40MB of data.

4. How do I monetize a podcast?
   - There are several monetization methods that you can explore. These include the following: coaching, affiliate marketing, sponsored segments, courses, advertising, donations, subscriptions, premium content, events, physical products, books, public speaking, and crowdfunding.

Myths About Podcasting

1. That you can't afford a home studio. When you're starting out, It's important to remember you don't need to buy the best of everything. You can easily set up a home studio that can get the job done for under $100 (provided you already have a computer)

2. That you don't have the time. Finding the time to do a podcast required good time management skills but you also want to be honest with yourself about why you want to do it. If your "why" isn't strong enough, you'll struggle to find the time.

3. That you don't have any radio or presenting experience. While its important to know how to use your voice, if you have a genuine passion for your content and want to share it with your listeners, the rest can be taught.

Inspiration #33

"Logic will get you from A to B. Imagination will take you everywhere."

Albert Einstein

Business #33

Start a Deals Newsletter

Before we proceed, it's important that we define what constitutes a deals newsletter. I am assuming that you are familiar with newsletters. These are online subscriptions which deliver to you messages on a certain topic or theme on a daily, weekly, or random basis. To subscribe to these services, you simply input your email address in a form and you'll start receiving messages and updates via email. A deals newsletter works exactly this way. However, the messages that are sent to you are about new deals, promos, discounts, and prizes on certain products and services.

Let's say that you are a customer looking for deals on auto parts. You come across a website that has a deals newsletter on auto parts. You input your email address and subscribe to the newsletter. With that completed, you will be receiving messages about the latest deals and discounts in auto parts in your inbox. That's basically how a deals newsletter works.

You can earn passive income by creating your own deals newsletter. Find a niche and scour the web for the latest deals, discounts, and promos relevant to the niche. Create messages about these deals and send these as a blast to those who subscribed to your deals newsletter. To create the newsletter itself, you need an email delivery service (i.e. MailChimp, Aweber etc.), which automates some of the process. To let people know about the newsletter, you should build a blog or a website that serves as the main entry point for your potential subscribers.

How do you make money from a deals newsletter? There are several monetization methods that you can explore. The top choice would be affiliate marketing. For example, look for the newest deals and promos on Amazon and inform your subscribers about these deals. If people buy products from Amazon through your referrals, you get to earn commissions. You can also do sponsored listing where businesses pay you to promote their offers to your audience.

Ratings Based on Our Criteria

A. Simplicity:

Maintaining a deals newsletter requires a little bit of work because you need to constantly scour the web for the latest deals. However, you can simplify this by hiring freelancers to help you find deals, which you then promote to your audience.

6/10

B. Passivity:

When done correctly, majority of your earnings from promoting deals will be passive.

7/10

C. Scalability:

To scale the business, either you create another newsletter in another niche or you increase the amount of messages you send to subscribers.

6/10

D. **Competitiveness:**

There are numerous deals newsletters out there so expect tough competition.

3/10

Tips For Success

1. Build a blog or a website first before you create a deals newsletter. Use the blog to attract readers which you then entice to sign up with your newsletter.

2. Focus on a niche. You are spreading yourself too thin if you target a general niche. For example, focus in iPhone deals instead of trying to find deals on all brands of smartphones.

3. Use an email automation software like MailChimp or Aweber. These services charge a fee but they're worth it because they take a lot of the burden off your back.

4. Don't exaggerate the deals you are promoting. If the discount in a product is 10%, don't claim that it's 12%. Lying to your subscribers is the easiest way to have them unsubscribe.

5. Offer an incentive for people to subscribe. It could be a free ebook, a piece of software, a free product, etc.

6. Promote your deals newsletter on social media. A quick post on Facebook or Twitter can potentially attract a few dozen subscribers if you have a decent following in your social accounts.

7. Sign up with the largest affiliate marketing companies out there like Amazon, eBay, Commission Junction, ClickBank, Rakuten, etc. These are some of the places where you can find great deals, which you can then refer to your subscribers.

8. Subscribe to other deals newsletters in your niche. This strategy is all about getting scoops from your competitors. It's not unethical at all. It's just business. It's similar to a TV station watching another station to get scoops on the latest news.

9. Try to replicate your success with another newsletter in another niche. This doubles the amount of work you do but it's worth it because you can potentially double your income from your newsletters.

10. Collaborate with other owners of newsletters. The trick here is to collaborate only with those who are in the same niche as yours. You can cross-promote each other's newsletters.

Myths About Deals Newsletters

1. That operating a deals newsletter business is very time consuming. This need not be the case. When you leverage auto responders to automate the email messaging process, hire virtual assistants to scour the web for deals, subscribe to company emails to get notified when they run discount promotions etc. you can free up your time to focus on other things you love doing

2. That a deals newsletter business is hard to monetize. On the contrary, there are many ways to monetize a deals newsletter business. The obvious one is via Affiliate Marketing. However, there are other ways like: sponsored listing, creating courses teaching people how to start their own deals newsletter business, consulting with businesses that want you to help them set up their own deals newsletter etc. You are only limited by how creative you're willing to get with this.

Inspiration #34

"Good ideas come from bad ideas, but only if there are enough of them."

Seth Godin

Business #34

Develop Wordpress Themes

Wordpress remains as the top content management system on the internet. Millions of websites and blogs use the platform because of its open-source management system. Needless to say, there's a huge market demand for all things related to Wordpress. These range from plugins to mobile applications. However, one of the biggest and most in-demand Wordpress-related products are Wordpress themes.

With that said, if you are a skilled and experienced web developer, you should consider creating Wordpress themes and selling them online. Thousands of developers make a full-time income from this endeavour. What's great about creating a Wordpress theme is that you can license it in the sense that people who download and use it have to pay you a fee. There's no limit to the number of people who can download and get your theme. If you create a popular theme, that's easy and recurring money going into your bank account.

Ratings Based on Our Criteria

A. Simplicity:

Developing Wordpress themes is not that difficult if you are a savvy web developer. Alternatively, you can hire someone to develop these themes for you.

7/10

B. Passivity:

Majority of the income you earn from sales of your Wordpress themes are passive in nature.

9/10

C. Scalability:

You can scale your earnings from the themes you created by making even more profitable themes or hiring a team of developers to create themes for you.

9/10

D. Competitiveness:

You will be competing with thousands of other developers who are creating Wordpress themes.

3/10

Tips For Success

1. Always code according to Wordpress standards. It makes customization easier for your users.
2. Always make sure that your code is up to date. Outdated code can cause a lot of problems for your users.
3. Create simple and uncluttered designs. Less is more.
4. Make sure that your theme is compatible with the most popular plugins within the Wordpress community.

5. Make your theme compatible to translation apps and plugins.
6. Always offer support to your users. This is very important considering the fact that you are commercially selling your themes.
7. Regularly perform quality checks of your themes.
8. Create a demo site so that potential users can test and see your theme in action.
9. Create a theme with a responsive design. This means it is compatible not only with laptops and desktop computers but with smart phones and tablets as well.
10. Make your theme easy to customize. Users tend to patronize themes that they can change and modify at a whim.

Myths About Developing Wordpress Themes

1. The more expensive the theme, the better. Generally speaking, paid themes offer you more support, more in-depth documentation than free ones. However, it's not always the case that a $300 Wordpress theme is better than a $50 theme.

2. That you have to pick a theme that looks like everything else on the market. On the contrary, it can be advantageous to be original. This will allow you to create a brand and an loyal audience

3. That Wordpress themes can't be fully edited and personalized. On the contrary, Wordpress offers a variety of options to adapt the selected theme to your branding or strategy.

Inspiration #35

"What do you need to start a business? Three simple things: know your product better than anyone, know your customer, and have a burning desire to succeed."

David Thomas

Business #35

Dividend Investing

Buying stocks that pay dividends can reward you over time if you are smart with your investments. What's great about dividend-paying stocks is that they offer steady payments. This is not to mention the fact that you get the opportunity to reinvest the dividends back in the company to purchase additional shares of stock. Many dividend-paying stocks usually represent enterprises that are considered as financially mature and stable. This means that the prices of the stocks of these companies may steadily increase, giving shareholders periodic dividend payments.

Companies that pay dividends also tend to be more stable and less volatile than the market in general. With that said, they may offer lower risks compared to companies who don't pay dividends and companies who have volatile price movements. Investing in dividend-paying stocks is a great option for young people who want to generate wealth during the long haul or for older adults who want to build a steady source of income during their retirement.

A very important benefit of investing in dividend-paying stocks is the power of compounding. This refers to the practice of generating earnings then reinvesting the earnings back into the business. Dividend compounding happens when you reinvest your dividends to purchase additional shares of stock from the company.

Ratings Based on Our Criteria

A. Simplicity:

You are dealing with shares of stock here so, at the very least, you should be knowledgeable of how the stock market works.

6/10

B. Passivity:

Nearly all of the money you make from dividend stocks are passive income.

8/10

C. Scalability:

To scale your earnings, you either buy more shares or use your dividends to purchase more shares or you can use both methods.

7/10

D. Competitiveness:

There's very little competition in the sense that competitors can't affect how much you earn from your dividend stocks.

6/10

Tips For Success

1. As much as possible, only invest in high-quality firms that have a proven record of growth, stability, and profitability.

2. Choose which stocks to invest in by ranking them based on their dividend histories. If a company's dividend payments have steadily grown for years, then it's probably a good bet.

3. Invest in companies that pay shareholders the most dividends per dollar they invest.

4. Rank stocks based on their dividend yields. Look for companies who have been trading below their 10-year historical average valuation multiple.

5. Don't get fooled by companies that pay out all of their income as dividends to shareholders. This may look good in the short haul but the company has no margin for safety. In short, investing in the company can be too risky.

6. Invest in companies that show a history of steady growth. If a company has maintained its growth for 10 years, the company will likely maintain such growth in the coming years.

7. Invest in the companies that attract people in times of panic and recessions. These companies are usually stable even during hard times.

8. If you can sell your stocks for much more than their worth, you probably should take the money. Get the funds and reinvest them in companies that pay higher dividends.

9. More often than not, when a company reduces its dividends, that's a red flag and you should consider options on how to cash out and exit from the company.

10. Diversify, diversify, and diversify. Spreading your investments is still one of the best strategies in dividend investing.

Myths About Dividend Investing

1. That dividend investing is just for retired people. Admittedly, dividend investing is very attractive for seniors, since typically their investing goals are income generation and capital preservation. However, younger investors also want the benefits from the dividend stocks, even when their portfolio value might not be as big compared to the seniors.

2. That dividend investing are safe forms of investments. Investing in general is risky. There is always the possible risk that you will lose money. However, there are some investments, which include dividend stocks, which have a tendency to be safer compared to others.

Inspiration #36

"The value of an idea lies in the using of it."

Thomas Edison

Business #36

Authority Sites

Before we proceed, it's important that we clearly define what constitutes an authority site. A general definition would go this way: *"An authority site is a website that contains the most valuable content about a particular topic. The content in the site is so good that people knowledgeable in the industry often refer to it or recommend it to their less knowledgeable counterparts."* For example, let's say you want to learn about starting a social media marketing business. Of course, your first step is to find information about it. It so happens that the websites with the best content about social media marketing are Search Engine Land and Social Media Examiner. So these two websites are perfect examples of authority sites.

Here are the core characteristics of an authority website:
- It contains the best content about a particular topic. The content can be in the form of articles, videos, images, infographics, etc.
- It's often cited by people knowledgeable in the field. In our example above, Search Engine Land and Social Media Examiner are often cited by social media marketers and experts. This means that they put a lot of value and respect on the contents of the two websites.
- It has dynamic content. Dynamic content means two things. One, it is always up to date. And two, it is very easy for readers to interact with the content. They can share it and they can copy it and post it in their own digital spaces.
- It is often cited as a source by other websites. For example, if you have a website about martial arts training that is often cited as a source by hundreds of websites about martial arts, then you are an authority site on martial arts training.
- It's frequently updated with new content. In the first place, it's hard to maintain an authority site if its content remains stagnant for long periods of time. The best authority sites are the ones that are regularly updated with new information, new data, new images, and new analysis (for opinionated authority sites).

As you can see, it's not too difficult to create and build an authority site. If a website meets the criteria listed above, then it passes as an authority site. However, in order to build an authority site, you must have patience and a penchant for exhaustive research. Always remember that for you to be considered as an authority in a specific niche, you must be the best at one or many of the following: the best content, the best articles, the best photos, the best videos, the best infographics etc.

The next obvious question now is how do you earn passive income from an authority website? There are several monetization methods that you can use. Most of these methods are discussed in this book. For example, you can use affiliate marketing. You can promote affiliate products in the articles that you post in the authority site. You can also make money through advertising. You can sign up with advertising programs like Google Adsense and display their ads in your site. Or you can deal directly with businesses and companies who want to directly advertise in your website.

Or better yet, you can create your own product or service and use your authority site as your selling platform. For example, let's say that you have an authority site about learning a new language. You can monetize it by creating an ebook or a video tutorial series about tips on how to learn a new language. You can sell these items as downloadable digital products. This is just one of several product ideas that you can explore.

Ratings Based on Our Criteria

    A. Simplicity:

    Building an authority website requires a lot of your time and resources. With that said, it can't be described as a simple business model. It only gets simpler if you decide to outsource most of the content creation and website management responsibilities to online freelancers.

6/10

    B. Passivity:

    Building an authority website can be difficult and time-consuming but the rewards are worth it. Most of the income you earn from it becomes more and more passive in nature as time goes by.

8/10

    C. Scalability:

    Your success in building an authority site can be replicated by building similar websites albeit in different niches. To make your life easier, you should consider hiring freelance writers to create the content that you publish in your authority sites.

9/10

    D. Competitiveness:

    Competition depends on the niche you have entered. However, generally speaking, there's great competition no matter what niche you enter these days.

4/10

Tips For Success

1. Focus on creating great content. High-quality content is the foundation of every authority site. Why would anyone recommend your site if you don't have valuable content? The general rule is that before you publish a piece content in your site, you should first ask yourself the following question: "Is this an article I would gladly share with friends if someone else wrote it?"

2. Create content that can be understood by an Average Joe. Being clear and understandable should be your topmost goal when writing a piece. You created the site to help people understand the subject. You didn't create it to impress people with your amazing prose.

3. Allow people to interact and engage with your content. You may think of yourself as an expert in the topic but there's always space for new or better ideas. Let people comment on your articles. Let them interact with each other. The more they engage in your site, the more attention your site gets.

4. Pay close attention to SEO. Here's something you should be aware of. Majority of authority sites get at least 80% of their traffic from search engines. Getting most of your traffic from search engines means people are voting for your content through backlinks and citations. You can boost this even further by optimizing your content with the right keywords and phrases. If you don't know how to implement SEO, you should start learning about it now.

5. Go beyond what others in your niche are doing. If a competitor is writing 1000-word articles, you should write 2000-word articles. If your competitor interviewed two experts in your niche, you should interview three or four experts. The point here is that you should strive to be always one step ahead of the competition. The moment you start lagging behind, you will slowly lose your reputation as an authority site.

6. Don't over-monetize your authority site. Too much advertisements or too much sales pitches can make you look desperate. It creates the impression that you are merely in the business of making money and nothing more.

7. Be honest and always stay transparent. This is very important if you run an authority site wherein you have to regularly offer your opinion on things. Honesty and transparency also means providing disclosures about the businesses, companies, and other entities that you have dealings with. For example, if a piece of content you published was sponsored by a company, you should disclose that it's a sponsored content.

8. Never stop promoting your site. Be active in social media sites like Facebook, Twitter, LinkedIn, Instagram, and even Pinterest. Never stop engaging with people who might be interested in looking at your content. Run advertising campaigns if you have the budget for it. In short, just keep hustling. Self-promotion is a huge aspect of building an authority site.

9. Build an email list. What you do is create a newsletter and invite visitors of your website to sign up if they want to be notified about the latest updates in your website. If you have amazing content, there's no reason why anyone should refuse to sign up with your newsletter. What's great about building an email list is that it can be automated using the right tools and resources.

10. Ask your readers what they want. Are there any topics they want clarified? What should you write about next? Asking questions is a great way to brainstorm for new ideas. Hell, you should also consider asking your readers to write a guest post for your site.

Myths About Creating An Authority Site

1. That people will come to your site once it's built and has quality content. That's not always the case. While having quality content on your site will attract some readers, you still need to actively promote your site on social media in order to scale it quickly.

2. That it's difficult to monetize authority sites. Well, I think by now we both know that's not true. There are so many ways you can monetize your site and we have already covered much of that when we discussed ways to monetize deals sites.

Congratulations!

The sixth character of the password required to unlock the business scorecard is letter z.

Inspiration #37

"The fastest way to change yourself is to hang out with people who are already the way you want to be."

Reid Hoffman

Business #37

Membership Sites

What is a membership site? This is a website the content of which can only be accessed by registered members. It's similar to a secret online forum, only this time you have to pay a membership fee to gain access to the content. Just think of a gated and exclusive club. To gain access to the entertainment inside the club, you have to pay an entrance fee. That's basically how membership sites work. These sites are filled with valuable content, which you can only access if you register as a member and pay the relevant fees.

How do you earn passive income from a membership site? Aside from the membership fee which you can collect monthly or yearly, you can further monetize the content of the site through various methods like affiliate marketing and advertising. You can also directly sell digital products to your members. Content in membership sites can include PDF files, ebooks, video tutorials, software downloads, webinars, exclusive forums, consultancy services, exclusive chat rooms, etc.

Now to the obvious question: How do you create a membership website? If you are an experienced web developer, you can do it yourself. If you know nothing about coding, you can always hire a freelance developer to get the job done. Additionally, there are numerous tools, resources, and apps out there that you can use to create membership sites with ease. Such tools and apps include MemberPress, Wild Apricot, Digital Access Pass, SubHub, WishList Member, Easy Member Pro, MemberGate, and SiteManPro.

Ratings Based on Our Criteria

A. Simplicity:

Building and maintaining a membership site requires a lot of work. This can be a full-time job especially if the site has a membership count that is in the thousands.

5/10

B. Passivity:

The recurring subscription income you earn may be passive but you have to take into account the immense amount of time and effort that you put into the business. Of course, to make this even more passive, some of the day-to-day management of the site can be outsourced to a virtual assistant manager.

6/10

C. Scalability:

To scale the business, create another membership website.

7/10

D. Competitiveness:

There seems to be a membership site for every conceivable topic these days.

3/10

Tips For Success

1. Take the time to research for a less competitive niche. You have a better chance of achieving success if there aren't already dozens of membership sites in the niche you want to enter.

2. Learn from the best. Check out the services of popular membership sites like Copyblogger, eDiets, and E-Course Lunch Formula.

3. Decide on the type of content you will put in your membership site before you start building it. It's easier to build the site if you know what's going to be published in it.

4. Use tools and apps to make it easier and quicker to build your membership site. We've mentioned some of these tools and apps above (i.e. MemberPress, Wild Apricot, Digital Access Pass, SubHub, etc.)

5. Consider offering a free trial period for new members. This is one of the most effective strategies in attracting new sign-ups for membership sites.

6. Offer a combination of free and paid content in your membership site. This means that all of your members will find something of value in the site.

7. Regularly update and improve the content of your website. If it remains stagnant for too long, that's when people will start cancelling their memberships.

8. Offer a variety of content in your site. Variety translates to enhanced engagement from your members. Put out ebooks, video courses, webinars, podcasts, online conferences, and Q & As. The more, the better.

9. Create a forum inside the site where all members can interact with each other. Building a forum is very effective in encouraging members to be more active in the site.

10. Regularly offer deals, discounts, promos, and contests to reward your members. They'll appreciate your efforts and give them even more reasons to stick around.

Myths About Membership Sites

1. That membership sites are easy money. Sure, membership sites can be a fantastic business to run as your recurring income builds month on month; however that doesn't mean it's easy. Unlike other forms of information products where the customer journey concludes with a purchase; with membership sites that's when your customer journey starts, and your responsibility is to continuously deliver a product that they'll pay for on an ongoing basis.

2. That membership sites are difficult to set up. This may be the case if you're not a web developer. However, in these day and age, this should not stop you. You can learn the basic skills required to build a membership site. Alternatively, you can outsource this process to a freelance web developer from upwork.com or fiverr.com

3. That you need to have all your content ready. This is not always the case. If your membership offers live training, ongoing coaching or is primarily community based, then your product isn't pre-created, static content – it's content that is produced in real-time; so until you have members onboard you're not actually creating any content at all.

Inspiration #38

"There are no secrets to success. It is the result of preparation, hard work, and learning from failure."

Colin Powell

Business #38

Putting Money into High-Yield Savings Accounts

A high-yield savings account is a bank account that earns you a much higher interest rate compared to a traditional savings account. Because of the higher interest rates, these accounts are also sometimes referred to as high-interest rate savings account. A traditional savings account usually yields less than 1% interest rate. High-yield savings accounts have rates that are between 1% and 4%. The difference in rates is quite substantial. Converted to cash, that's real passive income going into your bank account.

You might be asking: How can banks afford such high interest rates for deposits? Well, there's a catch for the bank when you put your money in high-yield savings accounts. For instance, you may have to pay monthly maintenance fees. There may be additional requirements to maintain a minimum balance. Banks also have to protect their interests. However, if you take into account these additional fees and requirements, they don't completely cancel out the extra earnings you generate from your high-yield savings account.

It's worth mentioning here that a lot of the banks offering high-yield savings accounts are internet banks (i.e. Synchrony, Ally, iGoBanking). The main reason internet banks can offer much higher interest rates is because they don't have the burden of spending money on physical branches and on hiring new people.

Ratings Based on Our Criteria

A. Simplicity:

The process of putting money in a bank is in itself very easy. The hard part lies in finding the types of accounts that will earn you the most returns.

8/10

B. Passivity:

The additional interest you earn from high-yield savings accounts are mostly passive income.

9/10

C. Scalability:

To scale, either you put more money into your account or you open more accounts in other banks.

6/10

D. Competitiveness:

You are not competing with anyone when you open a high-yield savings account.

10/10

Tips For Success

1. Always make sure that your high-yield savings account is covered by either the Federal Deposit Insurance Corporation or the National Credit Union Administration.

2. Try to look for an account that doesn't come with additional fees. The high interest rate means nothing if it's cancelled out by the additional fees.

3. Verify if the bank's high-yield savings accounts are truly worth it. To do this, you should read reviews and comments by people who have availed themselves of the accounts.

4. Find out about minimum balance requirements. If you don't meet the minimum balance, you will be charged a fee.

5. Ask if there's a required initial deposit. The general rule is that you should look for banks that offer lower required initial deposits.

6. Don't be fooled by teaser rates. These are rates that banks often advertise for their high-yield savings accounts. Sometimes, these rates are for a particular promo period only which means they only last for a while.

7. Take your time to shop around to look for the best deals.

8. Try internet banks. A lot of internet banks can offer high-yield savings accounts because they don't deal with high overhead costs.

9. Seek the advice of a financial consultant. It's always a good idea to seek recommendations from people knowledgeable about savings accounts.

10. Only put your money in stable and healthy banks. You will deal with less risks.

Inspiration #39

"Don't worry about failure; you only have to be right once."

Drew Houston

Business #39

Rent Out Your Car

Do you have a car that you don't drive most days? Instead of letting it sit idle, why not earn some money by renting it out? This is a business model that several companies have explored in recent years. The business model is straightforward. You sign up with the company, complete your profile, and then create a listing for your car. Your listing should include pertinent information such as the model of your car, its age, when it's available, and how much you charge per hour. Include inside and outside photos of your car. Communication between you and the interested renter depends on the system put forth by the company.

Basically, the set up here is that you list your car in the website and if someone is interested in renting it out, you'll get an alert or a notification. You then talk about how and where the renter can pick up your car. Of course, as the middleman in the transaction, the company gets a percentage cut from your earnings. That's how they make money on their end.

There are several companies that already offer this service. These companies include Turo, GetAround, RelayRides, JustShareIt, and Spride. Although they offer the same service, these companies differ from each other with regards to the way they manage transactions between car owners and renters. You should take the time to review each company's business processes so that you can choose the one appropriate for you.

Ratings Based on Our Criteria

    A. Simplicity:

    The business is very simple. Just sign up with the company offering the service then create a listing for your car.

9/10

    B. Passivity:

    Most of the income you earn are passive income.

8/10

    C. Scalability:

    To scale, you probably need to buy another car but that may not be economically viable.

5/10

    D. Competitiveness:

    This business model hasn't really caught on so you don't have to worry much about competition.

5/10

Tips For Success

1. Choose the right company. So far, the biggest names in the industry are HyreCar, Turo, Drivy, GetAround, and GoGet. Make sure that any of these companies are available in your location before you sign up.

2. Make your listing as descriptive as possible. Include important information like the model of the car, the brand, the color, etc. If there are any problems with the car, include the information in your description as well.

3. Thoroughly clean your car before you offer it for rent. Nobody wants to rent a dirty and smelly car.

4. Post high-quality photos of the car. People judge cars by how they look. If all you have is a grainy photo, no one will bite into your listing.

5. Make sure that the car is working perfectly before you list it to avoid unnecessary problems with both the company and the renters.

6. Give utmost focus to marketing

Inspiration #40

"Our greatest weakness lies in giving up. The most certain way to succeed is always to try just one more time."

Thomas Edison

Business #40

Rent Out Your Clothes

Check out your closet. Are there clothes there in perfect condition that you don't regularly use? What if I told you that you can take them out, offer them for rent to strangers, and earn some extra cash on the side? It's true. There are businesses today that allow you to rent out your unused clothes to complete strangers. Think of these companies as the AirBnb of fashion. Such companies include Glam Corner, Her Wardrobe, The Volte, Designerex, Girl Meets Dress, and Hire My Clothes. Although these businesses have their differences, their business model is similar. They serve as the middlemen between people who have clothes to rent out and those looking to rent them.

For example, let's say you have a lot of clothes that you want to rent out for cash. You sign up with Glam Corner. You take pictures of your unused clothes, upload them on the site, put a rental price on them, and click "create listing". A person wants to rent one of the dresses so she messages you to ask further questions. The customer eventually rents your dress and completes the transaction. To deliver the dress, you either meet up with the client or ship the dress to her residence. That's basically it.

Ratings Based on Our Criteria

A. Simplicity:

The business model is very simple. Sign up, list your clothes, and wait for customers.

9/10

B. Passivity:

You are receiving rental income and you're not actively exchanging your time for it so it's mostly passive income.

9/10

C. Scalability:

To scale, just add more clothes into your inventory and listings.

8/10

D. Competitiveness:

People tend to be squeamish in renting out their clothes to strangers so not many people are doing it. That means less competition for you.

5/10

Tips For Success

1. Provide as much detail in your listing as possible. This is especially important if you are renting out women's clothes. Women naturally ask a lot of questions. You can save a lot of time by describing the piece of clothing in detail.

2. Make sure that all of your items are in good to excellent condition. Even the smallest tear can disappoint a customer.

3. Price your items reasonably. Generally speaking, your rental price should largely depend on the cost of purchasing the clothing.

4. Lingerie and swimwear are a big no-no in clothing rental services. You know why.

5. Only list your best-looking clothes. Just because you have 50 unused dresses doesn't mean you should list all of them. You have to think if there's a demand for them before you put them up for rent. Too many listings can clutter your profile.

Inspiration #41

"Don't play games that you don't understand, even if you see lots of other people making money from them."

Tony Hsieh

Business #41

Rent Out Your Bike

Got a bike that you don't use too often? You should consider renting it out to make some extra cash. I'm not talking about knocking on your neighbor's door and asking if he would like to rent your bike. I'm talking about signing up with a legitimate online company that allows you to list your bike for rent. One of the pioneers of this business model is Spinlister. The company allows you to list your bike on the site. Anyone interested in renting your bike simply books it. You and the renter then talk on how and where he can pick up the bike.

There are several other companies that offer a similar bike rental service. These companies include Bike Sharing World, Bike Share, Travelling Two, Freewheeling France, Bike Bandit, and Liquid. These companies may have differences in their terms of agreement with clients or in the way they manage their business but they follow a similar business model. They all serve as a platform where you can list your bike for rent.

Ratings Based on Our Criteria

A. Simplicity:
Signing up with a bike rental company is easy and hassle-free.
8/10

B. Passivity:
Most of the money you earn are passive income.
8/10

C. Scalability:
To scale, you need to put more bikes to rent out.
6/10

D. Competitiveness:
Competition can be tough in highly populated and urban areas.
4/10

Tips For Success

1. Try including accessories in the deal to entice renters. For example, a helmet or a bike light can come with the bike.
2. Make your listing as descriptive as possible. Include important information like the model of the bike, the brand, the color, etc. If there are any problems with the bike, include the information in your description as well.
3. Thoroughly clean your bike before you offer it for rent. Nobody wants to rent a dirty bike.
4. Post high-quality photos of the bike. People judge bikes by how they look. If all you have is a grainy image of your bike, no one will be interested in renting it.

5. Make sure that the bike is in perfect working condition before you list it to avoid unnecessary problems with both the company and the renters.

Inspiration #42

"Timing, perseverance, and ten years of trying will eventually make you look like an overnight success."

Biz Stone

Business #42

Rent Out Your Garage or Parking Spot

In your neighborhood alone, chances are there's a lot of people looking for empty spaces to park their cars. Either they don't have a garage or they have one but it's not enough for their vehicles. There are two ways on how you can make money from people's parking problems. You can directly deal with the people and charge them rent by the hour or per month depending on how often they intend to use your empty garage or parking spot.

The second option is to use a company or business that connects you with people looking for garages and parking spots to rent. A good example of these companies is JustPark. This company allows you to create listings on their site advertising your empty garage or parking space. You determine how much you want to charge for your garage. Other companies with similar services include Share My Park, Elparking, and Your Parking Space.

There are also a ton of mobile apps that offer similar services. These apps include Parqex, CurbFlip, ParkingCupid, Spothero, ParkingSpotter, Spacer, SpotOn, Pavemint, Park Easier, and Rover.

Ratings Based on Our Criteria

A. Simplicity:

All you have to do is list your empty garage or parking space in any of the sites and apps mentioned above.

8/10

B. Passivity:

Most of the money you earn from this is passive income.

9/10

C. Scalability:

To scale this side business, you need more empty garages and parking spaces.

5/10

D. Competitiveness:

Most of these services haven't really caught on with the public so there's not much competition to worry you.

5/10

Tips For Success

1. List your empty garage or parking spot in more than one site.
2. The description of your spot is crucial. That said, list as many specifics as you can about your parking spot.

3. Find sites that allow you to update your spot's availability quickly so you don't miss out on potential renters.
4. Promote your spot in social media sites like Facebook and Instagram. Always remember that this is a localized business which means most of your clients will be people within your neighborhood.
5. Put restrictions on what renters can park in your parking spot. If you don't have any restrictions, some renters might turn your garage into a storage facility instead of just a parking spot.

Inspiration #43

"Ideas are easy. Implementation is hard."

Guy Kawasaki

Business #43

Get Paid to Watch Videos and TV

If you spend a lot of your time watching videos online, why not try to make money from it. There are actually several companies out there that will pay you just to watch videos and TV. Most of the time you will have to register with an app or sign up with a website where you get access to videos and television programs which you can watch and be compensated for your time in watching them. Below is a quick overview of some of these companies and apps:

- **Viggle App** – This is an app designed for both iOS and Android smartphones. After downloading the app, you get access to a list of videos and television programs which you can watch. You get one point for every minute of time you spend watching the shows. As the points accumulate, you can either encash them or use them to purchase products online.

- **Swagbucks** – You earn bucks by watching videos that range from world news reports, sports highlights, to funny animal videos. You can also earn bucks by taking online surveys and surfing the web. You can redeem your earning through PayPal or exchange them for gift cards.

- **Inbox Dollars** – This is a nice alternative to Swagbucks. Aside from watching videos, Inbox Dollars also pay you to complete surveys, play online games, sign up for promotional offers, and perform web searches.

- **Perk.Tv** – This is a sister site to Viggle. You earn points by watching trending videos, watching movie trailers, answering pop quizzes, shopping online, and downloading new apps.

- **HitBliss** – This service is unique in the sense that you get paid by watching mostly commercial advertisements. The platform even allows you to watch ads using multiple devices.

- **PaidtYouTube** – As the name of the company implies, you earn money by simply watching the YouTube videos that are featured in their site.

These are just some just of the apps and companies that pay you to watch videos and television shows. Other apps and companies that you might want to check out include National Consumer Panel, Slidejoy, Success Bux, Quikrewards, AppNana, Adfun, and SendEarnings.

Ratings Based on Our Criteria

A. Simplicity:

All you have to do is sign up and start watching videos.

9/10

B. Passivity:

You can watch the videos anytime you want.

8/10

C. Scalability:

To scale your earnings, you need to sign up with as many apps and companies as you can.

6/10

D. Competitiveness:

There's actually very little competition in this field.

5/10

Tips For Success

1. Sign up with as many apps as you can manage. More apps means more earnings and rewards.
2. Try using multiple devices if you are allowed to do so. Some apps allow you to sign in simultaneously with more than one devices.
3. Always bring your smartphone with you so you can watch just videos whenever you can.
4. Provide your login details to people you know and trust so they can watch videos using the app as well.
5. Refer the app to people you know. Most get-paid-to-watch apps have a referral program wherein you earn points for your referrals.
6. Focus on the apps that bring you the most money.
7. Subscribe to the newsletters of the app or company. You'll get notifications when there are new videos to watch or new surveys to answer.
8. Follow the social media accounts of the app. You get updates about the latest happenings in the app.
9. Make sure that you have a PayPal account. This is the most common payment method for get-paid-to-watch apps.
10. Log into the app daily. The more videos you watch, the more money and rewards you earn.

Inspiration #44

"I got lucky because I never gave up the search. Are you quitting too soon? Or, are you willing to pursue luck with a vengeance?"

Jill Konrath

Business #44

Vending Machines

Running a vending machine business may look simple but starting it requires planning and hard work. First of all, you need to decide on the machine type and what type of product it dispenses. The most popular and obviously most profitable vending machines are the ones that sell drinks and snacks. This doesn't mean that these are the vending machine types that you should pursue. You can try machines that sells specific products like coffee, popcorn, cigarettes, candies, ice cream, etc. Also keep in mind that some machines dispense individual items while other machines dispense these items in bulk.

In some states in the United States, you need a permit to start operating vending machines. So make sure that you have all the proper licenses before you start installing vending machines in your preferred locations. As to the machines themselves, there are a lot of these in the market that you can purchase. They are ready-made so all you have to do is stock them with the products they were designed to dispense. It's advisable that you get in touch with a supplier who can provide you with more machines should you decide to expand your locations.

Ratings Based on Our Criteria

A. Simplicity:

The process of starting a vending machine business needs a bit of work but once you're established, there much less work to do.

6/10

B. Passivity:

It's passive income but you have to take into account the costs you incur in purchasing supplies and in restocking the machines.

6/10

C. Scalability:

To scale, just add more machines in more strategic locations.

8/10

D. Competitiveness:

The vending machine industry is actually very competitive. Most shopping malls have them.

4/10

Tips For Success

1. Shop around for the best suppliers of vending machines. Only get those machines with a proven track record. Machines that break down too easily will eat away at your earnings.
2. Location, location, and location. The general rule is that you should install your vending machines in places that get a lot of foot traffic.

3. Vend the appropriate products in the appropriate places. It would be senseless to install a soda vending machine in an organic food store.
4. Offer prompt customer service to the establishments where you install your machines.
5. Only deal with reliable suppliers. Make sure that these suppliers are directly connected to the manufacturers of the machines.
6. Always see to it that your machines are restocked. You might need to hire someone who makes the rounds and see if all the machines are stocked and working properly.
7. Buy into a franchise. There are vending machine franchises out there that you can consider. What's good about this strategy is that you are using as leverage an already established business.
8. Test out products to see which ones sell well and which don't.
9. Keep your machines clean.
10. Provide your contact information for the location of your machines so you can be contacted when issues arise.

Myths About Vending Business

1. Running a vending business is easy and requires little effort. That's not always the case. While it is possible to make money with vending as a business, it also takes a good strategic plan as well as hard work on your especially in the beginning. Keeping the machines stocked is your number one key to making sure you have continual sales.

2. The vending machine business is a hands-off business. Not many people understand the level of maintenance that goes into keeping a vending machine in tip-top shape. Let's face it, people that use your vending machines are not going to be gentle, after all, it is not theirs, so many people will be rough with it. They are electronic and these parts can and do wear out.

3. You cannot make a full-time income with a vending machine business. This has been a myth that arose when many people went into the business and purchased too many machines too fast. It is wise to begin with one vending machine, once you start making money with that then look to purchase another. This way you start slow and gradually scale up as your cash flow grows.

Inspiration #45

"You gain strength, courage, and confidence by every experience in which you really stop to look fear in the face. You are able to say to yourself, I lived through this horror. I can take the next thing that comes along. You must do the thing you think you cannot do."

Eleanor Roosevelt

Business #45

Storage Rentals

Owning a self-storage facility is a profitable investment especially today wherein people tend to accumulate stuff that they barely need. More and more people are looking for spaces where they can store their belongings. According to Forbes magazine, the average profit margin for self-storage units and mini-warehouses is 11 percent. This makes them among the most profitable types of small businesses in the United States.

There are so many ways on how you can monetize a storage facility. Some of these ways are as follows:
1. Charge rents
2. Offer tenant insurance
3. Hold auctions
4. Create auxiliary sales opportunities
5. Partner with U-Haul
6. Set up vehicle storage
7. Add vending machines
8. Rent billboard space
9. Offer mail boxes

Needless to say, if you own idle land or space, you should consider building a storage facility over it. There are so many ways on how you can create a revenue stream from it. Although the initial capital needed is substantial, the maintenance cost isn't. Your main expenses will be on security and utilities. Everything else can be considered as miscellaneous expenses.

Ratings Based on Our Criteria

A. Simplicity:

Starting, running, and maintaining a storage facility can be difficult and complicated.

6/10

B. Passivity:

A good portion of the money you earn from operating a storage facility are passive income.

6/10

C. Scalability:

To scale, you need to add more storage rooms or build yet another facility in a separate location.

8/10

D. Competitiveness:

As I said earlier, with more people looking for storage spaces, more entrepreneurs are also starting storage businesses.

4/10

Tips For Success

1. Offer several levels of security for your clients. Hire security guards. Put up CCTV cameras. Do everything to assure the safety of all the items stored in your facility.
2. Train your staff. Train them on how to handle clients, how to handle stored items, and how to handle disasters.
3. Create an atmosphere of accountability within your operation.
4. Advertise your business in local papers, television stations, and radio stations.
5. Set up an online marketing plan that targets people in your area.
6. Offer insurance options to increase level of customer service and satisfaction.
7. Set up a website where potential customers can find all the information they need about your business and your services.
8. Enter into partnerships with other local businesses. Offer them affordable rates in storing their wares and products.
9. Offer discounts for your most loyal customers.
10. Allow potential clients to visit, tour, and check out your storage facility.

Inspiration #46

"The only thing worse than starting something and failing... is not starting something."

Seth Godin

Business #46

Licensing Music

If you have the chops for creating music, you can earn a good amount of passive income by licensing your songs and tracks. You don't have to be Ed Sheeran or Christina Aguilera to make a comfortable living from your music. In this case, we are talking about stock music licensing.

Stock music licensing is very similar to stock photography. The business model is exactly the same. You create the music, license it, and offer it royalty-free for anyone willing to use it. You make money by charging those who are going to use it. The good thing about this business model is that you still own the rights to your music and songs. People or businesses are simply paying you for the privilege of using them in their own content.

Ratings Based on Our Criteria

A. Simplicity:

Although the process of creating music is complicated, selling it through licensing is quite simple.

7/10

B. Passivity:

After licensing your music, majority of the income that comes your way is passive.

8/10

C. Scalability:

If you are a prolific music composer, you can have dozens or even hundreds of tracks licensed.

9/10

D. Competitiveness:

Music licensing can be considered a saturated industry because of the heavy competition.

4/10

Tips For Success

1. Get the levels and formats right. Make sure that your tracks are of the highest quality possible.
2. Only submit the best of your music for licensing especially if you are still trying to get some footing in the industry.
3. When sending your work, include everything that a music supervisor needs to know about your tracks.
4. Build networks and relationships with relevant and influential people in the industry.
5. Be patient. It takes time for people and music supervisors to notice the quality of your work.
6. Always act professionally when dealing with people in the industry. Don't let your ego get the better of you.
7. Always stay in touch with former clients. They might need more of your music down the road.
8. Always keep copies and files of your work.

9. Set up a website where people can hear samples of your work.
10. Never forget to include metadata in your music files. This will help with search engine optimization

---
Inspiration #47

"Anything that is measured and watched, improves."

Bob Parsons

Business #47

Network Marketing

Network marketing has earned a lot of bad press lately because of the unethical and often unscrupulous practices of some of those engaged in the business. However, you should understand that network marketing is in itself a good business opportunity if done right and with high-quality products and services. To be successful in network marketing, you have to be smart in choosing the companies you invest your money in. Don't be blinded by promises of luxury cars and instant riches. You should also familiarize yourself with the tactics of unethical network marketers to make sure that you don't ever fall into one of their traps.

Under network marketing, there are several business models that companies use. But all these models boil down to one or two systems. One, you have to grow your network. And two, you should be able to move products through your network. If you can master these two things, then network marketing is the perfect opportunity for you. Again, I have to remind you that the business models that network marketing companies use vary from company to company. It's important that you read and understand the company's business model before you even think of signing up.

In network marketing, you need to understand a variety of concepts like referrals, downlines, and uplines. It's important that you read the company's business blueprint to understand how they define these terms in the context of their business model. The term referral in one company may have a slightly different connotation in another company.

Top Network Marketing Companies Today Based On Annual Revenue

1. Amway
2. Avon
3. Herbalife
4. Vorwerk
5. Mary Kay
6. Infinitus
7. Perfect
8. Quanjian
9. Natura
10. Tupperware
11. Nu Skin
12. Primerica
13. Joymain
14. Jeunesse
15. Oriflame
16. Ambit Energy
17. New Era
18. USANA
19. Young Living
20. WorldVentures

This list is not exhaustive. There are dozens of other network marketing companies out there that register annual sales that range in the millions. Needless to say, there's money to be made in network marketing. The sheer amount of sales that these companies make every year is just astounding. Obviously, you have a lot of choices. So before you jump into any of them, you should take the time to do your research and weigh your options. The general rule is that you should choose the companies whose products you are actually interested in and you use yourself. It would be easier to sell them and you would be more comfortable pitching them to people you know.

Ratings Based on Our Criteria

A. Simplicity:

The business models being used by network marketing companies may look simple but they are actually complicated once you start implementing them. You have to learn how to crunch numbers. You have to learn how to compute if the money you are pulling out is more than the money you are putting into the business.

7/10

B. Passivity:

What's great about network marketing is that the income you earn become more and more passive as you grow your network. More people in your network means more passive income going to your bank account.

7/10

C. Scalability:

For sure, you can quickly scale your network marketing earnings by joining another company and applying the methods that helped you become successful in the other company.

7/10

D. Competitiveness:

In network marketing, competition is really tough. You must learn how to be patient. Keep in mind that there are thousands of other marketers out there offering the same products and opportunities as you. So you should be creative and smart in your approach. The main question is: "How do you differentiate yourself from the others?"

2/10

Tips For Success

1. Be genuine and ethical. There's so much negativity going on in the network marketing industry right now so a lot of people are wary of joining. That said, you need to play your cards right and focus on helping people understand the positive aspects of network marketing.

2. Don't fake it. This is very important considering the fact that the industry is about building networks of people who trust each other. Don't tell someone that you are earning $1000 a month if you are earning only half of that amount. Don't tell people that you bought a car with your network marketing earnings if it's not true. Please refer to tip #1. Always be genuine and ethical.

3. Leverage the power of social media. Social networking sites like Facebook, Twitter, Instagram, and LinkedIn are great platforms for promoting your business. These sites have a user base that is more than

a billion members. They are free to use so there's absolutely no reason why you shouldn't take advantage of them.

4. Make the business about your network and not about you. The business is about connecting with people and convincing them to be part of your network. This is very hard to do if all you talk about is you. You have to show people that the business is about themselves. That it's about creating better lives for them and their loved ones.

5. Find a company with products that you actually love. Here's something you should understand. It's a lot easier to sell something that you love than something that you have zero interest in.

6. Don't be too aggressive with your marketing tactics. Being too aggressive and intrusive are two of the biggest reasons why network marketing is getting a lot of flak from critics. Take the time to explain to people what the business is all about before you start with your sales pitch. Don't make the impression that you are desperate.

7. Understand your target market and where they are coming from. This is very important if you do most of your marketing and recruiting online. You have to be aware what types of people are more likely to sign up with your business. You have to be aware of where they usually hang out online.

8. Set up your own blog or website. This should be a mandatory strategy for online network marketers. Creating your own website and blog can do wonders for your business. You can use it to attract search engine traffic, which you then try to convert into paying clients. You can also use it to build your personal brand. If you have a personal brand, people are more willing to trust you and your business offers.

9. Always stay in touch with the people in your network and help them out whenever you can. This is very important especially if you are among those on top of the network. Always keep in mind that in network marketing, the success of the group is also your success as an individual.

10. Have patience. If you don't have patience, network marketing can easily burn you out. That's not an exaggeration. Don't go into the business thinking that you are going to get rich quick. Just like any kind of business, achieving success in network marketing requires hard work and a lot of patience.

Frequently Asked Questions and Answers

1. Isn't network marketing a pyramid scheme?
    - To be honest, some businesses out there that proclaim themselves as network marketing companies are actually operating a pyramid scheme. But you shouldn't let this discourage you. There are dozens of legitimate network marketing companies out there. This is why we always advice you to research deeply about a company before you join it.

2. Do I have to know a lot of people to earn money from network marketing?

- No. Of course, it helps if you know many people but majority of the income you are going to earn will come from people you don't personally know. Network marketing isn't about how many people you know. Instead, it's about how good you are in getting people to understand and join your business network.

3. Is network marketing a stable and sustainable business opportunity?
   - In technical terms, yes. If the product or service is good then there will always be a market demanding for it. This is why you should only go with network marketing companies that have a good reputation and a line of products that are in demand.

4. How much will it cost me to get started in network marketing?
   - It depends on the network marketing company you are joining. The membership package can be worth $50 or $100 or $10,000.

5. Is network marketing a passing fad?
   - Network marketing has been around for more than a century. There's absolutely no reason to believe that it will ever go away. Not in the immediate future, that's for sure.

6. Do I need training to get involved in network marketing?
   - A good training will always be valuable before you get started. However, it's often not necessary. Most of the time, all you need is an orientation to introduce you to the business, the business model, the products or services, and what you need to do to make money.

7. How much money can I earn from network marketing?
   - It can be a few hundred dollars a month. It could also be several thousand dollars a week. The point here is that the amount you earn depends on the nature of the company you joined and the amount of hard work you put into the business.

8. What types of products are sold through network marketing?
   - I'm pretty sure that you already have an idea about the types of goods being sold in the industry. To refresh your memory, the most common products in the industry include nutrition products, health care products, consumer durables, and cosmetics.

9. Can I join several network marketing companies at once?
   - Yes, of course. No one is stopping you from joining as many companies as you like as long as this doesn't break any of the terms of agreement of any of the companies you joined.

10. Can I work on network marketing part-time?
    - Yes. This is one of the good attributes of network marketing. Your time can be very flexible. You can work any time you want. You can work a full-time job during weekdays and pursue your network marketing business during the weekends.

Inspiration #48

"Stay self-funded as long as possible."

Garrett Camp

Business #48

Cashback Reward Cards

Most credit card companies offer a cashback reward program where a percentage of the amount people spend on their cards are paid back to them. Credit card companies offer these programs to encourage card holders to use their cards for shopping more often. Rebate percentages often range between 0.5% and 2% of the net expenditures of card holders. Needless to say, taking advantage of these programs benefits you in two main ways. One, you get discounts from products and services you purchase albeit these discounts are deferred. Two, the money going back to your card can be considered as passive income.

Credit card companies are able to pay cash back to card holders because merchants often pay an interchange fee on transactions made through a credit card. For example, when you purchase a television set with your card for $100, only $97 goes to the merchant. The difference of $3 is where the rebates and cashbacks will come from. Not all of it but a percentage of it.

Ratings Based on Our Criteria

    A. Simplicity:

        It's simple in the sense that it doesn't require a lot of work from you.

        8/10

    B. Passivity:

        The rebates and cashbacks you receive are basically passive income.

        8/10

    C. Scalability:

        To scale the rebates, you need to purchase more using your credit card.

        5/10

    D. Competitiveness:

        It's your credit card. You can use it any way you want. There's no competition whatsoever.

        10/10

Tips For Success

1. Align rewards with your interests and goals. For example, if travelling is your thing, you should get a rewards card for airline miles.

2. Make sure that the products and services you are purchasing are covered by your rewards card. Keep in mind that there are always exemptions.

3. Pay attention to the annual fees because cards with the highest rewards often collect the highest annual fees.

4. Skip cards with excess restrictions. An excess restriction means you can no longer earn rewards when you reach a certain amount of purchases.

5. Look for sign-up bonuses. A sign-up bonus basically means free money.

6. Use multiple cards if possible. More rewards cards means you have access to more products and services that have cashbacks.

7. Take advantage of bonus offers if these are offered by your credit card provider.

8. Make your purchases through online shopping malls because these often have partnerships with credit card providers.

9. Make the most of bill pay options. Use your credit card to pay for your bills if you get rebates on your payments.

10. Keep your spending in check. Getting more rebates doesn't always mean you are saving or earning money.

Inspiration #49

"When I'm old and dying, I plan to look back on my life and say 'wow, that was an adventure,' not 'wow, I sure felt safe.'"

Tom Preston-Werner

Business #49

Cashback Sites

A cashback website is basically a reward website that compensates its members by giving them a cut of the money it earned from goods and services that their members purchased through the site's affiliate links. Buying goods and services through a cashback site is called cashback shopping. Technically speaking, you are mostly saving money instead of making money when you use a cashback site. However, some cashback sites offer other services where you can earn some income. Such services may include online surveys and crowdsourcing tasks.

To illustrate how cashback sites operate, I'm going to provide you with a quick example. You sign up with a cashback site and use the site's affiliate links whenever you buy a product online. As you buy more products through the site's affiliate links, your points accumulate. During payday, your points are converted into rewards that you can claim. Cashback sites reward their members using various payment methods. You can be paid in cash (via PayPal, bank transfer, bank check), discounts in other products, or in gift vouchers.

Ratings Based on Our Criteria

A. Simplicity:
You simply sign up with the cashback site and use their affiliate links when you go online shopping.
9/10

B. Passivity:
Aside from saving some money, you get reimbursed for some of your purchases which can be considered as passive income.
7/10

C. Scalability:
To scale your earnings, you need to join as many cashback sites as you can.
6/10

D. Competitiveness:
More members in a cashback site don't necessarily mean there's more competition.
7/10

Tips For Success

1. Join several cashback sites at a time.

2. Regularly clear your computer's cookies. Most cashback sites verify if you have arrived at an online store through their site or through another website. Not clearing your cookies can cause tracking problems.

3. Transfer your money as soon as you reach the minimum payout.

4. Refer your friends to the cashback sites that you are using. In fact, many people make more money from their referrals compared to what they get as cashbacks.

5. Never use incognito mode when using cashback sites. Incognito mode can mess up how your purchases are tracked and recorded.

6. Read the details on the store to make sure that the items you are purchasing qualify for a cashback.

7. Don't surf other websites while shopping online because you might override your cookies without knowing it.

8. Add items to your shopping cart and check out immediately after adding the items. This is to make sure that the cashback site recorded your purchases.

9. Turn off ad blockers in your browser. Again, these blockers can mess with the cashback site's tracking system.

10. If you have several browser windows open, see to it that you make your purchase on the shopping site from the window that was opened through the rebate website.

Inspiration #50

"Success is the sum of small efforts – repeated day in and day out."

Robert Collier

Business #50

Refinance Your Mortgage

I know exactly what you are thinking right now. Can I really earn passive income by refinancing my mortgage? Oh yes, you sure can. Let me explain in brief how this works. Let us say for instance that you are making monthly mortgage payments of $1,500 for your home in the moment. Now, let us say that you can reduce that monthly payment from $1,500 to $1,300 a month through mortgage refinancing. That basically means you will be pocketing the difference of $200 every month. It may not be much but $200 is $200. Technically speaking, that amount can be considered as passive income.

At this point, you might be saying: "But mortgage refinancing isn't free. You have to pay for and settle the closing costs." Yes, you are absolutely right. This is why refinancing your mortgage as a source of passive income only applies to certain situations. If you are planning to live in your home long enough to more than break even, refinancing your mortgage is a great idea. It's worth it.

For illustration purposes, let's say that your closing costs will amount to $6,000. Let's also say that you are going to save at least $300 every month from the refinancing agreement. In this scenario, you are going to break even in a period of twenty (20) months. That's less than two years.

Ratings Based on Our Criteria

A. **Simplicity:**

I would not go as far as to say that this is simple because refinancing a mortgage can be very difficult and arduous. If you are unlucky, you might not even be able to secure a refinancing agreement.

6/10

B. **Passivity:**

The difference between the new interest rates and old interest rates definitely produces passive income.

8/10

C. **Scalability:**

This is almost impossible to scale unless you have more than one home. If you have several homes, you should get into real estate investing instead of trying to make money from refinancing.

1/10

D. **Competitiveness:**

Who would be competing to have your home refinanced? None. So competition in this arena is basically non-existent. You just have to be smart in negotiating your mortgage.

10/10

Tips For Success

1. Prepare your credit profile. This is the first thing that a financial company would look into if you were to shop around for a refinancing deal.

2. Clearly identify your objectives. What's your end goal in refinancing? Is it to take equity or to reduce the monthly payments?

3. Get appraisal. This provides you with a better understanding of how much your home is worth.

4. Go over your application numerous times before submitting it. One mistake can ruin all of your chances.

5. Use rising home prices to your advantage. You might want to consider tapping into your home's equity through a cash-out refinance.

6. Compare APRs, not APYs. When looking around for a deal, you should pay more attention to quoted annual percentage rates (APR) than annual percentage yields (APY).

7. Pick the right length. Just think about how long you want your mortgage to last before you enter into a refinance deal.

8. Don't fall for no-cost refinance offers. There are always costs associated with a refinance deal. The company offering the no-costs deal is either lying or is trying to mislead you.

9. Consider paying points. Sometimes, you can lower your interest rates by paying points. A point is usually equal to 1% of your loan value.

10. Consider a rate lock. A rate lock is when you lock in an interest rate and cost structure with a particular lender regardless of whether the rate change from the period of the rate lock to the closing date.

Frequently Asked Questions and Answers

1. What is a mortgage refinance?
   - Mortgage refinancing is the process of replacing your mortgage(s) on your property with a new mortgage, generally with different terms than the original mortgage. Mortgage refinancing will provide new money to the borrower, and used to pay off the original mortgage, usually with better mortgage terms

2. What is the purpose of refinancing?
   - Common reasons for refinancing include taking advantage of lower interest rates, reducing monthly payments, converting adjustable rates to fixed rates, and choosing to cash-out.

3. How much equity do I need to refinance?
   - It depends on the lender and the type of loan you originally acquired.

4. How much does it cost to refinance?
   - The costs can range from two percent to five percent of the balance of the mortgage.

5. Is it required to have good credit before you can refinance?
   - It depends on the new lender. However, keep in mind that there's an approval process with regards to refinancing. The better your credit status is, the better chances you have in getting a favorable refinancing deal.

6. When should you consider going through mortgage refinancing?
   - It could be any of the following reasons. Your current mortgage has a rate that is above current market rates. You have an adjustable rate and you want to convert it into a fixed rate. You wish to improve cash flow by lowering your monthly payments.

7. How much can I save if I refinance?
   - It depends because very situation is different. There are a lot of factors that must be considered. It's advisable that you seek the help of a financial or loan consultant.

8. Can I really reduce my payments by entering into a mortgage refinancing deal?
   - Yes because you can negotiate for a lower interest rate or for an extended maturity date.

9. Can I refinance if I've had bad credit in the past?
   - It is definitely possible. The new lender will have to look into your employment history, income trend, as well as your debt and cash reserves.

10. What are the closing costs involved in refinancing a mortgage?
    - Closing costs vary per lender and your mortgage type and your place of residence determine these. Closing costs may include lender fees, third-party fees, appraisals, and title insurance.

Myth Busters About Refinancing Your Mortgage

1. You're supposed to be an expert. People always tend to assume that you should know how to refinance your home if you've been paying for it for too long. That's not always the case.

2. Refinance applications require a lot of documents. The process is actually often faster and less of a hassle.

3. That you need cash to cover closing costs. Most of the time, cash isn't necessary.

4. That it's all about getting a lower rate. Lowering the rate isn't always the reason why people refinance their mortgage.

5. That your current lender can offer you the best rates. Nope, that isn't always the case.

6. That you haven't reached the break-even point of your current loan. You can still refinance if you haven't reached the break-even point.

7. That you need 20% equity to refinance. This is not always the case. While loans with less than 20% equity may require mortgage insurance, you are still 100% eligible to apply for a refinance. Even with the addition of mortgage insurance, refinancing could still be a good move for you, particularly if it saves you money in the long run.

8. That you won't save that much money by refinancing. You can save a lot of money by refinancing if you are smart about it.

Affiliate Marketing

Learn

How To Make

$10,000+ Each Month

On Autopilot!

Introduction

Are you looking for an online business that you can start today? If so, affiliate marketing is for you. This method of earning money through the Internet has been around for more than two decades and people are still using the same model today as 20 years ago.

This book will teach you everything you need to know about affiliate marketing. It discusses how it all started and evolved to the multi-billion dollar industry that it is today.

In this book, we will discuss how you can get your slice of the affiliate marketing pie. You will learn how you can start with this business and build your affiliate marketing assets from scratch. You will also learn how to develop content and drive massive amounts of traffic to them through organic (free) and paid methods.

Lastly, we talk about the different strategies on how you can become successful as an Internet marketer and how you can **earn a lot of money** with Affiliate Marketing. With the help of this book, you will be on your way to earn a *six-figure* monthly income.

Start building your affiliate marketing empire today!

Inspiration #1

"There are no secrets to success. It is the result of preparation, hard work, and learning from failure."

Colin Powell

Chapter 1

What Is Affiliate Marketing?

Affiliate marketing refers to programs that aim to sell more products for a company through partnerships with third party online sales people called affiliates or publishers. Unlike traditional Contextual Advertising, affiliate marketing programs allow content publishers to connect directly with advertisers.

A successful affiliate marketing campaign can lead to a higher income to publishers compared to publishing contextual ads from services like Google AdSense. From an advertiser's standpoint, affiliate marketing is an efficient way of promoting one's products because the reward system is based on the publisher's productivity. The advertiser only needs to pay if the publisher successfully facilitates a sale.

History of Affiliate marketing

The affiliate marketing business model is not new. It has been around shortly after the first few businesses started offering products and services in the web. The affiliate marketing commission system was likely inspired by the commission payment system of offline sales people. In the sales world outside the internet, sales people have been paid via commission or a percentage of the payment amount for the longest time. In particular, it is a common sales model in the cosmetic, homeware, car and pharmaceutical industries.

The first recorded transition of this business model to the online world happened in 1994. It was a flower selling business called PC Flowers and Gifts. Its founder, William J. Tobin, designed and patented the use of revenue sharing and tracking of visitor's activities. The first affiliate network was the Prodigy Network, an IBM owned subscription service that offered online services like access to news, games, polls and many more. Subscribers of the network were given the opportunity to earn commission for facilitating a PC Flowers and Gifts sale to other members of the network.

In 1996, Amazon launched what we now call Amazon associates. At the time, Amazon focused on selling tangible books. A website owner can post a banner ad or a link that leads directly to the product page of a specific book. Commission is paid if a visitor who used the link purchases the book.

In the years that followed, many other affiliate marketing schemes were launched but Amazon Associates became the most popular among them. Since then, the popularity of affiliate marketing as a website monetization method has increased. In 2006 for instance, sales generated by affiliate marketing in the UK, amounted to $2.92 billion.

The popularity of affiliate marketing increased even more when more and more people took part in online content creation. In the early 2000s, Web 2.0 types of content became increasingly popular online. People turned to blogs and forums for answers when they face problems. Some of these blogs and forums monetized their online properties using affiliate marketing programs. By positioning affiliate products as a solution to people's problems, they were able to earn from the content they post on their websites.

Around 2011, Google cleaned up its search engine results pages with what is commonly called the Panda update. This update in the search algorithm penalized websites with poor content. This was largely due to the fact that many website owners gamed the process of ranking in Google's search result pages. This process is called Search Engine Optimization or SEO.

By doing practices frowned upon by Google, webmasters with websites that hardly have any useful content in them managed to reach the top spot of search result pages. Practices like stuffing a webpage with keywords or creating thousands of fake links that point to a websites allowed these webmasters to raise their spam webpages in the rankings. Most of these spam webpages were monetized by affiliate links and banners. With Google cracking down on webpages like these, the black hat days of most affiliate marketers came to an end.

After the Google Panda updates, websites that provided useful and engaging content rose to fill the top positions of the search result pages. Because of this, websites with excellent content managed to get the affiliate marketing sales.
In the following years, affiliate marketers saw the emergence of social media websites. Together with this, smartphones and other mobile devices replaced personal computers as the primary tools used for accessing the internet. With these changes in the internet marketing world, affiliate marketing strategies also evolved. The internet became a truly multimedia experience. Text content no longer ruled the internet. Instead, videos and images dominated the screens of internet users.

This gave way to a new breed of affiliate marketers. Some of them do not even own a website. They only use their Facebook pages, YouTube Channels and Instagram accounts to generate affiliate sales. These days, people no longer spend countless hours surfing the web. Instead, they stick to one or two apps, fully engaged in the content in these apps. This is the current state of affiliate marketing. The old ways of succeeding in this business still has some value. You could still earn by posting useful content in your website. However, if you want your affiliate marketing game to improve, you need to master the social media-marketing world as well.

The Affiliate marketing business model

As we discussed above, affiliate marketing is a revenue sharing business model designed to increase the sales of a particular product or service. Before we talk about how you can take part in this business model, let us first discuss the different players in this type of business:

The Advertiser

To understand affiliate marketing, one needs to understand the three parties involved in this type of marketing program. The first one, is the advertiser or the business that wants to promote its products or services. They set up their own affiliate marketing program or they sign up with an affiliate network to manage the marketing program for them. The advertiser's goal is simply to sell more products and to reach new markets through the internet. Most of the time, they set up this kind of program because they want to reach online markets that they normally cannot reach by traditional online advertising.

Affiliate marketing also has other benefits for the advertiser's online presence. By setting up this program, more content creators will be talking about their products. Some of these content creators have thousands of fans. Each one of these followers will be exposed to their products. Even if these followers do not purchase a product now, they will still become familiar with the promoted product. They may choose to look for the product in the future, without passing through the affiliate marketing channel.

The advertisers should provide the tools needed by the publishers. For instance, they could provide marketing materials that the affiliate publishers will use to promote their products. They should also provide the platform to make it easier for the publisher to participate in the program. Most affiliate programs come with an account to the affiliate marketing website. This website serves as source of all the tools provided by the advertiser. It also comes with a dashboard where the publisher can tract their performance.

The consumers

The next party in the affiliate marketing business model is the consumers. The consumers refer to the people who buy the products of the advertiser. The advertisers want the right types of consumers to see their marketing materials. If they like the advertiser's product or service, they can click on the link provided with the marketing material and start the purchasing process.

The internet is filled with people who can become consumers. However, the best types of consumers are those that are willing and able to buy the advertiser's products. A willing consumer is interested in the product or service. He or she has a personal reason for wanting or needing the product. A consumer is able to buy the product if he or she can complete the purchasing process. First, the consumer needs to have the technical knowhow on completing an online purchase. He or she should also have enough funds to pay for the product or service offered.

The Publisher

The last party is the publishers. Publishers are the people who post the marketing materials of the advertisers so that the consumers can view them. Affiliate programs usually require their publishers to have an online asset that they can use to attract the attention of consumers. Most affiliate programs require that you have a website where you will promote their products or services. While a website is usually required when signing up, the publisher is not limited to promoting the advertiser's marketing materials in there. Depending on the affiliate program guidelines, the publisher can use contextual advertising, social media marketing, and other means to bring attention to the affiliate offer.

If you want to earn money in affiliate marketing, the best way is to become a publisher. It will be your role to generate leads towards the websites of your affiliate advertisers. This means that you need to attract people who are likely to buy the products of the advertisers and encourage them to go to the advertiser website and make a purchase.

This part however, is easier said than done. Though billions of people use the internet every day, you will not be able to reach the majority of them. A big chunk of the online population does not speak English. Among the English speakers, only a small percentage is interested in the topics you are discussing in your blog, your videos or your podcasts. Even among people who are interested in the topic you are discussing, only a small percentage have intentions of buying online. The majority of people still prefer to buy things through brick-and-mortar stores if they are available. Many of those who habitually buy things online have their preferred online stores. Many of them just buy from the popular sources like Amazon.

The most successful publishers earn through affiliate marketing consistently by establishing themselves as authorities in their chosen fields. You may also follow this path. Most of these people are already experts in their fields and they only use online marketing as a source of extra income. If you want to create content related to your job for example, you can brand yourself as an expert. A trainer in a gym for example, can create a website where he puts contents that gym goers can do when they cannot go to his classes. In the process, he can promote fitness related products that the visitors of his website can make use of. Because the gym trainer is an expert in his field, the visitors in his website are likely to follow his advice.

You can also take the same approach by starting an affiliate business based on what you do for a living or on a hobby you like to do. By doing so, you can establish yourself as an expert in that field. It will also be easier for you to find your first website followers. You can encourage the people you meet in your job to visit your website. In there, you can provide free advice to keep the visitors coming back to your website. In the process, you can monetize the website by suggesting products and services that you use yourself. You could then use affiliate links to direct your visitors to these products and services.

A carpenter for example, could provide free carpentry lessons in his website and his social media accounts. Together with his content, he could provide Amazon Associate links to the product pages of the tools and other products that he uses in his carpentry lessons.

To establish yourself as an expert, you will need to provide evidence to the visitors of your website. For instance, you can create an about page where you put your credentials and your achievements in the field. You could also provide photos where in you are working to show people that you are who you say you are.

While it is easier to convince people to buy the affiliate products if you are an expert, there are other approaches to become a trusted source in the affiliate marketing business. For instance, you can also become a successful publisher even if you are just a beginner at your chosen topic. Instead of providing advice based on your personal experience, you can also give them as you learn a new topic. A beginner carpenter for example could show people his journey in learning to become an expert. In the process, he could share the lessons he learned together with the tools he uses to learn.

Many people who go to the internet are beginners who want to learn something. It is rare to see a free website that will teach you everything you need to know to learn a skill. Most websites that teach specific skills tend to be paid and often demand a high price. You can give the audience a free version of these websites. Instead of charging the people for the information, you can earn through the affiliate marketing income instead.

Chapter 1 Quiz
Please refer to Appendix A for the answers to this quiz

1. What do you call productivity-based programs that partner with online sellers to encourage the sale of products and services?

   A) Contextual marketing
   B) Affiliate Marketing
   C) Cost Per Click Marketing
   D) Search Marketing

2. What do you call the third-party sellers that promote affiliate products to consumers?

   A) Advertisers
   B) Online Sellers
   C) Affiliates
   D) Programmers

3. Where did the commissions payment system used in affiliate marketing originate?

   A) Real-world sales industry
   B) Online contextual advertising industry
   C) Email marketing
   D) The bakeshop business

4. When was the first affiliate marketing program started?

   A) 1994
   B) 1996
   C) 1991
   D) 1998

5. When was Amazon Associates launched?

   A) 1994
   B) 1996
   C) 1991
   D) 1998

6. What are businesses that set up affiliate programs called?

   A) Affiliates
   B) Advertisers

C) Business Partners
D) Consumers

7. What do you call the percentage of the purchase price paid to the affiliate?

   A) Success Rate
   B) Commission Rate
   C) Conversion Rate
   D) Payment Method

8. Who are the general target audience of affiliate programs?

   A) Children
   B) Business owners
   C) Advertisers
   D) Consumer

9. What are the two requirements of an ideal product consumer?

   A) Willingness and capacity to buy
   B) Social media and search engine usage
   C) Facebook account and credit card
   D) Computer and twitter account

10. How are affiliate marketers paid?

    A) Commission System
    B) An agreed upon fixed amount
    C) Based on the cost per click rate
    D) Based on the number of impressions

Inspiration #2

"If you really want to do something, you'll find a way. If you don't, you'll find an excuse."

Jim Rohn

Chapter 2

Low Ticket vs. High Ticket Affiliate Marketing

If you want to become an affiliate marketer, there are many products and services you can choose from. Veteran affiliate marketers classify these products based on their prices. The price of the promoted product is important to the affiliate marketer because the commissions they earn are usually a percentage of the product's selling price. With this in mind, affiliate marketers classify low cost products as low-ticket affiliate products and those that are more expensive to be high-ticket affiliate products.

As you start in the affiliate marketing business, you need to decide whether you want to promote cheap or expensive items. Most affiliate marketers choose to promote low-ticket affiliate products because they think that it is easier to convince people to buy cheap items. However, this also means that you need to sell **A LOT** more items to reach your income goals.

Let's say you have a website that promotes small bedroom items. The average price of the products you promote is $5 and you earn a 10% commission for each sale you promote. That means that for each $5-item you sell, you make only $0.50. If the minimum payout amount is $100, you will need to sell 200 $5-items to reach your goal. You will need a *massive* amount of traffic to make this number of sales in a month.

High-ticket items on the other hand are those that sell for $100 and up. These items are harder to sell because they require a bigger financial commitment from the consumer. However, you only need a few sales of these items to reach your income goals. If you are selling a $100-item on your website for example, and your commission rate is also 10%, you only need to sell 10 items to earn the minimum payout amount of $100.

It is not wise to make the decision of going for high ticket or low-ticket affiliate programs right now. You will need to consider many factors when making this decision. First, you will need to consider the industry or niche market that you wish to take part in. After that, you will need to consider the types of content that you enjoy creating.

You cannot expect to be successful promoting gadgets and tech-related stuff if your content is all about sports. The product you choose should fit seamlessly with the content you create. They should be aligned with the needs of the visitors of your website. The types of people who visit your website will depend on the content that you have in there and the marketing efforts you put in.

The types of offers available in the market will also limit your options for affiliate products. If you are promoting tangible products, you will always have the option of selling Amazon products through the Amazon Associates program. The majority of products in Amazon are low-ticket. In addition, the commission rate for almost all categories start at 4%. This rate is low in the affiliate marketing industry.

Most people who stick with Amazon however, do so because of the company's reputation and reliability. Most people who go to your website already know what Amazon is and you no longer need to upsell the retailer. On the other hand, if you are selling a product from an unpopular source, you will first need to introduce the retailer, talk about their track record and why your readers should buy from them.

Chapter 2 Quiz

Please refer to Appendix B for the answers to this quiz

1. What do you call inexpensive affiliate products?

    A) Low-Ticket Items
    B) Cheap Affiliates
    C) Clickbait
    D) Affiliate bargain

2. What is one advantage of selling an inexpensive affiliate product?

    A) It has a high commission
    B) It always comes with a high commission rate
    C) It is easy to sell
    D) It requires higher financial commitment for the consumer

3. What is one disadvantage of selling an inexpensive affiliate product?

    A) It does not come with a warranty
    B) It is too easy to sell
    C) You need to pay a lot in advertising fees to promote it
    D) You need to make a lot of sales to reach the payment threshold

4. How do you earn big with this kind of products?

    A) You need to have high quantity of sales
    B) You only need to sell two or three items every week
    C) You need to pay more on advertising
    D) You need to focus your efforts in search marketing

5. What do you call expensive affiliate products?

    A) High-ticket Items
    B) Low-Ticket Items
    C) High rollers
    D) Golden affiliate products

6. What is one advantage of selling an expensive affiliate product?

    A) It comes with a lot of freebies
    B) It can come with a one-year warranty

C) It is easy to sell

D) You only need to make a few sales to reach the pay out

7. What is one disadvantage of selling an expensive affiliate product?

   A) It is easy to sell
   B) It is faster to sell
   C) It comes with a lot of disclaimers
   D) None of the above

8. Why is it harder to sell this type of item?

   A) It requires higher financial commitment for the consumer
   B) It is difficult to ship
   C) It comes with a high shipping fee
   D) It does not look appealing to the buyer

9. What factor should you consider when choosing between inexpensive and expensive affiliate products?

   A) The need of the consumers
   B) The price of the competitor's products
   C) The reach of your marketing efforts
   D) The state of the world economy

10. What example of low-ticket market was mentioned in the chapter?

    A) Amazon
    B) ClickBank
    C) Shopify
    D) eBay

Inspiration #3

"Don't let the fear of losing be greater than the excitement of winning."

Robert Kiyosaki

Chapter 3

How To Become An Affiliate Marketer

To become an affiliate marketer, you only need to become a member of a good affiliate marketing program and start spreading the affiliate link. To make money consistently however, you need to be smart in your approach in the business.

Here are the things you will need to start with this business:

A website

As stated in the previous chapters, most affiliate programs require that you have a website before you will be accepted. Advertisers check the website to see what types of content you have. Some advertisers are extremely picky when choosing affiliates. They only accept those whose websites can bring in huge amounts of traffic. Don't worry though, because there are also beginner level affiliate marketing programs that will accept even publishers with new websites.

A profitable niche

You cannot just create any type of website if you want to become a successful affiliate marketer. In particular, you need to be careful in choosing the niche market. We will discuss how you can choose the right niche market in future chapters. For now, just remember that the types of affiliate marketing products that you can sell will depend on the niche market you choose to participate in. If you want to sell only high ticket items for instance, you need to make sure that the niche market you've chosen have high-ticket affiliate marketing programs.

An organic source of traffic

In the world of internet marketing, there are two ways for you to get traffic, organic and paid. While some affiliate marketers do use paid methods to earn through affiliate marketing, these methods exposes you to a higher financial risk. Those who use these methods have developed their skill over years of trial and error.

For now, you should focus on building assets that will help you gather organic visitors. This includes social media accounts and pages, forum memberships, accounts in niche specific online communities, offline traffic sources and other similar assets. You will need to think about where you will get your traffic for your website if you want to be successful from day one.

A membership to an affiliate marketing program

There are tons of affiliate marketing programs in the web. However, not all of them will be suitable to offer to the type of traffic that you can get. You will need to choose an affiliate program that fits the needs of the audience. We will discuss how to choose the best affiliate marketing programs for your audience in the following chapters.

The four factors above are the minimum requirements for becoming a successful affiliate marketer. After choosing an affiliate marketing program, you can apply directly from the web. Most of the application processes just require you to fill up a form with your personal details. In addition, the application form may also ask how you plan to generate traffic for your affiliate offers and what types of products you wish to promote. The form may also ask you how much traffic your own website gets a day and what other monetization methods you use in the said website.

In addition, you may be asked to fill up a tax form. This part will depend on the requirements of the country of origin of the affiliate program. When signing up for Amazon Associates for Amazon.com for instance, US citizens will be asked to fill up a US tax form. A different form will be required if you are applying for Amazon.ca (Canada) Associates program.

How hard is the application process?

For some affiliate programs, getting in is easy. Some may even automatically approve your application. There are more specialized programs though, that will ask for more requirements after you apply. The most demanding programs will have their employees scan your website for the quality of the content. If they are not satisfied with the design or the quality of the content of your website, they may reject your application.

These extremely selective programs usually do this for different reasons. The majority of them do it because they want to protect their brand. Big brands only want to be associated with websites that have good quality content. Some of them will only accept websites that have been around for a long time with hundreds of archived content. Some brands will also reject your application if they see that your website or your contents are not aligned with their target consumers. If your website is in English for example and you apply with an affiliate program for Spanish people, you are likely to be rejected.

My application has been approved, what now?

It is after the application process that the real work begins. Now that you have a product or service to promote, you can now start gathering traffic and funneling them towards your affiliate links. There are multiple methods on how you can do this.

First, you can use paid methods as a source of traffic. You can use advertising platforms that allow affiliate links and pay for the clicks or the views that your ad gets. With this method, you are spending money to make money. You will need a bankroll of hundreds, if not thousands of dollars to make this strategy work. You will also need to make sure that you follow the guidelines set by the affiliate advertisers.

Most of them will restrict you from using certain keywords in the advertising targeting. If you are selling Nike rubber shoes for example, the affiliate program contract may restrict you from using the keywords like Nike. They do this to prevent affiliate marketers from competing with the mother company in the advertising bidding.

The second method of sending traffic is to spread the link around the web. In the past, people used to do sleazy techniques to get clicks on their affiliate links. Some of them for instance, put their affiliate links in the signature part of their forum accounts. This way, when people see their forum comments, they also see the affiliate links. Many forums learned about this technique and now ban the use of links in the signature.

Some affiliate programs also allow the use of redirects and pop-ups to gather traffic. An affiliate marketer using redirect for example, may set up a page that will automatically redirect to the affiliate website. When the visitor visits that page, they are automatically transferred to the affiliate program's landing page. The problem with this strategy is that most people who go through the automatic redirect are sent to the affiliate program's website unwillingly. The majority of them will bounce (i.e. leave rather than continuing to see other pages on the website). This excess traffic of non-buyers will eventually take its toll in the advertiser's website. This is the reason why many affiliate programs ban the use of redirects.

Some people also use link pop-ups to send people through the affiliate link. They may set the pop-up to appear after a certain link in the website is clicked. Upon clicking the said link, another window or tab will open. This works both for desktop and for mobile browsers. When the pop-up opens, the affiliate link is triggered and the affiliate landing page starts to load.

This process of sending traffic to affiliate programs is also problematic. Aside from being prohibited by most affiliate programs, browsers also tend to have pop-up blocking technology. This prevents most of the pop-ups from opening even when the right link is clicked.

The recommended way of gathering traffic for your affiliate programs is through the use of content marketing. Simply put, content marketing is the process of gathering internet user's attention by using different types of content media. One has the option of using text, audio, images, videos or a combination of all these to invite people to go to your website.

News websites are a classic example of websites that use content marketing. They create news articles and accompany them with videos and relevant images. After creating them, they post their content in their social media properties. They spread their news articles through Facebook, Twitter, and other social media marketing platforms. When a person interested in the news sees the article, the headline and the accompanying image should compel them to click on the link of the article. This will lead them to the news website.

After reading the article, they may press the up-vote button for the content. Some may even share a link of the content to their friends. By doing this, they are spreading the news and increasing the reach of the news article.

Other people interested in the news may also click on the article. Afterwards they may also share the content with their own social media followers, continuing to spread the news.

Some people who may be looking to read that specific news article may also go to Google and do a search. Because of proper search engine optimization practices, the article landed in the top spot of the search result page with its relevant keywords or key phrases. Because of this, more people from Google manage to read the content. Some of the readers who are interested in the content of the article may also choose to share it with their friends.

While this may seem like a simplistic illustration of how content marketing works, this is how it happens for most content on the web. Content creators simple make the content and share them in the relevant online hotspots. They develop their skill in getting people's attention over thousands of hours of practice.

You could also do the same with your affiliate marketing business. You could lure internet users to go to your website by creating and sharing content that are relevant to their interests and needs. In the process of viewing your content, they should also see the affiliate ads that you share in your website. A percentage of them will click on these marketing materials and make a purchase. You will receive a percentage of the sale amount that your referred customers spend.

Chapter 3 Quiz
Please refer to Appendix C for the answers to this quiz

1. What is the primary marketing asset of the affiliate marketer?

    A) Website
    B) Money
    C) Affiliate program
    D) Friends

2. What do you call a topic that the affiliate website is focusing on?

    A) Preferred topic of interest
    B) Featured Topic
    C) Favorites
    D) Niche Topic

3. Why does a website need marketing?

    A) To send massive amounts of traffic to the advertiser's landing page
    B) To help the website become popular
    C) To increase the chances of winning affiliate promotions
    D) To prevent spammers from infiltrating the affiliate networks

4. How do demanding affiliate programs judge your application?

    A) They ask you to sell them a pen
    B) They email your referrals to check if you are a real person
    C) They use bots to look up your information online
    D) They check your website manually

5. Why are some affiliate programs strict in accepting affiliates?

    A) They are protecting their brands from Spamming marketers
    B) They do not want to accept low-ticket marketers
    C) They do not have enough slots for more marketers
    D) They reserve their slots only for high-ticket marketers

6. What are the two general ways of sending traffic to your affiliate website?

    A) Paid and Free
    B) Social and Search
    C) Email and Search

D) Ads and Search traffic

7. What do you call the strategy of using content to attract traffic to a website?

   A) Search Marketing
   B) Content Marketing
   C) Social Media Marketing
   D) Banner Marketing

8. Where is content marketing most effective?

   A) Social networks
   B) Email Marketing
   C) Offline Marketing
   D) Banner Marketing

9. What do you call the process of making your content rank well in search engine result pages?

   A) Social Engine Marketing
   B) Search Engine Optimization
   C) Search Media Optimization
   D) Traffic Source

10. What is an example of a type website that uses content marketing routinely?

    A) Software support website
    B) Purely Ecommerce website
    C) Membership website
    D) News Website

Inspiration #4

"If you can dream it, you can do it."

Walt Disney

Chapter 4

The Top 20 Affiliate Marketing Programs

There are hundreds of affiliate marketing programs to choose from. However, to become successful, you need to find the one with the best potential for earning. You need to consider many factors such as the stability of the company running the network. You should also consider what types of advertisers and products they have in their network. In this chapter we will discuss some of the biggest affiliate programs right now.

1. Amazon Associates

Amazon is probably the most commonly used program by beginners. It allows you to earn from any type of item sold in Amazon, aside from digital kindle products. The program though, covers all tangible products. The commission rate varies for each product, depending on the type of product your associates account sells. Most items start out at 4% for the first six sales of the month. The rate for the seventh until the 30th item on the other hand is 6%. The rate increases as the number of products you sell also increases. In this affiliate program, affiliates are rewarded for selling a high quantity of items. The more items you sell in a month, the higher your commission rate will be.

Unlike most affiliate marketing programs, Amazon does not have a fixed landing page for their products. They allow the affiliate marketer to choose a product and use the product page as the landing page.

The best part about selling through Amazon Associates is that the affiliate marketer will be credited for any item bought by a person that clicked their link. The person you referred to Amazon does not need to buy the product you suggested. As long as they clicked your link, you will receive commission for everything that they buy in the website.

A person who clicks your regular Amazon Associates link has 24 hours to make a purchase for it to be credited to your account. If they do not make a purchase after 24 hours, the cookie will expire. Any purchase they make after the cookie expires will no longer be credited to you.

A special type of link that you can generate in your Amazon Associates account automatically leads to the clicker's cart page after they log in to their Amazon account. If you use this kind of affiliate link, the affiliate cookie extends to 90 days. As long as the item is kept in their cart in the 90-day period, you will be credited for the sale. In addition, if the person buys other things from Amazon in addition to the item in their cart, the sale of these items will also be credited to you.

Apart from the lower commission rates based on the industry standards, the only downside with selling through Amazon is that it will not redirect the Amazon links for you based on the visitor's location.

2. CJ.com

CJ or Commission Junction is one of the longest running affiliate network in the world. CJ is an affiliate network that connects affiliate marketers with advertisers. After signing up to CJ.com, you will be able to apply to the different advertisers they have in the website. Some of the advertisers allow immediate approval of applications. Others however, will manually check the application and may reject it depending on their acceptance standards.

CJ.com provides the tools that you will need for setting up the affiliate links in your website. They will also provide you with a dashboard where you can check how many clicks your affiliate marketing efforts get. This is also the place where you will see the amount you earn from the clicks you get.

The links that you will get from your CJ.com console will go straight to the advertiser's landing page. It is important that you choose the landing pages that you use. Choose a landing page, that you think will have a high chance of converting visits into sales.

The commission rates for affiliate programs in CJ vary per advertiser. This rate is usually written in the description of the program. While Amazon Associates rates are capped at 7.5%, it is normal for some advertisers in CJ.com to offer 10%. If you prove that you can send a good quantity of high quality leads, you may even request the advertiser for a higher commission rate.

3. Clickbank

Clickbank is also popular among affiliate marketers, mainly for its high commission rates. They sell a variety of products and services, from arts and entertainment to travel and leisure. Just go to their website at clickbank.com and go to the Affiliate Marketplace. In this page, you will see the different categories of affiliate offers that they have. Upon clicking on one of these categories, you will see a list of products and services. After choose a product or service that you would like to promote, you will need to sign up to the program by clicking the "Promote" button.

Most of clickbank's affiliate advertisers sell digital product and online services. Because of this, they can offer extremely high commission rates. Some of them offer up to 70% of the price of the purchase. These types of rate are only possible with online products and services. Because of the high commission rates, affiliate marketers prefer to promote clickbank content.

4. Rakuten Linkshare

Rakuten Linkshare is also one of the most popular affiliate programs. The sign up process for this program is fairly simple. You only need to fill up the usual information fields as well as complete the tax form. After which, your account will be registered and you will be allowed to sign up.

Once logged in, you will be able to select a category of products. The number of products available in Rakuten Linkshare is significantly fewer compared to the other affiliate networks discussed above. However, Linkshare has the reputation of being reliable for fast payments for both US and non-US based affiliates.

5. JVZoo

JVZoo is new to the market but it is one of the fastest growing affiliate program in the industry. It offers features that are not commonly found in other affiliate programs. For instance, they are the only program that commits to timely payment delivery. This is a common issue among many programs. It usually takes them time to validate sales reports to make sure there are no sales frauds in the records. Some of the longest running programs like CJ.com and ClickBank still take weeks and even months to deliver payments for members with large volumes of sales.

6. Avantlink

Avantlink is less popular than the first few programs we've discussed above. However, its wide range of advertiser categories and its beginner-friendly user interface also makes it a great affiliate network.

7. eBay

EBay tends to be forgotten in the affiliate marketing world because of its strict approval process. Because eBay does not sell its own products and does not take responsibility in the quality of their products, affiliates tend to avoid promoting products from there. It's brand however, makes the network an easy sell to the average shopper. The shop is particularly popular among bargain hunters. If your website attracts of bargain hunters, eBay affiliate may work for you.

8. Shareasale

Shareasale's competitive edge is the size of its network. It offers more than 4,000 advertisers in various categories. Its user interface is also easy to use and it collects some types of analytics data not available in other networks. It is also one of those networks that pay on a monthly basis.

9. Avangate

Avangate exclusively offers affiliate offers from software. They offer the best brands in software downloads and online services. As with other technology-based affiliate programs, Avantgate advertisers tend to offer higher commission rates.

10. Affibank

Affibank.com is also a newer player in the market but they are making a name for themselves among affiliate marketers because of their high commission rates. Many of the offers in the Affibank give out commission rates of 75%. This means that a big chunk of the money you refer goes back to you. The offers in this marketplace are similar to those found in ClickBank. The only downside is that they are currently offering few offers and most of them are in the Health, Beauty and Fitness Categories.

There are hundreds of other affiliate marketing programs available for you to explore. Here are ten more that you can look into if you cannot find a program you like in the marketplaces listed above.

11. Maxbounty

12. RevenueWire

13. ReviMedia

14. Flexoffers

15. Commission Factory

16. PeerFly

17. ClickFunnels

18. Tradedoubler

19. AffiliateWindow

20. BankAffiliates

While these marketplaces are the best places to start, you can also look into in-house affiliate programs in specific companies. Some online companies maintain their own affiliate marketing programs. If you have a company whose products you wish to promote, you can search their company with the key phrase "affiliate program" added to it.

If they do have an affiliate program, there is no doubt that it will show up in the search result pages. Think of the products and services that you have been using in the past and check online if they do have an affiliate marketing program set up. One example is Shopify. You can promote it to people who want to start an online store and earn while doing it.

Chapter 4 Quiz

Please refer to Appendix D for the answers to this quiz

1. What types of products can you sell with Amazon Associates

    A) All tangible products sold in Amazon.com
    B) All products in Amazon.com and eBay.com
    C) Products in Amazon.com, Amazon.au and Shopify
    D) All digital products in Amazon.com

2. What affiliate program consistently offers high commission rates

    A) CJ.com
    B) Affibank
    C) Amazon Associates
    D) eBay

3. Why is Shareasale a strong network?

    A) It has lots of advertisers and offers
    B) It has a strong social media following
    C) It is recommended by celebrities
    D) It offers a high commission rates

4. What is JVZoo's defining feature?

    A) High number of offers
    B) Fast payment processing
    C) Longest running affiliate network
    D) Multinational reach

5. What type of products does a Avantgate offer?

    A) Sports equipment
    B) Software
    C) Computer Hardware
    D) Cars

6. What is eBay's best feature?

    A) Brand recognition
    B) Product quality
    C) Business process

D) Superior customer service

7. What is Amazon Associate's best feature?

    A) High commission rate
    E) High volume of products
    F) Superior customer service
    G) Fast payment processing

8. What is CJ.com's best feature?

    A) High commission rate
    B) High number of advertisers
    C) Superior customer service
    D) Fast payment processing

9. What is an example of a company that offers in-house affiliate program

    A) Shopify
    B) Nike
    C) Under Armour
    D) ESPN

10. What do you call a company that hosts its own affiliate program without passing through a network?

    A) Affiliate network guru
    B) Business process outsourcing
    C) Virtual Assistants
    D) In-house affiliate program

Inspiration #5

"Many of life's failures are people who did not realize how close they were to success when they gave up."

Thomas Edison

Chapter 5

How To Choose An Affiliate Marketing Program

Choosing an affiliate marketing program is an important factor in becoming a successful affiliate marketer. If you choose the wrong program, you may end up not making any money from all your efforts. You need to align the content you created with the right types of products in the affiliate marketing program. You also need to make sure that the commission rate in the program you've chosen is big enough. Lastly, you need to make sure that the company behind the program provides excellent customer support and fast payment processing.

Check the advertisers

The advertisers should be the primary reason why you should join an affiliate program. If you find an advertiser you like in an affiliate network, you should join that network. Not all advertisers you would like to partner with will all be in one program. To be able to sell all the products and services that you personally like, you may need to work with multiple advertisers. This means that you will need to work with multiple affiliate accounts.

Find the programs with the best commission rate

Aside from the types of advertisers they have, you should also join programs based on their commission rates. The commission rate of a program varies depending on the type of product sold. Usually, the commission rate goes up when the product is digital (such as in the case of software) or when the product is hard to sell. Companies that are having a hard time selling their product tend to add a high commission rate to their product to increase the motivation of online marketers to sell them.

You should also watch out for the types of products that also offer residual payments. In affiliate marketing, residual payments happen when the people you refer to the program renew their membership in a merchant. This type of payment usually applies towards services that require customers to become members. Many web hosting affiliate programs for example, offer this kind of deal to people. With this type of commission payment, you will continue to make money from people that you referred even years ago.

Based on the quality of backend services

Lastly, you need to consider the quality of service of the affiliate program. Most affiliate programs tend to offer a do-it-yourself approach to marketing. However, they do offer one-on-one support when the affiliates need help with technical parts of the website. Choosing a company that has good customer support is important so that there will be someone to help you in the future when problems in your account arise. Whenever you find a new program that looks promising, look into the reputation of its customer service online.

If the company has a poor customer service, you will hear about it in the forums and blog posts. Check other people's experiences about how fast the company responds to queries and reports. More importantly, you should also research on how fast the company delivers payments and what types of payment methods they use.

Chapter 5 Quiz
Please refer to Appendix E for the answers to this quiz

1. What should be the primary reason for joining an affiliate program?

    A) The advertiser
    B) The competition
    C) The email marketing service
    D) None of the above

2. What determines the amount paid to the advertiser?

    A) Success rate
    B) Commission rate
    C) Popularity of the product
    D) Customer service

3. What do you do if the advertisers you want are in different affiliate networks?

    A) Apply in both networks
    B) Abandon one network over the other
    C) Find an alternative advertiser in your preferred network
    D) Create to websites to promote different products

4. What is a common problem among affiliate programs?

    A) High bounce rates
    B) Slow internet connection
    C) Slow payment processing
    D) Spam marketing content

5. What usually determines the commission rate of the program?

    A) The popularity of product
    B) The type of product sold
    C) The number of annual sales
    D) The popularity of the website

6. What do you do when you encounter a technical issue with your affiliate program?

    A) Transfer to another affiliate program
    B) Replace all your affiliate links with working ones
    C) Contact the affiliate program support group

D) Wait for the problem to be solved on its own

7. What makes a good affiliate program support team?

    A) Making excuses for not solving problems
    E) Presence of email support
    F) Fast and accurate responses from the team
    G) Great reviews from online bloggers

8. How do you check if the affiliate program support group is any good?

    A) If they are available in multiple communication channels
    B) If they are good at upselling products from the affiliate program
    C) If they are available during business hours only
    D) If do not respond through emails

9. How do you make sure that an affiliate program pays?

    A) Find program reviews in YouTube and in personal blogs
    B) Wait until you reach the payment threshold
    C) You cannot have any guarantees
    D) Buy the affiliate products yourself to reach the payment threshold

10. From a payment standpoint, what should you check before you apply with an affiliate program of network?

    A) The past earnings of other people
    B) The total revenue of the affiliate advertiser
    C) The methods of payment offered by the program or network
    D) The cost of contacting the affiliate support team

Inspiration #6

"The secret of success is to do the common thing uncommonly well."

John D. Rockefeller Jr.

Chapter 6

Writing Content For Affiliate Marketing

To start your content marketing campaign, you should begin with the product or products that you wish to promote to your visitors.

Promote products you've used in the past

Ideally, you should share products that you have used in the past, so that you can share your firsthand experience in using them. This will make your content authentic. Online authorities usually use this kind of approach. A welding teacher for example, uses his website together with YouTube to create a multimedia content experience. In his articles and videos, he shows people how to do welding techniques and projects. In the process, he shows them the tools that he is using. By showing the people that he is using the tools, he is more likely to convince them to buy from his affiliate marketing sources.

If you choose to present yourself and your website as an authority in the subject you are using, you can also use this strategy. When thinking about the topic that you are going to discuss, also research on the possible products that you may promote to your online visitors. It's better if you already have some of these products so that you no longer need to buy them.

Presenting products you haven't used

Some affiliate marketers in the market also suggest the use of products they have never used in the past. This type of affiliate marketing suggestion usually works for generic products that people will still buy regardless of the price or the brand you present. Weight plates for dumbbells are an example of this type of product. Even if you do not show that you are using weight plates, you can talk about them, show photos of them and present an affiliate link for them.

Because they are common products, your readers are familiar with what these products are. They will also be willing to buy them even if you do not show yourself using them. If you post a link to an Amazon product page with an acceptable price range, some of your uses will make the purchase.

When presenting products that you haven't used yet, you should do all the research you can about it. The web today is rich in information, you can do your research about any product out there. If the product can be found in Amazon, you can even use the review section as your source for doing product research. The people posting these reviews mostly have firsthand experience in using them.

Beginners make the common mistake of being too positive about the products they present. This makes them sound as if they are doing a sales pitch; you do not want people to see you this way when you are talking about your content. Instead, people want hard facts about the products you are presenting. Show them both the pros and cons of using the product.

What type of content should I create?

When choosing the type of content you will create, choose the ones where in you can actively and naturally suggest the products you use. Listicles (list articles), tutorial articles and tips articles are some of the types of contents where in you can naturally plug a product in. Ideally, you should create three types of content. An article in your website for people who prefer to read, a video in YouTube and an audio version of the video for iTunes. You can embed the video and audio files in your article page to make all your content come together.

In addition, you can also create additional content such as behind-the-scenes videos and photos. You can then post these photos in your social media accounts or your website blog. By doing so, you will be able to keep your accounts active. Some of the people who see your social media content will also be interested in what you are up to. If you show a photo doing a project for example, your followers may become interested in knowing what project you are working on.

By posting these behind-the-scenes footage and content, you will be able to build excitement in your audience base. This increases the potential views of your different contents from the different platforms you use.

All these pieces of content have one important purpose, to redirect the attention of the visitor towards the affiliate links and buttons. Your target market will be minding their own business, using social media or doing a Google search. In the process, they may stumble upon your content and spend some time to watch, read or listen to it. This is what you are fighting for when doing content marketing, your potential visitors' time and attention. You want to keep them tuned in to your content long enough so that they will see or hear your product pitches.

Putting the Tips into Action

Now that you know how the basic content marketing process works, let's consider an example of a successful content marketing campaign for an affiliate marketing program.

Mary is a stay at home mom and she wants to start doing affiliate marketing to supplement the household income. In her free time, Mary likes to work on her garden and she has had some success in growing both flowering and fruit-bearing plants. Because she enjoys gardening and she has the experience to teach people how to do it, she decided that this will be her niche topic.

Mary begins by researching about the types of information that are already in the market. As she expected, there are already a lot of content about general gardening. Because of this, she decided to make her niche narrower. She looked into creating content only for specific aspects of gardening such as organic gardening, composting, and similar contents. She found that while there are already a lot of content in this area, she has some article ideas that no other website have discussed with depth.

With her niche market set, Mary begins to craft her content marketing strategy. In the beginning of the website, there will not be a lot of traffic because people will not be aware yet that the website exists. This gives Mary the opportunity to create and refine her content. She starts by creating a series of posts focused on planting lettuce in her backyard. She did her research and outlined her content so that everything will be organized and easy to follow.

While researching, she also followed the tip of listing down all the tools she will need for her series of articles. In her list, she included both generic garden tools and some brands that she personally uses. After creating the list, she looks for these products in Amazon and uses her Amazon Associates account to generate links for each one of them.

Now that the information for the content is ready, Mary starts to create. To create her content, she works on her garden and uses her smartphone camera to take photos and to record videos. She plans to edit these videos and share them in YouTube. She also takes photos and short videos and shares them in Instagram, Pinterest, Twitter and Facebook. In the process, some of her friends start interacting with her content, asking her what she is up to. She lets them know that she is working on her garden and creating an article about it. With her initial social media content, starts to pique the interest of her natural audience.

After her gardening project, she managed to create 5 articles about plating lettuce, one video about how to plant them from seeds and multiple social media posts about it. These become her first contents for her website and her YouTube Channel. In both her articles and her YouTube video, she actively discusses the tools and planting products she uses. She then tells her content viewers that they can also get the same products through the link she provides. In her articles, she posts the link directly after mentioning them. In her YouTube video, she puts all her affiliate links in the description of the video. She also includes a link towards her articles so that people from YouTube will be able to go to her website easily.

Now that her first set of contents are ready, Mary begins the second part of her content marketing effort. She now starts to spread her content around the web. She continues to post in her social media platforms about the progress of the growth of her plants. In Instagram she posts photos of the sprouts coming out of the ground, she also posts about the different plants in her garden.

She also shares the same content in her Twitter account. In there, she also talks with other Twitter users about gardening. Every now and then, she mentions her articles and her videos. In Facebook, Mary posts her articles and uploads a copy of her video. In the beginning, only her friends and family talked about it. Mary entertained her audience in the comments. With people engaged in her articles and her video, the reach of her content increases. Because of this, other people outside of Mary's social circles start seeing her contents. They press the up-vote button while some leave a comment and share the content.

Aside from social media marketing, Mary also optimizes her content so that it ranks high in search engine result pages. She uses her target keywords in the title of her content as well as in different paragraphs in the article. In her YouTube video, she also created a long description with the relevant keywords included to make it easier to find for people looking for videos.

All these marketing efforts increased the views of Mary's articles and video. Out of the thousands that viewed her content, some clicked on the Amazon links she provided. The purchases of these referred visitors allowed Mary to earn some cash from Amazon Associates.

In this example, our protagonist did all things right to make money through Amazon. Here are some of the content marketing best practices she did right:

Pick a topic you enjoy working on

You are stuck with the topic you pick until you see success or until you give up on your affiliate marketing business. To make sure you do not get fed up making content on the same topics, you should pick one that you love doing, in our example, Mary chose to work on gardening, one of her natural interests. If you have a long-term interest or hobby, you can also pick that topic for your content marketing.

Create specific types of content based on your marketing platform

Right now, the Google and Facebook are the two biggest sources of website visitors. They are so influential that they are rumored to be used for important political events like elections. While they are both excellent places to share content, not all types of content will work in both of them. For Google, it's best to use keyword-rich instructional contents. People go to Google when they have problems or when they are looking for specific information.

For Facebook on the other hand, the best types of content are those that provoke certain emotions on the readers. They do not need to be necessarily useful. In fact, many of the contents in Facebook are purely for entertainment purposes. Content in Facebook become popular if people engage with it. Engagement in social media marketing is defined as any positive action done by the user towards the content. In Facebook, reactions such as "Likes" are examples of engagement. Comments and Shares are even more powerful forms of engagement. The Facebook content management algorithm will show your content to more people if it received a lot of these positive reactions in the first hour of posting.

Encourage followers to engage with your content

In our example, Mary knew that engagement is important in her content marketing game. Because of this, she entertained the comments of people in the content she shared. The more comments and reactions the content gets, the higher the number of people that gets to see it.

You should also do the same when doing content marketing is social networks. Make your content rise in the newsfeeds of your friends and family by entertaining comments. Also encourage people to share the content by directly asking them to do it in the content description.

State a clear call-to-action to go to the affiliate website

People will not just click on your affiliate link just because you added it to your content. They will only click on it if you directly invite them to do so. In our example, Mary directly invites her viewers and website visitors to click on the affiliate links she provides. Even better, she shows people that she is using the affiliate products she invites them to buy. Affiliate marketing is more than just a selling business. It's about helping your community solve their own problems. You can only earn if you convince people that your way of solving the problem is better.

Do not be afraid to over use your call-to-action statements and buttons. The business is all about directing the attention of your audience towards your links. If you are shy with making people click on that affiliate link, you will fail in achieving your goal. If you believe that the product you are selling will solve the problems of the people viewing your content, you should not be afraid of sounding to salesy.

Chapter 6 Quiz

Please refer to Appendix F for the answers to this quiz

1. Ideally, which type of product should you promote?

    A) Products that other bloggers are promoting
    B) Products with high ratings on Amazon
    C) Products you have used in the past
    D) Products that look great

2. Why should you promote products you've used in the past?

    A) To increase your credibility as a reviewer and product ambassador
    B) So that it is easy to find out what qualities to upsell
    C) To make it easier to fool consumers
    D) To sell more products

3. What makes a good content in promoting products and services?

    A) Showing people that you use the product
    B) Showing stock photos of the product
    C) Writing only positive qualities of the product
    D) Showing that the product is on sale

4. How do you present yourself and your website as a content authority?

    A) Make up information about your achievements
    B) Show content on how to use a product
    C) Talk about how good you are in your niche topic
    D) Build a visually appealing website about the topic

5. What is the best way to find information about products you've never used before?

    A) Copy content of other affiliate marketers about it
    B) Make things up about the product
    C) Buy the product yourself to test it
    D) Use the information written in the marketing flyers of the product

6. Which of the following is a good source of user information about the product?

    A) It's website
    B) Other blogs
    C) Amazon's review section

D) Magazines

7. What type of content would probably do well in Facebook?

    A) A link post to your latest content
    B) An emotional video related to your content
    C) An image of your website's front page
    D) A rant about your competitors

8. How do you make sure that your content does well in social media?

    A) Post your content in other people's pages
    B) Buy social media up-votes
    C) Create a specific type of content for your chosen social media platform
    D) Post your content in as many groups as possible

9. How do you encourage users to engage with your content?

    A) Put more videos in your content
    B) Entertain people's comments in the website
    C) Talk about how good your content is
    D) Make a pop up that forces people to make a comment

10. How do you convince people to click on your affiliate link?

    A) Fool the user to thinking that he is going to a different website by clicking the link
    B) Fill your webpage with affiliate links
    C) Rant about how bad other products in the market are
    D) State a clear call-to-action to click on the link

Inspiration #7

"The only place where success comes before work is in the dictionary."
Vidal Sassoon

Chapter 7

Using Social Media Platforms For Affiliate Marketing

As mentioned above, social media is one of the best sources of traffic right now. Next to Google search, social media apps will probably become your best source of traffic. Learning how to funnel traffic from these sources can lead to a significant increase in your earnings. To learn how to make use of the different apps in the market, use the following steps:

1. Find the social media website or app where most of your target audience spend their time

There are hundreds of social media apps out there. However, you do not have to participate in all of them. Instead, you only need to find the online communities where most of your target audience hangs out. If you are targeting adults between the ages of 25 and 40, Facebook, Pinterest, Twitter and LinkedIn may be the best options for you. For young adults between 20 and 25, Instagram and Snapchat are the more popular options.

There are more social media options available depending on your target country and the interests of your audience. If you can clearly define what demographics your target audience belongs to, you will be able to choose the right network.

2. Identify what content to share in each network

Each social network favors different types of content. You want to know what type of content each social network requires before you start your social media marketing campaigns.

Facebook is a truly multimedia social networking platform, in that you can post any type of content in there. However, since the time video content was allowed, it has dominated all other types of contents in terms of engagement and reach. You will still need to mix it up though by posting images, text content and links from time to time to add variety to your page.

Instagram on the other hand is focused on hosting images and short videos. Pinterest is used as a tool to collect images from around the web. If you have a project for example, you can use your Pinterest account as a vision board of inspirations.

LinkedIn is just like Facebook. However, the users in this network prefer content that are related to careers, professional networking, finance and personal growth. If you post so-called viral content in LinkedIn, most users will unfollow you. They just do not want their feeds to be filled with distractions.

Twitter is ruled by short text content. You will also find some pictures and videos in there but text conversations dominate this network. You can post your opinions and your thoughts in twitter as long as you make your message fit in the character number limit of the network. You can also react to other people's tweets by pressing or tapping on the heart icon under each tweet. The retweet option however, is the primary sharing feature for tweets. The most popular tweets in the worlds are retweeted millions of times.

Businesses are fond of twitter because they can use it to communicate directly with their fans. It works both as a customer service and a marketing platform.

3. Find out how content is spread in the network

Each social network has a unique way of spreading content. Most social networks use a system where in users can follow other users. When a user follows you, they will see every public post you share in your account. This system is used in almost all the popular social networks today such as Facebook, Twitter, Instagram and Snapchat.

A user with millions of follower is considered an influencer or authority. They hold a lot of power in the social network because any of their posts can be seen by millions of people. As an affiliate marketer, you want your social network accounts to reach this kind of status. You can do this by sharing excellent quality posts.

Aside from increasing the number of followers, you can also share your content by encouraging engagement. This is a second feature common to all social networks. They allow users to engage with content. In Facebook for example, the network allows the users to select a reaction for the content shares. The thumbs-up icon is called the like button.

This is a form of an up-vote towards the content. In recent years, Facebook also added other reactions to convey the user's emotion towards the content. A person who finds the content funny for example, can choose a laughing emoji. If the content is sad, the user also has the option to use the sad emoji. All these reactions however, count as a form of engagement. The more reactions a content gets, the higher the likelihood will be that the content will spread.

Aside from reactions, Facebook can also leave a comment below the content. Facebook comments are powerful engagement signals because sometimes, they encourage other users to also engage in the discussion. The tagging feature of Facebook also helps content spread wider through the comment feature.

In Facebook, the newsfeed is the primary sharing feature among users. When a user shares something on Facebook, that user's followers will see the shared content in their newsfeeds. As an affiliate marketer, you want your shared content to show in the newsfeeds of your target audience. Driving the engagement up in your contents will help you achieve this. More people will discover your content if other users are engaged with the content.

Instagram also has an up-vote feature in the form of a heart. By double tapping an image in Instagram, you are able to up-vote a content. Just like Facebook, Instagram also allows users to comment and to tag other users. While Instagram also has feeds that shows the shared content of the users you follow, this is not how other people will discover your Instagram account.

Most of the content discovery happens in the search screen of the app. When the user taps on the magnifying glass icon in the bottom of the app, the search screen will show. In this part of the app, the user can search for accounts, hashtags, and places. In the same part of the app, they will also see suggested images and video content. The suggestions in this part of the app are based on the perceived interests of the said user. This perceived interest is based on many factors like the accounts followed by the user, the types of images and videos they clicked on or up-voted in the past and past searches made by the user.

For your content to be shown to the right people on Instagram, you should establish your accounts identity. You can do this by controlling the types of content your share. If your Instagram account is about gardening, you should post mostly images and videos about your garden. You can also post about significant events, but you should still increase the frequency of posting content related to your affiliate marketing topic.

You could also establish what your content is about by putting a detailed description of your account in the account Bio. This is the part just below you profile picture and your name when you are looking at your profile page. To make your content spread, you should also add descriptions below your content that are relevant to your affiliate marketing topic. Your content will also reach many other users if you include the right hashtags to it.

Twitter also uses many of the social networking features discussed above. Users in this network can follow one another to subscribe to each other's tweets. However, one does not need to be a follower to participate in the public conversations of other people. Just like with Instagram, people use the search feature to find content here. They can also find related tweets by clicking on hashtags.

Twitter is well known for its high click-through rate. Users in this network are more open to clicking on links. If many of your target audience are twitter users, you may have the opportunity to earn big.

4. Completely create your account and start sharing

If you do not know where to start in using social media, start by choosing a platform where most of your users are found and create an account there. To be successful, you will need to complete all the details of your account. In most cases, you will be required to add a profile image and a larger cover photo in the case of Facebook, Twitter and LinkedIn.

You will also be asked to write a description about yourself or your page. Just fill in whatever form the account creation process gives you.

After creating the account, you should plan how and where you will get your content. It is possible to grow your social media accounts by using other people's images and videos. However, you will find more success if you have an option to create your own content.

5. Facebook and LinkedIn groups

One of the best ways of using social media to keep your audience tuned into the content you create is by using the group feature of social networks. Networks like Facebook and LinkedIn have features that allow you to create groups where network users can join. These groups are effective in keeping your audience engaged with the content you are promoting.

A gardening blog owner from Canada for example, can create a group in Facebook about the topic for his home town. He could then ask his friends and relatives who are interested in gardening to join the group. In the group, he could create conversation topics regularly. An active group can have hundreds to thousands of new content per day. What matters most however, is not the actual number of posts but the amount of engagement of the group members in those posts. Among the different ways to engage in post, comments are probably the biggest newsfeed ranking indicator. The more comments your content gets, the greater its reach will be.

There are two steps to social media group marketing. The first step is the process of growing the group. You can start building the group by talking adding the people you actually know to the group. If you know for sure that a person you know is interested in your affiliate marketing niche, talk to them about it and ask them if they want to join your group.

After tapping your natural circles, you can start using your other marketing tools to promote your group. You can begin by talking about it in every other post in your website. You could then leave a link to your group. You could also promote your group in your different social media accounts. If you have a Facebook page, you should link it to your group.

The easiest way to increase the number of member of your group is by introducing it to the people you meet every day who are also interested in the niche topic. If you meet a coworker for example who also likes your content, you could tell them about your group. This group is an effective way for you to create a place for all your followers to meet each other. Your follower can be from different social networks and some may even find you on Facebook. By having a group in Facebook or LinkedIn, you will have a place where they can all meet and have a conversation amongst themselves.

If you are not familiar with how social media groups work, you could begin by joining one first. Ideally, you should join one that is related to your chosen affiliate marketing niche. Observe how the manager or administrators of the group keep the users engaged. Take note of the types of content that he or she is posting in the group. The purpose of these groups is for people to have meaningful conversations about the common topic that they are interested in. However, it could also be for other purposes. Sometimes, people use these groups to build relationships. Others do it to solve problems. They do this by posting a question in the group, hoping that group members will be able to answer it.

While you are in the group, start participating in the conversation. If you see a question that you know the answer to, answer it for the person asking. Also, while you are there, observe how different types of content rise up in the groups newsfeeds. Just like in any other type of social media newsfeeds, the content in social media groups are usually shown based on the amount of engagement they get. In short, contents with a lot of comments and reactions tend to be shown to more viewers.

Also, take note of how the members interact and how they react to posts. In places like Facebook, you are more likely to see people talking in a casual manner, sometimes even using informal writing to communicate. In LinkedIn, people tend to communicate in a more respectful and politically correct way. You will need to set the tone with how people communicate in your own group in the future.

The group will only continue to grow beyond the people you add if the community becomes active. To do this, you could make the group come alive by keeping the conversations going. You could do this by sharing content to it. You may also appoint some of the most active members of the group to become your co-administrators. These people will help you police the group and to make it a pleasant place for the members. They can also help in keeping the community members active. You should not worry if the progress of growing your group seems slow. As long as you keep adding content and keep participating in your own group, it will continue to grow.

The content that you share in the group does not have to be always your own. You could put content from other sources as well, as long as they fit the purpose of the group. Every time you post a new content in your website however, be sure to post it in the group.

If the group grows, you can even use it as a way to drive some affiliate sales. The members of a group about professional networking for instance, will be interested in new books about the topic. If the group owner sees an interesting book, he could make a post about it in his book. He could then use Amazon Associate links to promote the book in the group. If some of the group members buy from Amazon after using the link, you may earn commission from it.

Chapter 7 Quiz
Please refer to Appendix G for the answers to this quiz

1. Which of the following statements is true?

    A) You should create accounts in all social networking websites and apps
    B) You only need to learn how to use Facebook
    C) Instagram is the best app to use right now
    D) The choice for the best social media platform to use depends on your target audience

2. From a marketing standpoint, what is the most important aspect of a social networking app or website?

    A) The visually appealing content
    B) The underlying technology
    C) The community of likeminded individuals
    D) The ease of entry to the app

3. What is the best way to communicate your website to social media users

    A) Communicate with the social media users in a natural but charismatic way
    B) Flood your account with promotional content
    C) Pay other users to do the marketing for you
    D) Attack the beliefs of others users to gain attention from the rest of the community

4. Which social network should you use if you have a great video content to share?

    A) Instagram
    B) Twitter
    C) LinkedIn
    D) It depends on the topic of the video

5. Which social network is great for promoting products for professionals?

    A) Instagram
    B) Twitter
    C) Pinterest
    D) LinkedIn

6. How does content spread in Facebook?

    A) People share them
    B) They naturally spread through newsfeed algorithm
    C) They only spread through ads

D) Only private contents are allowed in Facebook

7. Which of the following has a high impact in the spread of content in Social Media?

    A) Mention of brand names and celebrities
    B) Time of posting
    C) Hashtags
    D) Engagement with the content

8. What feature of Facebook allows people of the same interest to meet?

    A) Facebook Live
    B) Facebook groups
    C) Newsfeeds
    D) Messenger

9. What feature in groups will have the biggest impact in helping the spread of content?

    A) Likes
    B) Comments
    C) Spam
    D) Pinning of content

10. What is the best part of having a successful social media group?

    A) Being liked by the members of the group
    B) Being popular in the social network
    C) Instant likes in your posts
    D) Access to a homogenous audience

Inspiration #8

"Success is not final; failure is not fatal: It is the courage to continue that counts."

Winston S. Churchill

Chapter 8

Common Affiliate Marketing Mistakes

Many people who try to build an affiliate marketing business fail because they make common mistakes that end up ruining their business. In this section, we will discuss the most important mistakes so that you will be able to avoid them when you do start your own affiliate marketing career.

1. Thinking that a website is the only way to sell affiliate products

Many affiliate marketers make the mistake of focusing too much on their website and not finding other opportunities outside to promote their affiliate products. Every now and then, your followers will forgive you if you promote to them through Facebook, Twitter or even Instagram.

When guest posting in your friends' website, you can also post affiliate links relevant to your topic. Make sure that you get the permission of the website owner first. Few will actually allow you to do so. However, if it is possible, you should take the opportunity.

2. Not building a community from day one

The biggest affiliate marketers in the industry can demand certain discounts, freebies and other promotions. They can do this because tens to hundreds of thousands of people follow their content. This is your goal and it makes sense to start building this goal for day one.

From your first article or video, you should already start considering your audience as a part of that community. If you have this kind of mindset, you will be able to avoid making some of the basic mistakes in this list. With a community building mindset, you will put your community member's interest first. You will not focus on factors like commission rates of your products or conversion rates of your marketing tools. Instead, you will be able to focus on helping the members of your community. You can do this by providing useful content to your audience (community members) and opening them to exclusive offers that only you can give them.

In the beginning though, try to help your community members by providing them with the information they need. As your community grows, you will be repaid by the love they show your content. They will talk about it, not only in the comment areas of your website but also in other places online.

3. Becoming too salesy by claiming exaggerated results

Many affiliate marketers think that selling is all about highlighting the positive parts of the products they promote. This is far from what is actually happening in reality. The population of internet users is becoming smarter each year. They are becoming more mindful of false information. This is especially true with internet buyers. With thousands of products available online, the average consumer have options on where to get their products.

If you make exaggerated claims regarding the features and benefits of the product you are promoting, most people will call you out for it. People are more vigilant now with these types of schemes. If they think that you are fooling people with your claims, they may make a post about it in social media. It is common nowadays for regular people to attack business by posting negative things about them online.

When posting about your products in any of your content, you should make it a habit only to talk about the facts. When using a product for instance, you should only talk about how you like to personally use it. Talk about the pros and cons of the product based on your experience. If you set an extremely high expectation, your audience will be disappointed when the product actually arrives in the mail. Because you have a website, they will be able to go back to your claims and leave negative comments. They may even call your entire business a scam. You do not want this to happen to you.

4. Not working with a partner

An affiliate marketing business is easy to start. You can definitely fund it and work on it on your own. However, it is also the ease of entry that makes it easy to let go. Many of people who fail at affiliate marketing give up on the task before they even start making money. When they fail to see results in the first few weeks of creating content, they start to doubt the process and consider quitting. Many of them give up on their project before the sixth month period.

One way to avoid this is by working with others who believe in your vision. I am not talking about hiring an employee. Instead, I am talking about working with a partner. A business partner motivates you to work on the business even when you do not want to. It also has the same effect on your partner. They will also be forced to work on the business because you are holding them accountable.

A partner not only increases the amount of work hours put on a business but also gives it a longer financial runway. In startups, the runway refers to amount of time that the capital fund of a business can fund its operations. If all business partners chip in to fund the affiliate business, the financial risk will be divided.

In the beginning, the first few people you will convince to use your affiliate links are your family and friends. Your friends and family members will be the first group of people who will see the content and marketing materials you share in your social networking accounts.

With a partner, the reach of your organic marketing will significantly increase. You will be able to double the amount of people who sees your marketing materials if both partners share the content with their personal social media accounts.

5. Shiny Object Syndrome

Another reason why most affiliate marketers fail is because of what is known in the industry as the "shiny object syndrome". This phenomenon is common among entrepreneurs. The minds of entrepreneurs are so active in looking for business opportunities that it continues even when they are already working on a business. Many of the entrepreneurs who lack discipline jump from one business opportunity to another. In the middle of working on an affiliate marketing project, they decide to abandon it and start doing another type of business. This usually happens when the first idea takes too long to start showing progress.

You can avoid this common mistake by plotting the steps that you need to take to reach your goal and holding yourself accountable for reaching these goals. Consider that if you start with another project while you are in the middle of another one, you will go back to square one. Instead, you should just take note of your business ideas for you to start later on. For now, put all your focus, energy and effort on the current project you are working on. The more time and resources you put on this project, the better its chances will be of becoming successful.

6. Not delegating tasks

Affiliate marketing is a business. All businesspeople need to use the power of delegating to be successful. Creating a successful community for your affiliate marketing offers will require a lot of work. You will need to write hundreds of thousands of words of content. You will also need to create hundreds of hours' worth of video and audio content.

Creating content is more than just writing or recording. You also need to do a lot of research before writing, proofread your articles, edit your videos, create featured images for your blog posts, and create thumbnail images for YouTube.

The point is that your success depends on thousands of hours of work. To become successful, you will need help. This is where a VA can help you. VA stands for virtual assistant. To hire a real assistant, you will need to consider many factors like his or her pay, benefits, tools for working and other things. A VA on the other hand, is hired by a third-party company. You only pay the company a fraction of what you would normally pay a full time personal assistant. In turn, they will provide you with an assistant that has the skills that you need for your business.

Today's Virtual Assistants come in different forms. Some of them are jack-of-all-trades. They can do pretty much everything from writing your content to editing your YouTube videos. There are also some types of VA with specialized skills. Some can act as a personal assistant, answering emails and scheduling appointments for you so that you no longer have to deal with these kinds of tasks. Some specialize in specific industries, like real estate, accounting, finance and many more.

You can also use VAs to get some of your tasks off your plate. If you do not have the skills for editing your own videos for example, you can look for a VA with this kind of skillset. You can agree on a price and start on a per-project basis. If they deliver in terms of the quality of work and deadlines, you could hire them again for future projects. If their quality of work or work ethic is problematic, you have the choice to give them another chance or to let them go.

Finding a good employee is just as complicated online as it is offline. It may take you a few tries before you find one that works well for your business process.

7. Failing to track results

After building your affiliate marketing assets, you cannot just sit back and wait for the business to make you money. You need to continue observing the system you've developed and examine how it could be improved. Examine each step that your customers take before they end up making a purchase and find ways to improve their success rate. In some cases, you may need to improve your activities in gathering traffic. There may also be some improvements needed in converting your traffic into paying customers.

You can only learn what improvements are needed if your track the important data in your website. Luckily, you can do this free with tools like Google Analytics, Google Webmaster Tools, Twitter Analytics, Facebook Pixels and other forms of website activity tracking technology. They are easy to set up but the insights they provide can be the different between success and failure.

Chapter 8 Quiz
Please refer to Appendix H for the answers to this quiz

1. Which statement is true?

    A) You can only promote affiliate links in your website
    B) You can only promote affiliate links in your blog posts
    C) You can only promote affiliate links by spamming social media
    D) You can promote affiliate links in many places online

2. What do you call a person who trusts your vision enough to invest in your business and work with you to make it succeed?

    A) Virtual Assistant
    B) Business Partner
    C) Angel Investor
    D) Affiliate

3. What is an advantage of having a partner?

    A) Bigger operational capital
    B) Easier working process
    C) Larger affiliate sales numbers
    D) Faster spread of content in search engines

4. How do you track your sales numbers?

    A) Through the affiliate dashboard stats area
    B) Through the commission you receive
    C) Through Google Analytics
    D) Through Social Media Insights

5. What do people hate when they are looking for good content about a product?

    A) Engaging videos
    B) Images of the product in use
    C) Exaggerated claims
    D) Formal grammar

6. What is an example of an exaggerated claim?

    A) This laptop has 4GB of RAM
    E) This phone can be submerged until six inches of water

F) The casing is made from aluminum
G) This chair is the best computer chair I've ever seen in my entire life

7. How does the "Shiny Object Syndrome" affect your success?

    A) It allows you to accomplish more tasks in lesser time
    B) It doubles you productivity at night
    C) It prevents you from finishing projects
    D) It prevents you from selling affiliate products

8. What do you call workers who can do specific tasks for you over the internet?

    A) Virtual assistants
    B) Drones
    C) Crowdsourcing
    D) Ghostwriters

9. Which of the following statements is true?

    A) Virtual assistants are good only for menial tasks
    B) Virtual assistants will steal your ideas
    C) Some virtual assistants have specialized skills
    D) Virtual assistants are too expensive for the affiliate marketing business

10. Which of the following statements is true?

    A) You can succeed only by delegating all your tasks to virtual assistants
    B) You can succeed by doing everything things on your own
    C) You can start delegating tasks to lessen the workload on yourself
    D) Virtual assistants cannot be trusted

Inspiration #9

"Don't be afraid to give up the good to go for the great."
John D. Rockefeller

Chapter 9

Choosing the Right Niche

Choosing the right niche is just as important as choosing the right affiliate program to join. Many beginners start out just making affiliate marketing websites for the first topic that enters their minds. Three months into the project, they are no longer motivated to work on the topic. This is one of the primary reasons why beginner affiliate marketers quit on their project. In this section, we will discuss how you can choose the best niche for you:

Make a list of your hobbies, interests and passions

First, you will need to make a list of the hobbies, interests and passions you have in life. Consider the things that you spend the most of your time in. You could also include a topic about your occupation if you enjoy talking about it. Also, think about the topics that you would like to learn. Choose at least 15 topics and list them down.

Arrange the topics you've chosen according to how much you enjoy talking about them

Next, you should arrange the topics based on how much you enjoy it. Right off the bat, you will notice that there are some topics that you enjoy more than others. Look into these topics first when you are deciding on an affiliate marketing niche.

Survey other people's interest about the subject

Starting with the first topic on your list, you should start researching the interest of other people in the topic. You want to start working on a topic that people are interested in. You can start by surveying the content in your big traffic sources (Google Search, Facebook, Twitter, and Instagram). You could do a quick Google search about the topic and take note of the content that comes out. You could also look into the content marketing accounts in social networks that deal with this type of content. You can guess the popularity of a topic based on the number of engagement they get in social media.

Survey the competition

If you are satisfied with the amount of interest that that a topic gets, you should check the competition in the market about it next. You probably already encountered some of your content marketing competition when you were doing the previous step. Any website that is doing some sort of content marketing is one of your competition because they are trying to take your target audience's attention away. The more competition you have, the harder it will be for you to stand out in the content market place.

Ideally, you should pick a topic with the least amount of competition. However, at times, you can succeed in a high-competition niche by narrowing your content's focus only on the more profitable topics. With the topic recreational running for example, you could choose to focus only on the topic of running gear. You could share content about the latest and best running shoes, clothing and gadgets in the market.

Find the most commonly searched problems about this niche

Now that you have a niche in mind, start planning the types of content that you will create. You should start writing about the content before you even set up your affiliate marketing website. This way, you will be able to start promoting the moment the website is live.

To find topics to talk about, you should start with the problems that people interested in the niche face. If you are just learning about the topic yourself, you should look into the problems that beginners tend to run into. This way, you will also be writing with a beginner's point of view.

Find affiliate products that can solve the problems in these niches

After choosing the niche based on its popularity and the amount of competition in the market, you should look into the available affiliate products you can sell in that niche. You could start by looking for products that will solve the problems established in the previous step.

The easiest way to start is to look for products and brands in Amazon. Amazon sells pretty much everything. If you cannot find the product that you would like to promote in other companies, there is a good chance that it will be available in Amazon.

Amazon though has a low commission rate. To get better commission rates, you should check if the product you want to promote can be found in other affiliate networks discussed previously.

Chapter 9 Quiz
Please refer to Appendix H for the answers to this quiz

1. What do you call a small segment of a larger market where certain products can focus their marketing efforts?

    A) Finance market
    B) Business to Business Market
    C) Niche Market
    D) Open Market

2. How does focusing on a niche market help your website?

    A) It attracts a group of people with specialized needs
    B) It allows the website to attract a bigger number of visitors
    C) It gives the websites opportunities for special promotions
    D) It increases the number of possible content

3. How do you start finding the right niche for you?

    A) Ask the people around me for the best niches
    B) Explore my own hobbies and interests
    C) Look for products online
    D) Build the website and see which content ranks well

4. How do you check if other people are interested about the niche topic?

    A) Visit popular news websites regularly
    B) Ask your friends and family if they will be interested about it
    C) Check related content in social media and the amount of engagement they get
    D) Do an initial ad campaign about the topic

5. Which topic should you take?

    A) Topic with the most competition
    B) Topic with no competition
    C) Topic that has more products associated with it
    D) Topics that has one expensive product associated with it

6. How do you differentiate your website from the strong competitors in the niche market?

    A) Copy the content of the competitors
    B) Pick a specialized niche topic that few people have talked about

C) Post 5 or more contents every day
D) Use a catchy domain name

7. How do you look for content on your chosen niche topic?

    A) Make things up
    B) Research on the common problems that people encounter when researching about the topic
    C) Research on the ways on how you can promote products to visitors
    D) Buy products in your niche and review them

8. If you are writing how-to contents about the niche topic, who are likely to come to your website?

    A) Random people
    B) Experts in the topic
    C) Beginners in the topic
    D) People who need to solve the how-to problem

9. If you are writing news content about the niche topic where will your content be most effective?

    A) Search engines
    B) Social Media
    C) Forums
    D) Question and Answer websites

10. If you've chosen the basketball sneakers niche, which type of content should you create and share?

    A) Articles about the latest sneakers in the market
    B) Articles about girlfriend of basketball stars
    C) Videos about basketball highlights
    D) Videos about rumors and gossips in basketball

Inspiration #10

"Successful people do what unsuccessful people are not willing to do. Don't wish it were easier; wish you were better."

Jim Rohn

Congratulations!

The eight character of the password required to unlock the business scorecard is letter p.

Chapter 10

Building your Email List

Many of the people who go to your website will not necessarily click on the affiliate link. Most of them will just leave without taking any action that helps your business. You can use an email marketing campaign to keep a percentage of these people coming back to your website. Email marketing is effective because it makes you part of one of the most common habits among professionals, checking emails.

People treat emails with a higher level of priority compared to other forms of communication because it is usually used for work. Checking one's emails is one of the first things that most people do when they get to work. By setting up an affiliate marketing campaign, you will be able to put your affiliate marketing business in the screens of people who do have the power and the willingness to buy the products you promote.

To implement an effective email marketing campaign, you will need to learn the steps on how to make people sign up and how to use email newsletters to keep them coming back to your website. The basic steps of an affiliate marketing campaign come in three basic steps:

- ❖ Capturing emails
- ❖ Automated response
- ❖ Sending out newsletters and email-exclusive promotions

Experts say that it takes at least seven interactions with your brand before the average new customer decides to buy. If you want new visitors to come to your shop and buy using your affiliate links, you will need to make them keep coming back to your website, constantly. An email campaign is an effective way to do this. First though, you will need to convince your visitors to give up their email addresses.

You can do this through your content marketing campaign. In your website, you could set up an email capturing tool that appears together with the content. The placement of these email capturing forms is important. Here are the places where you should be placing them:

Before your content

An email form before the content will ensure that the visitors see it. In this position, more people will see it and a higher number of visitors may sign up. Make sure though that it occupies only a small part of the screen and it can be dismissed.

In-content

Most online readers have developed a habit to skip everything above the fold and go straight to the content. Their eyes go from the title of the article straight to the first paragraph. For visitors with this kind of habit, you can put your email capturing tool inside the article. This strategy works because you can use the text in the content or the other types of media to bring attention to the email subscription form.

In pop-ups

Pop ups can be good or bad depending on how you use it. If you use it to promote unwanted ads, then people will hate your website. In the case of email subscription popups on the other hand, you are actually offering something that people may like.

The best part about popups is that you can choose an action that will trigger it. For instance, some popups are triggered after you have spent a considerable amount of time in the website. Some of them are also triggered by activities like clicks or pressing the close button to leave the page. With these triggers, you can capture the emails of visitors based on their intended activity in the website. You can have it triggered for example by a call-to-action button. Or, you can also capture it when the person is about to leave.

In the Sidebar

In the past, bloggers and content marketers mostly put their email subscription forms in the sidebar. This makes the form easily visible, especially if it is placed above the fold. Unfortunately, because of the use of the sidebar for placing ads, internet users have generally developed the habit of avoiding looking at the sidebars. Because of this, the effectiveness of forms placed in this section has decreases.

The increase in the use of mobile devices to view websites has also made sidebars less effective. In a mobile-responsive theme, the sidebars are placed under the content. This means that your forms at the sidebar will only be viewed after the visitor read the content. Unfortunately, between 40-60% of readers never get to the bottom of articles. If you post mostly long articles, expect that the sidebar forms will be ignored. If you post short posts on the other hand, a large part of your traffic may reach the bottom of your content and more people will see your forms.

AMP Pages and Facebook Instant Articles

Facebook and Google are both promoting the use of stripped down pages for mobile devices to increase the speed of webpage loading. Google calls this type of webpage AMP or accelerated mobile pages. Facebook has its own version of this and they call it Facebook Instant Articles.

Both of these traffic sources have guidelines on how to create these types of pages. For Google, you only need to create a special part of your website dedicated to AMP. This type of page is stripped down its usual features. Any extra code is removed and only the essentials are left.

For Facebook Instant Articles, you will need to create alternate versions of your content inside of Facebook. The Instant Articles will be hosted by Facebook themselves and you will need to pass an application process to be able to use this feature.

These types of pages are effective in collecting emails because they are fast loading and they tend to have higher capturing rates compared to the average webpage. The lack of distractions in the AMP and the Facebook Instant Articles makes it easier for people to see the email form you set up. In the case of Facebook instant articles, the email address of the Facebook user is already typed in the form. A user only needs to click the subscribe button to sign up to your email newsletter.

Other social networks

You can also get more email newsletters from the other social media assets you have. If you have an Instagram page for instance, make use of it by mentioning your email newsletters in your post descriptions. You could then add the link to your email subscription form in the bio. This is a much better approach than just to drive Instagram users to your latest content. It will consistently create a call to action that can lead to returning visitors.

Aside from Instagram, you could also mention your email newsletters in your personal and business twitter page. Together with your regular marketing posts, you could include a call-to-action link leading to your subscription form pages. It will be challenging for you to craft a good copy in twitter because of the limit in the number of characters that you can use. You can use other types of media though, like images and videos, to capture the attention of your audience better.

Above, we talked about Facebook Instant Articles. This is not the only way though to collect emails from Facebook. You can also put your email subscription link in the description of your Facebook content. While Instant Articles can also be effective in spreading the news about your website, contents like videos and viral images will have an even greater reach to your audiences in Facebook.

To start, you should pick one piece of content that you will use as your carrier. Ideally, you should choose the type of content that has no other call-to-action feature. For example, you can use a how-to video in your niche. You could also use an image that you think your target market can relate to. If you are satisfied with the content, you could then post it in your Facebook page.

In the description section of your content, you could then add a paragraph for promoting your email subscription form. In this section you could state some of the benefits that they can get for signing up. Together with the text marketing copy, you can then add a link to your sign up form.

Creating a Lead Capture/Squeeze page

A lead capture page is a type of landing page designed to capture opt-in email addresses from potential subscribers. The goal of a squeeze page is to convince, cajole, or otherwise "squeeze" a visitor into providing one of their most sought-after and coveted pieces of personal data: the email address. An example squeeze page is shown below:

To be successful collecting leads, your capture pages need to have the right balance of "ask" and "reward." The "ask" are the form fields you use, and the "reward" is the offer you're promoting.

A lead capture page that asks visitors for irrelevant information to the offer is abandoned because a poorly-optimized lead capture form is one of the leading causes of landing page friction. Ideally, your form should not ask for more than basic contact information on the user's first interaction with your company.

A number of companies provide softwares that help you design these capture pages. One of the good ones out there is clickfunnels. Below are the reasons why:

- Clickfunnels provides you with a LOT of pre-built funnel templates. For those who have never designed a funnel before this will be perfect for you!
- Great visual drag and drop editor which is very beginner friendly
- Huge selection of page elements (name field, telephone number, countdown timer etc.)
- The ability to share your funnels with your friends and clients!
- Amazing onboarding process - Wrapping your head around all that ClickFunnels can do may seem daunting at first. But this is helped by a fun on-boarding process. When you first sign up, you're presented with the 7-day challenge. It consists of 4 different games with each one having a number of steps to complete. Every step features a task and a short video clip of Russell explaining what you need to do to finish it.
- If you're interested in getting a 14 days free trial, go to the clickfunnels website or my website at www.MichaelEzeanaka.com (disclaimer – I am an affiliate)

Limit the number of times you ask for visitors' emails

People do not like it if you keep pestering them with intrusive call-to-action features. You do not want people to leave because your marketing campaign is too aggressive. With this in mind, you should limit your popups to just one per session. You can even program popup plugins in WordPress to stop showing to repeat visitors. This will ensure that your visitors will not get the wrong impression from your aggressive ways of capturing emails.

Ask for emails in a natural way

The language you use when asking for email addresses affects the effectiveness of your tools. Ideally, you should talk in the language of your average visitor. If you are talking to professionals for instance, you can use formal English to talk to them so that they are more likely to engage. If you are talking to young adults for instance, try to use modern colloquialism that young adults use. Your familiarity of your target audience plays a big role in your ability to create your call-to-action statements.

State your email campaign's unique value proposition in your email subscription forms

People will not just automatically sign up to your email newsletter service just because you have your forms set up. You still need to convince them to sign up by promising them the right things. We call this part your unique value proposition. This is a paragraph or a statement that comes with you subscription form where you state the benefits of signing up. You could tell them what they will get for signing up to your website.

Think of different ways for you to get the attention of your viewers towards your signup forms. Some affiliate marketers for instance, give out free digital products like a free eBook or a free trial to a service, to encourage people to sign up to the email campaign. You can also do the same. One way to do this is to create an awesome eBook that fits the interest of your niche market. You could then sell the eBook to Amazon and other eBook selling platforms. Doing this will allow you to establish the value of your books. After setting it up in these websites, offer a free version of your book in your website, telling them that they will be able to read the book for free if they sign up to your email service.

In the process, you could also explain the other things that they can get for signing up to your email newsletters. You could state what types of content you send out and how often you send them out. For instance, you could tell them that you have a video tutorial series that are available only to email newsletter subscribers.

Creating many types of lists

As your website grows, you will eventually find that you have multiple categories of content. This can lead to attracting audience that has different interests and goals for coming to your website. If you are attracting a heterogeneous traffic, you may need to create multiple types of email lists, categorized according to the interests and goals of your market. If the person first arrived in an article about planting green leafy vegetables for instance, you could have him sign up in a newsletter that promises content about planting green leafy vegetables. You also notice that great deal of your visitors is attracted towards your articles and videos about composting. You can create a different type of list exclusively for these people.

It goes without saying that you will need to craft very different autoresponder messages for these two lists. The welcome message and future messages should be related to the interests of your subscriber. You could also create a different list based on the buying stage of the subscriber. You could create an email list for beginners for instance. You could create another one for those who are interested in advanced level contents. Beginners for a topic will need a different set of content and affiliate offers compared to those who are already in the advanced or expert levels.

You could then create a sales funnel. In a sales funnel, you try to convert passive readers of your email newsletters into buyers of your offers. You can do this by adjusting the content that you send to your subscribers, from entertaining and informational to contents that suggest buying products and services.

Engaging with the customer

You should capitalize on the hype that the visitors get when they sign up with your email campaign. The energy and enthusiasm of subscribers are highest at this point. When they sign up, they are eager to see what types of content you have to offer in your email marketing campaign.

Creating your autoresponders

The signup process for email newsletters is pretty straightforward. After signing up with your email subscription form, your subscribers will expect a welcome email. You can set this up with your autoresponder service.

Create your content with your chosen email marketing management service. The email should read in a warm manner, making your new subscribers feel welcome. If you made any promises in the sign up process, you can start fulfilling them in the welcome email. If you promised a free eBook for instance, you should have the link to your eBook in the welcome email of your newsletter.

In addition to the welcome email, you should create more content related to your unique value proposition in the email subscription process. If you promised unique types of content in your email, you could craft them ahead of time and have them sent out daily through your autoresponders. Let's say that your website is about home keeping. You could begin by creating list article where in you talk about 5 ways to keep the home organized. Instead of showing the entire article to your audience however, you could have the content drip in the email newsletter auto responder. You could then have them scheduled to be sent out twice a week so that people will anticipate them.

Make sure that the content in your welcome emails and in the succeeding auto-response to be substantial so that people will find them valuable. If your email subscribers do not view these emailed content valuable, they may end up ignoring your emails or they may choose to unsubscribe.

To automate the process of sending out these autoresponders, you could use email campaign management services like Aweber. With this tool, you can create prepared emails with the names of the future subscriber in the content. You can also set up the emails to send every week. As at the time of writing, they do an initial 30-day free trial. Alternatively, feel free to check it out at my website (disclaimer – I am an affiliate).

Choose your email marketing approach

There is more than one way to craft your autoresponders and email newsletters. In this section, we will discuss the different approaches and email layouts you can use to create your emails.

The personal approach

If you website is heavily reliant on your personality, you may need to use the personal approach in creating your emails. With this method, you are communicating towards your subscribers as if you are writing a letter to them. The goal of any content you add is to create a personal relationship with the subscriber.

This method requires that you show your face throughout the email marketing process. It begins with the sign up process. In your sign up form, you could enhance the effectiveness of your opt-in tools by putting your own smiling face beside it. People love to join email marketing campaigns wherein they know who is behind it. By putting your own image with the marketing materials, you are establishing the trust between you and the subscriber. Remember that you are asking them to give up their email address at this point. For most people, giving up an email address is a sign that they are giving you're their trust. The best part about this is that you will significantly increase the success rate of your opt-in tools. People are more likely to signup if they see a familiar face.

The personal touch continues with the rest of the content that you send to the subscriber's emails. It begins with the welcome email. Together with your picture, you could also write a letter that sounds welcoming and personal. The idea is to thank your news subscribers by personally welcoming them into the program.

To continue this approach, you should aim to write personalized letters to your subscribers as a way to introduce your email content. The more interactions you have with these people, the better your relationship with them will be. With this kind of relationship in place, they are more likely to follow your suggestions and your recommendations. This will lead to higher sales numbers.

The brand approach

If you do not like putting your face in all your marketing tools, you may also choose to use the brand approach. In this approach, your aim is to have your subscribers trust your website, rather than your real persona. While many big businesses use this approach, it may take time for you to develop a brand name and to have people trust that brand.

With this approach however, you will be able to distance yourself from the business. With the personal approach, you need to be present to continue creating email content for your subscribers. They expect personal treatment from you.

With the brand approach on the other hand, the trust is with the brand that you have developed. Because of this, it will be easier for you to delegate task to the people around you. You can send out an email to your list with a less personal note and no one will notice because they trust the brand rather than your persona.

To start with this approach, you need to create uniform way of presenting your brand. To start with, you should decide on a brand name, a tag line and a logo. The brand name will be the name that your visitors will use when talking about your website. The tagline is a short phrase that tells new audiences about what your brand is about. The brand name and tagline should be easy to understand and say. They should roll off the tongue easily. You will also need to design a logo that represents what you stand for. Make your logo characteristics match the overall theme of your brand. If your website is about gardening for instance, your logo could be green and it could have images related to gardening. You can have such a logo professionally created for $5 in Fiverr.com.

To develop your website's brand, you need to show people that your website is a reliable source of information. To do this, you need to make sure that the website is already complete by the time you launch it. There should be no lacking aspect of your website. This will show that the website is backed by competent professionals. Next, you will need to add content to your website in a consistent manner. The content in both your website and your social media marketing assets should be professionally done. Ideally, they should be unique and not copied from other website.

Now that you have established that you run a professional website, the next step is to make this reflect in your email marketing campaign. While people using the personal approach can get away with sloppy newsletters, brands cannot. It is easy to forgive a person for common mistakes but it is significantly harder to forgive brands.

Chapter 10 Quiz
Please refer to Appendix I for the answers to this quiz

1. What is the primary purpose of an email marketing campaign?

    A) Increase affiliate sales
    B) Keep people coming back to your website
    C) To send people unwanted messages
    D) To reach strangers who have never been to your website before

2. What do you call the emails that are automatically sent after a person signs up?

    A) Autosender
    B) Autorepeater
    C) Autoresponder
    D) Autoblogger

3. What is an example of an email campaign management service?

    A) GoDaddy
    B) Aweber
    C) Facebook Pixels
    D) Google AdWords

4. What do you call the faster, stripped down version of webpages used by Google for displaying content in mobile devices

    A) AMP
    B) CBS
    C) BBD
    D) Instant Articles

5. How do you share your email subscription form in Instagram?

    A) Put a link of it in your bio and mention the link in your posts
    B) Put a link in your bio and the description of your posts
    C) Use private messaging to reach random people
    D) Comment the link in the images and videos of celebrities

6. In which placement position is an email form most likely to be engaged with?

- A) In the sidebar
- B) In-content
- C) In the footer
- D) In a new window pop-up

7. This is the part of the email subscription call-to-action that states the offer that only you can give the audience. You offer this feature to them in exchange for giving up their email addresses in the form...

- A) Free products
- B) Instant promotion
- C) Email newsletters
- D) Unique value proposition

8. Which practice should you avoid when showing your email subscription form?

- A) Put the form in the body of the article
- B) Show the form in 3 pop-ups for each visitor
- C) Put the form in your social media accounts
- D) Talk about the unique value proposition in the sign up

9. What is a good example of a freebie that you can give people to encourage them to sign up?

- A) Free eBook
- B) Membership to an exclusive websites
- C) Free coffee beans
- D) Discount with one of your promoted affiliate programs

10. What are the two approaches for talking with your audience through email?

- A) Brand and Personal approaches
- B) Business and Social approaches
- C) Single and Married approaches
- D) High-ticket and low-ticket approaches

Inspiration #11

"Don't let the fear of losing be greater than the excitement of winning."

Robert Kiyosaki

Chapter 11

Affiliate Marketing Strategies

An effective affiliate marketing strategy should be efficient. One way to ensure this is by keeping the number of clicks between the traffic source and the affiliate marketing landing page as few as possible. The fewer clicks it requires to reach the affiliate marketing website, the higher your conversion rate will be.

If you post your affiliate link directly to Facebook for example, there will be only one click between the source and the affiliate landing page. This is the shortest route between the traffic source (Facebook) and the landing page.

The model looks something like this:

Facebook > Affiliate Marketing Landing Page

In most cases however, this marketing model is not effective because most people are likely to avoid your content if it only contains an affiliate link. It may work to some degree in the beginning. Eventually though, your success rate will go down. Your audience will eventually catch on with what you are trying to do and they may avoid your post.

In addition, convincing people to move from a traffic source to the affiliate marketing landing page can be difficult. Most people do not want to move away from their social networks or their preferred websites. People only willingly click away from these websites or apps if they are motivated to do so. Most people would only move away from their Facebook or Twitter apps if there is an article they want to read or a video they want to watch.

The most successful content marketers use a different approach. They first send their traffic to their website content, where they can convince them to buy the product. They use the content marketing strategies, similar to the ones discussed in this book, to drive traffic from the traffic source to their websites. The model looks like this:

Facebook (Sample Traffic Source) > Website Content > Affiliate Marketing Landing Page

In this model, the process is still somewhat efficient because there are only two clicks between the traffic source and the affiliate marketing landing page. With this model, it will be easier for you to lure your target audience from the traffic source with the use of the right types of contents.

Track the movement of your users

When you are successfully sending traffic to your website through the various traffic sources, you need to set up your analytic tools to track how people move in your website. In the beginning, a big portion of your traffic will bounce. Bouncing refers to the act of leaving a website after viewing just one page. People usually bounce when the content in the website did not pique their interest. This is common with news websites where the average bounce rate is just above 80%. This means that 80% of the traffic leaves the website after reading just one news story.

As an affiliate marketer, you want your viewers to keep reading your content, transferring from one page to another. If this happens, it means that your contents are effective in keeping the attention of your website users. With this method, you will be able to track the movements of the users and identify the types of content that they are likely to click on.

You could also track the total number of clicks that your affiliate links get. The most accurate number will be posted in the statistics portion of your affiliate marketing account. In affiliate programs like Amazon Affiliates and ClickBank, these clicks are shown directly in your account dashboard. You can get the total success rate of your website in sending people to the affiliate landing pages by dividing the total number of clicks on your affiliate links by the total number of unique visitors to your website in a given period. You could then multiply the quotient by 100% to get the percentage value.

Let's say that you want to get your website's success rate for an entire week. You should take the total number of clicks on your affiliate links (found in your affiliate account) and the total number of unique visitors for the week (found in your website analytics) for the said period. You could then use this formula to get the effectiveness of your website in converting users:

Success rate = (number of clicks/total number of unique visitors) * 100%

Let' say that for that week 2,500 unique visitors went to your website. Of that number, 50 people clicked on your affiliate links. Using the formula above, we will get a success rate of 2%. With the success rate, you will be able to predict how well your website performs in sending people to an affiliate landing page in the future.

Judge each affiliate program based on their landing pages

The success rate metric alone however, is not enough to predict how much you will earn in the future. To get this prediction, you will need to get the average conversion rate of the landing page. The advertisers' landing pages are supposed to be designed to increase conversion. A 2-4% conversion rate is normal for a non-optimized affiliate landing page. These numbers can significantly increase to 10% and up if the advertisers test different pages and stick to the page layouts and designs that lead to the most conversions.

Online advertising professionals put a lot of time, working on increasing the conversion rates of their landing pages. However, some landing pages just work better than others. If all other factors are equal, you will earn more if you promote an affiliate program with an excellent landing page. Because of this, you want to stick only with advertisers whose landing page performs well. Unfortunately, you can only check how well a landing page performs by sending leads to it and measuring the results.

The conversion rate of a landing page is usually shown in the analytics section of your affiliate marketing account. If this is not the case however, you could calculate this yourself. To do this, you first need to find the total number of leads (unique visitors) you sent to a particular landing page. This should be reflected in the number of clicks that a particular affiliate link gets. You will also need the total number of sales generated for that particular link. You can usually get this number in the sales report section of your affiliate account.

You can then divide the number of sales by the number of leads you sent and multiple the result by 100%. A higher percentage means that the landing page is effective in converting leads into customers. Sometimes, different websites will have completely different conversion rates even if they are sending traffic to the same landing page. This happens because many factors affect the success of a landing page. We will discuss them in the following section. You can check these factors whenever you are inspecting a new landing page of an advertiser

Factors that affect landing page conversion rate:

The design and layout of the page

You can choose advertisers based on the design and layout of their landing page. If a landing page has no published conversion rate, you may need to base your decision to use it based on these two superficial factors.

Ideally, the design should focus on the purchasing features of the page. The landing page's sole purpose is to convince the people viewing it to make a purchase. If the page has too many distractions or if the purchase buttons are too small to be seen, this may lead to a low conversion rate.

An effective way of checking the design and layout of an affiliate landing page is by using the help of your loved ones. Before you use a landing page, let the people you know check it out first. You could have a questionnaire ready when they check these landing pages. You will need to ask them the following questions:

1. From a scale of 1-10, how likely are you to buy from this page?
2. Do you see a purchase button or link immediately?
3. How do you find the design?
    - Distracting or too cluttered
    - Helpful for buyers
    - Unattractive or outdated
    - Informative or educational
4. If you like the product being promoted, are you going from this page or are you going to find another source of the same product? Why?

By letting the people you know check the landing page and answer the questions above, you will be able to get an idea of how an average person with no marketing background views the page. You will be able to get multiple opinions on the quality of the page. If you just base your judgment on your own opinion, you may have personal biases that may prevent you from choosing the best landing page. Knowing what other people think about the page will help make your decision of choosing a landing page objective.

The quality of traffic that you send to it

At times, an affiliate marketer may get a lower conversion rate than the published rate of a landing page. The affiliate network metrics for example, may say that a landing page gets 7% conversion rate but it only converted 3% of the traffic you sent to it. This may happen when the quality of the traffic you send to the landing page is not at par with the industry standards.

Here are the qualities of the visitors that you should send to your affiliate marketing landing pages:

They should have a buying intent

Landing pages work best if you send people to it who are already in the verge of buying the product. This factor is most important to people who are buying something pricey. Low-ticket items are open to impulse buys. A person with no buying intent may buy a $5 shirt from an online retailer without thinking too much about it. Everything changes when more money is on the line. Consider your own personal process when buying something expensive. Do you research first or do you buy impulsively?

Before an average person buys a new laptop for example, they first look around for the newest models from different brands. They then, collect information on the features that are important for them. A person on a budget for example, may take note of the prices of the different models. A computer gaming enthusiast on the other hand, may not be as interested in the prices as he or she is in the performance specs of the laptop. Only after people have collected enough information are they likely to make a buying decision.

You can make sure that the people you refer to your affiliate links have buying intentions by adjusting the types of content in your website. If you already have a website with a lot of articles and other contents, check each of them. Assess your website contents and check whether they are important in the beginning, middle or end of the buying process. Plot the normal buying process for the products you promote. Then, you should create content that will capture more people who are towards the end of the process.

Let's say you are promoting action cameras in your website. You use a GoPro to record your activities like playing with your dog, playing sports, going on vacations, etc. With the content you share in social media, you are able to attract a lot of users from social networks.

The problem with this method of gaining traffic is that the people you attract do not necessarily have buying intentions. They are only there to view the photos and videos you took with your GoPro. Because they do not have a buying intent, they are less likely to click on your affiliate links. To convert these people from being passive audiences into buyers, you will need to create multiple contents (articles and videos) where you can naturally promote the action camera. For example, you can film your trip to a local vacation spot and make a how-to article and video about how to get there and what to do when you are there. In the process, you can write that their experience will be greatly enhanced if they bring an action camera with them. You could then include an affiliate link in your article. In the video you create, you can talk about the same thing and mention that you have link in the description of the video for the item you are recommending.

Aside from these types of contents, you can also create series of contents that are designed to highlight the product you are promoting. For example, you can write an article of record a vlog talking about your own buying decision when you bought the action camera. You can also make a comparison article or video, comparing the product you are promoting with competing brands. Lastly, you can talk about the prices of the product from different sources and the discount coupons they can use to save money when purchasing.

As a recap, here are the types of contents that you should create:

1. Articles and videos to a local tourist spot where you use the action camera
    - Target Audience: Beginners and Social Media Users
2. Article and video about your personal buying decision
    - Target Audience: Beginners and Social Media Users
3. Comparison article and video against competing brands
    - Target Audience: People with buying intent, Google Searchers
4. Article and video talking about the price and the best sources of the product
    - Target Audience: People with buying intent, Google Searchers

These are only some ideas on the types of content you can create for this particular product. You can create all these articles and videos in a matter of weeks. You should also consider not stopping with these four contents. You can create more articles and videos about going to the different tourist attractions in your area. Aside from the action camera itself, you can also make product reviews about its different accessories. Just keep creating content about it and how to use it and people will eventually buy it.

They should be capable of buying the product

There is no use promoting your website in places where the majority of people are not capable of buying your product. If you are promoting products from Amazon.com for example, you should make sure that you are promoting to people from the US. Make sure that the tips and recommendations you post on your articles and videos are significant to US consumers. The same goes for the coupons and other promotions you offer.

Aside from ensuring that you are promoting to people from the right location, you should also make sure that the people you are promoting to have the necessary tools for purchasing. This means that they should have access to a credit card or any other method of payment allowed by the retailer you are promoting.

Promoting affiliate products towards children for example, is not just against that law but also ineffective. Children do not have the financial freedom to purchase the product themselves.

Shopping seasons and the level of competition in the market

The conversion rate of a landing page will also be affected by the season. A landing page that has a high conversion rate in regular days may experience a dip in its effectiveness during the holidays when there are many other competing offers in the market. In the US for example, the time around thanksgiving and Christmas is usually considered shopping season. People love the promotions in these days. If the products in the landing page that you are using are still offered at their regular prices in these times of the year, your visitors may choose to buy the competing brands or from others sources of the item where there are discounts.

As a response, you should always keep track of the different competing offers in the market. Check the different source for the products that you are offering. If you see that the other sources of the products are offering discounts, you can talk to your affiliate marketing manager about it.

Chapter 11 Quiz
Please refer to Appendix J for the answers to this quiz

1. How do you keep your affiliate marketing strategy efficient?

    A) Keeping ads expenses low
    B) Using a cheap hosting package
    C) Keeping the number of clicks low between the traffic source and landing page
    D) Using hosted blog platforms like blogger

2. Why is posting affiliate links directly in public ineffective?

    A) It may be copied by other people
    B) People will go directly to the website without going through the link
    C) People will avoid clicking on it, thinking it's spam
    D) It is against the rules

3. What motivational trick can we use to make people click on shared content?

    A) Use great headlines and featured image
    B) Promise free gifts
    C) Offer them money for clicking
    D) Use bright colors in the post

4. What do we call the event wherein the person leaves the website after viewing just one page?

    A) Trounce
    B) Bounce
    C) Once
    D) Exit

5. How do you make an intelligent guess if an affiliate link has a high conversion rate before even making it live?

    A) Examine the landing page
    B) Buy the affiliate product yourself
    C) Ask your friends to clock on it
    D) Test it with children

6. What two factors affect the quality of the visitors you send to a landing page?

    A) Intent and capacity to buy
    B) Credit card brand and location of visitor

C) Country of origin of the product and the visitor
D) Religious and political orientation of the visitor

7. How to you improve click-through rates in your landing pages?

    A) Gather the right type of traffic
    B) Build more websites
    C) Post more often in social media
    D) Buy ad placements in popular websites

8. Which type of visitor has the highest intention of making a purchase?

    A) Search engine users who arrived with a product related key phrase
    E) Facebook users who clicked on your content
    F) Instagram users who clicked the link in your bio
    G) A user that came to check images

9. How does the shopping season affect the performance of landing pages?

    A) People don't buy online during holidays
    B) Bargain hunters spam landing pages to make them unusable
    C) People like to shop during this time of the year therefore, increasing the price
    D) The level of competition increases during this season, making regular offers obsolete

10. What should you do to have a competitive landing page during high volume traffic seasons?

    A) Find landing pages for competitive offers and promotions
    B) Stop affiliate marketing during the holidays
    C) Use more ads during this time of the year
    D) Keep expectations low during this time

Inspiration #12

"The way to get started is to quit talking and begin doing."

Walt Disney

Chapter 12

Tips to Become a Successful Affiliate Marketer

Success in affiliate marketing can mean earning millions of dollars every month. The very best players in the market achieve this level of earnings on a regular basis. How do you reach this level of success? Check out these tips to start:

Sell things and services that you are knowledgeable about

It is easier to become an effective affiliate marketer if you know what you are talking about. If you create a website about a niche topic, experts in the industry will eventually check your websites and view your content. The experts in the industry will know if you are only posing as an expert. If an expert in the niche exposes you, you may end up losing credibility with your audience.

As we've discussed earlier in the book, it is easier to have people obey your suggestions if they see that you are an expert in the topic. Because of this, it is ideal if you start your affiliate marketing career in a niche topic that you are an expert on.

In the beginning, focus on providing good quality content and getting traffic. Many aspiring affiliate marketers focus too much on earning their first buck. If you have this mindset from the beginning, you will be disappointed when the income is slow as you are just starting out. Instead of focusing on the income, shift your focus on the process of creating high quality content first. After you've created your first few articles and videos, turn your attention to getting people to see them. This book provides you with the tools on how you can do this part of the process. All you need to do is avoid worrying about the first few bucks and shift your focus on catering to the needs of your audience.

Keep your online assets active

Aside from creating content and driving traffic to them, you should create a system for keeping your online assets active. You will need to work hard and work smart to achieve this. In the beginning, you will not have a lot of funds to work with. You will be using your personal funds to pay for the business. Because of this, you will need to do much of the work yourself in keeping your website and your other social media assets active.
As you start to earn money, you can reinvest part of it back to the business. Instead of spending all of it, you could use part of the income to hire a VA, as suggested in earlier chapters. Hire them to do simple projects like creating a series of related articles or for managing your social network posting schedule.

Hiring a VA is worth the money if he or she can take tasks that you hate doing. If you do not like communicating with other website owners and bloggers for guest posting, you could have a VA do the email tasks for you. All you have to do is to instruct him or her on what to do, state the steps for his or her work process and supervise everything he or she does every day. By letting your VA do some of the work, you will be able to shift your focus to getting more traffic and continuing to grow your business with high quality content.

Don't stop with one website

There is a limit to the potential of a niche topic. Let's say that your website is about scuba diving and your content is focused on diving related articles and videos. In the process, you use your content to promote scuba diving related gear and equipment. Even if you do get the top spot in Google and your social media pages and accounts become super popular, your success will be limited by the number of people who are interested in scuba diving. If something happens that makes people want to avoid scuba diving (like news about scuba diving accidents), your business may suffer.

To prevent these types of events from damaging your business, you should diversify and explore other niches when you are contented with your first website. This way, you will be able to earn from other niche markets.

You will need to make sure that your first website is earning and self-sustaining before you commit to working on another one. This way, you can leave the operations of that one to one of your VAs and only go back to it once or twice every week.

Learn to cross sell related products

In each of your affiliate marketing websites, you will have one bestselling item. Sometimes, the product that sells best is something that you are not promoting. A scuba diving website for instance may sell more Go Pro accessories than actual scuba gears and equipment. To maximize the growth of these websites, you need to learn about which products are most effective to promote. You also need to learn how to promote related products. When showing a video in your website for instance, you could mention the type of camera that you used to shoot that video and have an affiliate link pointing to that camera in Amazon.

Create a core team to grow your business

The most important part of growing your business is having people around you that you can trust to help you out. As you become more successful, you can hire people to do the work for you. Whether they are virtual assistants or real employees, you should try to keep them if they can do good work.

Each person in your group should play an important role in the group for increasing the income of the business. Keep a core team of great performers and compensate them well so that they will stay with you. You can even take in business partners if they are willing to chip in with the capital of building the business.

Reinvest profits to growing your business

With affiliate marketing, you are using your money to earn more money, especially if you start using paid methods of gaining traffic. In the beginning, the risk is high and there is good chance that some of your ad campaigns will lead to losses. Everything changes however, if you manage to match the right group of people to the right affiliate program. By following the tracking practices discussed in the previous sections, you will be able to make your ads target and reach the right kinds of people.

When you find success with your ad targeting and affiliate program, you should try to maximize profits by increasing the scale of your add campaign. To do this, you will need to reinvest the amount you earn from your affiliate marketing ad campaigns. Use it to fund more ad campaigns or to promote new products to the same audience. If you successfully promoted a camping tent to a group of audience for example, you could cross sell other camping equipment to them. You could then use part of the profits from past campaigns to fund this one.

Renegotiate the terms with the advertiser

If you experience success in promoting a specific product, you may be able to find some leverage to negotiate with the advertisers. You will not be able to do this with big online retailers like Amazon or eBay. However, you may be able to do it with some affiliate networks.

You will be able to contact the advertiser through the support team of the affiliate program. When negotiating, you can ask for special perks that are not available in the regular affiliate marketing program. For example, you can ask for higher commission rates to keep promoting their products. You will need to have a long relationship with the advertiser to be able to ask for something like this. You also should be bringing in a lot of sales for you to be able to demand a pay raise.

You could say for example, that a competing company has contacted you to promote their products and that they are offering a higher commission rate for products of the same price. You could then ask the advertiser if it is possible for them to match the offer.

You could also ask for other types of requests from your advertiser. For example, you could ask for a special promotional coupon that is specific to you website. When a person uses your coupon, the sale is automatically assigned to you. This is a common practice among affiliate marketers who create video content. For this type of affiliate marketers, links are ineffective because they cannot just put links on their videos. YouTube linking features for example, usually do not show in the same way when viewed from mobile phones.

Because of this, many video content creators miss some affiliate sales. Instead of using links to validate a sale, they use coupons because they can mention the coupon code in their videos. The viewers are also likely to use the coupon because it will give them a discount. If you show strong sale numbers, you may be able to ask for this kind of set up from your advertiser.

Don't just create websites, create brands

Your website just serves as the headquarters for an entire network of content marketing assets. The entirety of your online business spreads far beyond the webpages of your website. To make the most of your online assets and all the expenses you put into building and developing it, you should create a brand.

A brand is a business entity that is easily recognizable to the consumers. When your website becomes familiar to the average internet user, you no longer need to write your website name and your tagline for them to know what your website is about. Instead, you only need to show your logo and the visitors will understand what your brand is about. Together with being easily recognized, brands are also associated with certain qualities that are unique to their products, services and company culture.

In the same way, you can also build your website and all your other assets to represent your brand. While your primary method of earning is called affiliate marketing, your business is actually called a content marketing business. With this type of business, you are using your content to drive attention towards your online assets. In the process, you make suggestions in your content that lead to affiliate marketing sales.

A branded content marketing company is not new. All news websites and online magazines are considered content marketing companies. You can also transition your small affiliate marketing website to become a strong content marketing brand. To do this, your audience needs to see positive qualities that they will be able to associate with your brand. Start by making sure that your website and your social media assets are updated in a consistent manner.

You could include a blog in your websites for example, where you talk about tips regarding your affiliate marketing niche. The constant addition of new content will improve your SEO ranking in some keywords. It will also give you something to share organically in your social networking pages. If people expect your website to update regularly, they will remember to go back to it every now and then. While not all of these people will buy from your affiliate links, many of them will help in spreading your content, increasing the reach of each post in your website.

Aside from posting content consistently, you should also aim to continuously improve the quality of your content. If you post spam in your social networking pages, people will associate your brand to spamming. To prevent this from happening, you should only post high quality content in your website. You should not just create and post content for the sake of checking the task off your to-do list. Instead, you should focus on making content because it will be useful to the people who regularly visit your website.

To further establish your brand, you want to maintain a consistent image in all of your online marketing assets. Your logo, name and website tagline should be the same in all these assets including your website, your social media accounts and even your offline presence. The way you talk in these assets should also be the same. If you are using professional English in your website to attract professionals, you should also use the same way of talking in your social media communications. If you choose to make changes in your brand identity (like changing the logo), you should do it simultaneously in all your online assets.

Lastly, the most important quality of a brand is its staying power. Most of us do not actually know how profitable our favorite brands are. Because of this, most people judge whether a brand is successful or not based on its staying power. Brands that still exist are considered strong and those that are becoming less relevant, are considered weak. To establish that your content marketing brand is strong, you should maintain your consistency of posting and creating content. Every now and again, you could create promotions and special events for your readers.

With consistent content creation and marketing, people will look up to your brand as a reliable source of information. If they see your brand's domain name in the search result pages, they are more likely to click on it even if there are other search results entries above yours. They are more likely to trust your content when they see it in their social networking feeds, whether it is in Facebook, Twitter or LinkedIn. Every now and again, they will see your content in apps like Instagram or Pinterest. This may motivate them to give your website a visit. With continued exposure to your content, they will eventually click on your affiliate marketing links when they need the product or services that you are suggesting.

Chapter 12 Quiz

Please refer to Appendix K for the answers to this quiz

1. What can happen if you pose as an expert in a niche you have no experience in that may damage your business?

    A) You will get more sales
    B) People will see you as an expert
    C) Someone may call you out as a fraud
    D) Your brand will look stronger

2. What two activities should you focus on in the beginning of your affiliate marketing career?

    A) Social media marketing and making ads
    B) Gathering traffic and building high quality content
    C) Finding people to work with and passing the work to them
    D) Collecting and sending emails to strangers

3. What is the risk with depending on just one website?

    A) People will not trust your website
    B) You will not have enough domain names for promoting multiple products
    C) People will view your website as amateurish
    D) The business may suffer when the niche market has negative news

4. When negotiating with an affiliate, what should you use as leverage?

    A) Your excellent sales performance
    B) The size of your website
    C) The number of followers you have in Instagram
    D) The number of employees you have

5. What is one factor that makes up the brand identity?

    A) Social media ads
    E) Content length
    F) Website Logo
    G) Website color scheme

6. What make great brands unique from other generic companies?

    A) Unique, recognizable and positive company culture
    B) Low prices

C) High product demand
D) Unique color schemes

7. What is an example of a positive quality that people can associate with a good content marketing brand?

    A) High quality content design
    B) Video content curation from YouTube
    C) Long articles
    D) Timely and consistent posting of content

8. What is an example of an activity that can hurt your brand?

    A) Creating contents with no videos
    B) Posting long articles
    C) Posting Spam
    D) Removing the comment section

9. Which of the following characteristics contributes to a strong brand image?

    A) Removing the comment section in posts
    B) Posting memes every day in your website
    C) The presence of employees
    D) Consistency in website and social media marketing

10. What is the most important brand quality?

    A) Staying Power
    B) Great Logo
    C) Long articles
    D) Funny videos

Inspiration #13

"The successful warrior is the average man, with laser-like focus."

Bruce Lee

Chapter 13:

Proven Ways to Improve Website Traffic

Success in affiliate marketing can mean earning millions of dollars every month. The very best players in the market achieve this level of earnings on a regular basis. How do you reach this level of success? Check out these tips to start:

Gaining traffic is probably the most difficult part of affiliate marketing. You will need to attract massive numbers of the right types of people to your website. You want the types who are likely to be interested in the products you promote and the content your offer. Here are some of the tested and proven ways of gaining traffic:

Guest posting

This method of getting traffic is one of the most intimidating for most internet marketers. In this section, we will discuss how to do it properly so that you will be able to push through with it.

The first step of guest posting is always to create an excellent article. You want to write content on something that you are confident writing about. You want to write about something that is related to the topic of your affiliate website.

When creating the content that you will offer for guest posting, you will need to make sure that it is well researched and it is pleasant to read to the readers of the other website. The readers will judge you based on the quality of content that you will share. If they like your content, they may go to your website and check out your other articles. If they do not like your content, they may ignore you, or worse, talk about how bad your content is in the comments.

After creating the new content, it's time to look for a website where you will share it. To begin with, make a list of websites where some of your target audiences may regularly visit. Ideally, it should not be another affiliate marketing website. Instead, find websites that are considered as authorities in your niche industry.

One option is to approach real world publications and offer your services as a freelancer. You can find a write-for-us section in websites like the Huffington Post or Bleacher Report. These popular website get thousands of requests from aspiring writers every day. You do not want to go after these general publications. Instead, you should focus on the big publications or online magazines that cater to your niche.

Make a list of at least twenty of these online publications. After creating the list, you will need to contact these companies to ask if you can write in their website. To achieve this, you will need to email the administrators of the websites. Most of them have a contact-us page or a write-for-us page. Do not expect that you will be compensated in any way for your guest posting. You will need to do this service for free.

In your email, be courteous and go straight to the point. You could use the same emails for all your applications, changing only small details. In the email, you could provide a link back to your website so that they will be able to see samples of the articles you have written. This will allow them to inspect your content easily, giving them an idea of the type of content that you can share in their website.

If you have confidence that the content you created will stand out and increase the chance that your offer will be approved, you could also mention it in the email. You could talk about what the content is about and how it can be valuable to their website.

If you hear back from them, you may need to ask for the terms of the partnership. In exchange for writing for their website, you need to ask to have a link back to your own website. The link will help your own website in terms of search engine ranking. If the website you will be writing for has a strong marketing arm, you may even get some traffic from the link.

If you are accepted and you agree on the terms of the guest posting, you will be asked to submit a file of the article that you will post. In most cases, the administrators of the website will have suggestions on how you will change the content. The changes are not always significant. They will mostly be done to make your content fit the other types of content in their website.

After some editing, your content will be posted in their website and you may see some traffic come out of it. Make sure though that the terms that were agreed upon are followed. Your name should be mentioned as the author of the content and there should be a link going back to your affiliate website. If there is no traffic surge to your website, you will still get some SEO juice from the link in your content. Once your guest post is up, do not think too much about it. The content is there for everyone to see. If the website has a strong SEO presence, you may have your guest post rank well.

Now that you are done, you should shift your focus on working on a new guest post. You should do one of these guest posts a month. The overall goal is to increase the number of contents you have from other websites. With each guest post you set up, you will get a legitimate backlink to your own website and you may get some traffic.

Some of your contents will be more successful than others. If you see that one of your articles get a lot of attention in one website, you can ask the administrators if they would like you to do another one. You should do this for the websites where your guest posts get a lot of positive results like great search ranking and a high number of referred traffic.

Guesting on a Vlog

Guesting opportunities online do not only apply to online articles. They can also be applied in podcasts and in vlogs. You could follow the same strategy discussed above to book other promotional events. For instance, you could message a YouTube channel manager if you could talk in one of their shows or if they would like you to become a guest in their shows.

If you have a tech website for instance, you could ask to guest in tech shows and news websites. You could also look for podcasts about your topic. The best part about this type of guesting is that you get your name and your work out there without the need for excessive preparations. This allows you to reserve your writing talents to your own contents. Becoming a guest in internet shows can be fun and it does not take a lot of work.

You do not have to travel to the exact place of the vlogger either. You can set up your own working place so that it is suitable for internet videos. News agencies use skype all the time to talk to their guests in the show. You and the vlogger can also do this. This way, it will not cost you much to appear in the shows of other influencers in your circles.

To become a guest, you will need to meet in person or virtually with the vlogger and review what you will talk about in the show. Most vloggers will only invite you in their shows if you are already an established expert in your niche and your inputs in the show matches the needs of their audience.

Search Engine Optimization

The best way to get traffic to your website is through search engine optimization. Search engines are the primary tools used by internet users to get around online. Unlike social media, these tools are used not just for entertainment and communication. They are used to look for specific types of content in the searchable web. Search engines "crawl" and collect information all public websites online. They organize the websites based on the data they collect about it. Mostly, they are concerned with the information found in the website. However, they also collect information related to user experience such as website speed, server uptime and the presence of malware or other dangerous types of codes.

If your website is found to be safe, legal, and easy to use, it will be added to the search database. To match the information in your website the needs of internet users, Google and other search engines use keywords and phrases.

When the internet user enters a word or phrase in the search bar, the search algorithm uses this information and searches all the websites they've crawled for matching information. Because multiple websites have the same type of information, reaching the top spot of the list in the search result pages will require you to deal with intense competition, especially in the most popular topics.

If you do manage to outrank all the other pages in your niche topic, you will manage to attract the people in your niche market. This type of traffic is considered by most affiliate marketers to be superior in quality compared to the ones coming from social networks because they are using the internet to deal with a specific need. If you happen to have the solution to their needs, you can earn by suggesting affiliate products to them.

How to optimize content for search engines

Search engine marketing comes in many phases. The first phase starts in the building and development of your website. In this part of the process, you need to decide on the identity of your website. To establish your website's identity, the search engines will check factors like your domain name, your website tag line and the different internal links (links that lead to other pages inside the same website) you offer in your website's primary menu. Secondary to this, your website identity will be determined by the headlines of your posts.

Ideally, these headlines should have an H1 tag. Ideally, you should start adding the most important keywords in your niche at this part of the process. If possible, you can include your keyword and phrase in the domain name. You should also use related keywords and phrases in the relevant links in your website, especially the ones in your menus. This makes up the basic parts of your site-level optimization.

The second phase of search engine marketing involves page-level optimization. This is the more crucial part of the two because it will be your pages that will be individually ranked in the search result pages. It all starts with the keywords you use in the title of your article. Ideally, the keywords or phrases should be placed in the beginning of the headline. Also make sure that the title includes 50-60 characters only. Google displays this range of characters in the search results.

Next to the title, you should also consider what to write in the meta description of the page. The meta description is the paragraph that will be used below the SEO title. This part should help establish the information in the page to the internet user. You do not have to overthink this part. Just tell the reader, in a conversational manner, what information is included in the page. Ideally, you should make this paragraph be around 320 characters long. You should also include the relevant keywords or phrase in this paragraph.

Next, you will need to create the body of your content. From an SEO standpoint, the body should be at least 350 words long for short content types like news, blog posts and updates. For posts that require instructions and steps, the word count should be north of 750 words to be competitive. The text components of the body should include paragraphs (with a <p> tag) and headings (h2, h3…). You should mention the keyword or phrase multiple times in the paragraphs. It should also be included in at least two paragraph headings.

If the content is intended to show a process, like how-to contents, you will need to use the list tags (<ol> or <ul>). This will tell the search engines that you are presenting a list to the intended audience. Aside from using the list content as your paragraph headings, you should also include multiple types of media to make the content easier for the eyes.

The first type of media that you should add is the text. The text portion of the content is easy to optimize for the search engine because you can simply write the keywords and phrases as they are needed in the paragraphs.

Ideally, the keywords and phrases should comprise 1-2% of your text content. The first one should be included within the first two sentences of the first paragraph. If you have a 1,000-word long article, you should use your keyword or phrase ten to twenty times. You should not allow the content however, to contain more that 4% of the keyword or phrase. More than that, Google may flag you for keyword stuffing. This may have your content penalized for gaming the search engine algorithm.

Next to text, the second most important type of content is the image. The presence of images in the page indicates a break in the wall of text content. By breaking the content into chunks with the use of images, you will make your content easier for the eyes of the user. To make the images help in your SEO efforts, you should include the keyword or phrase in the alt-attribute of the image. In most website content management systems, the option to change the alt-attribute is present when the image is uploaded or edited. Adding a caption also helps to establish the nature of the image.

Lastly, you will need to add a video whenever there is a need for it. The video should complement the content of the website. Of the three types of content discussed in this section, you should be least worried with optimizing the video content. Focus your SEO on the other two types of content.

With these three types of contents, you will be able to establish what the page is about. The next step is to use links to establish how it relates to the other contents in the web. Links come in two types, inbound links and outbound links. You could use your outbound links to link to other pages that may be useful the user. You should do this when the linked page has information that is not included in your own page. The links in your page are either internal (going to other pages in the same website) or external (going to pages of other websites). Feel free to use internal links as you see fit.

However, you should be more careful when linking externally. Make sure that the third party website that you are linking to is safe to use and hosts legal contents. Ideally, the page you are linking to should be related to the topic that you are talking about in the page. Linking to other websites is supposed to supplement the knowledge of the user about the topic. The search engine crawlers (robots that check your website) will use the content that you are using to guess what type of content your website has.

Linking externally should be done naturally. If you mentioned a technical term that a few people may not understand for example, you can add a link to a page with the definition of the said word. Adding the right links is important in affiliate marketing. By making your readers become accustomed to the use of links, you may increase the chances of clicks to the affiliate text links you add to your content.

Now, let's talk about the SEO functions of inbound links. Inbound links are used by the search engine algorithm as a metric for how popular and useful a website is. Inbound links refer to the links from other websites that lead to the webpages in your website. You can use tools like the Google Search Console (sometimes also called Google Webmaster Tools) to check which websites are linking to your pages.

Each link that points to your webpages has a different value. The search engine ranking algorithm considers factors like the age of the domain, its Page Rank and many other different metrics to decide whether a link adds value to the webpage it is pointing to. Many online marketers for instance, believe that links from difficult to obtain domains like the ones with a .gov or .edu extensions are more valuable than those from .com domains.

There are multiple legal ways for you to get inbound links to your webpage. The first one is to do your professional networking in your industry. If you are in the gardening industry for example, you should look for other webmasters in the same industry. Links from their websites or blogs will tell the search engines that your webpages are also about gardening. If most of your links are coming from US based websites with US-centric contents, this will also signal that your content is also for US audiences.

Aside from obtaining links from the websites of people you know, you could also get them by doing guest posting. This is the reason why you really need to negotiate to have a link pointing back to your website every time you do your guest posting. As suggested in the guest posting section of this book, you should choose the websites that you guest post to. They should be related to your niche, they should have access to a market that does not currently go to your website, and they should have a good search rankings. It is ideal if you could get your guest posts from websites with better search engine rankings in keywords that you are interested to compete in.

Marketing in forums and other online communities

Aside from social networks and the search engines, you will need to work with other types of websites that have a big online community. To do this, you will need to look for the types of websites where your average target audience spends a lot of his in. This could be a forum, a membership website or an online app.

If this website has lots of contents, you could also ask to guest post in it. Some blogs for example, has a high following of people that post a lot of comments. With this type of blog, the community it mostly concentrated in the comment section. You may use this section of the website to communicate with your prospect website visitors. Ideally, you should add useful comments in this section to answer other commenters' questions. You could then suggest links for suggested sources of information. In the process, you could also add your own content in here.

Forums are also great sources of traffic. However, forum members tend to be avid internet users. Because of this, they are warry about salesy people online. Before you can convince others to go to your website, you should first gain their trust. In the forum culture, this usually means that you need to contribute content to the forum while following the forum rules. Many forums have point and ranking systems. Active members tend to get more points, increasing their ranking in the website. This gives them certain perks that less active members do not have.

When you have developed a strong relationship with the people in the forums, you can now start promoting your own content. Even if you are already a trusted member in the forum, you should still only suggest your content in the context of the conversation in the forums.

You could also consider looking for Q&A websites. Websites like Quora and the once popular Yahoo Answers, are examples of websites like these. Q&A sites can either be general, like in the case of Quora, or specific. Specific Q&A websites allow only answers related to the topic. There are some Q&A websites for example that focuses on questions related to solving Windows Personal Computer problems. If your content is related to solving PC problems, this may be a good community for you to work with. There are also some that only allow questions about fitness. You will need to find a Q&A website that fits your niche. Only work with it if it has an active community. You can check this out by going straight to their website and checking out the website activity.

Using ads to get traffic

When your website is ready to accept traffic, it's time to start use paid methods to pump traffic into it. It is common to make the mistake of relying solely on organic means of getting traffic. This process takes too long. Let's say you work hard to build your content base and your social media presence. After your done setting everything up for getting organic traffic, the newsfeeds algorithm changes for Facebook, making all your previous efforts futile. A similar event happened to many affiliate marketers back when Google launched its Panda and Penguin updates. The majority of people who depended only on organic traffic were affected the most when pages were penalized.

To learn why you need to use paid means of getting traffic, let us first discuss the differences between free and paid traffic.

Free versus paid traffic

As mentioned above, free traffic is known in the industry as organic traffic. Any visitor coming to your website because of your free efforts in social media and search engine optimization can be considered organic. In the beginning, this will be your primary source of traffic. In fact, it is highly encouraged by affiliate marketing experts that you master the skill of gaining free traffic first.

Free traffic however, is harder to get than most beginners think. The first big factor that works against free traffic is competition. Regardless of what niche topic you choose, there will always be people who will be competing with you. They will compete with you in competing for the attention of your target audience.

If you are promoting a special type of food supplement in your website for example, there will be other people who will be promoting the same product. And you are trying to attract, the same group of people that you are attracting. In the online world, it is easy to track what your competition is doing. You simply go to their websites or their Facebook pages to see what type of promotions they are running. When you become successful, you should expect that your competitors will also be doing the same thing.

With paid traffic, there will also be some competition. However, the number of competing websites will not be as high those competing in free traffic channels. In most websites, there is usually a place for ads, separated from the other types of content. In Google's search result pages for example, the ads are usually located at the top part of the search results. Before the organic search results, you will see two to four ads placements first. Because it is seen first by the search engine user, they are likely to click on it first.

The second big factor to consider when deciding whether to use paid traffic sources, is the speed of business progress. Because of the high level of competition with organic marketing methods, it usually takes an affiliate websites some time before a significant amount of traffic starts coming in. This can be a problem for affiliate marketers with a small capital. The sales come with the traffic that you funnel towards your website. The more traffic comes in, the higher the chances of sales will be. In the beginning, you will only get between 0-10 people coming into your website daily if you rely only on passive and organic means. This is the amount of traffic that you should expect if you are only adding one article in your website and posting one or two contents in your social media channels per day.

The amount of traffic that you get through organic means depends on the number of users you can reach in social media and your search ranking in Google. In the beginning, you will not fare well in both of these marketing factors. With less than 10 people coming to your website daily, you cannot expect to get a substantial income from your affiliate website.

Paid campaigns enhance organic marketing efforts

You should not approach your paid campaigns as separate from your organic marketing efforts. Any success you experience with your paid marketing will also trickle down towards your organic marketing channels. If you make a Facebook ad for instance, some people who do not click on your ads may choose to click on your page and follow it, instead. Some people who do not click on your call to action button in your landing page may choose to surf around your website and they may choose to return at a later date. While behaviors like these do not show as a success in your ad campaign tracking tools, they still have a positive effect on your business.

Using Ads to Get Traffic

Getting few daily visits does not mean that your business model will not work. It just means that you are not getting enough traffic to make the system work. It also means that you are not reaching your target audience with the organic traffic marketing that you are using. You will eventually reach these people with organic marketing methods however, it may take you years to reach your goal.

There are multiple ways to get the amount of traffic that you want. However, the best and fastest way it so use paid methods. Using this method can be risky, especially if you do not know what you are doing. The risk is highest in the beginning when you have no experience of using the advertising platform. You can prepare for your first marketing campaign as much as you can through books and YouTube tutorials but you will learn most of the best practices in marketing with experience. Even if you have decided to use ads to drive traffic to your website, there will still be a lot of planning needed to make sure that you succeed in carrying out an effective and efficient campaign.

First, you need to choose a platform where you will use ads. There are various online platforms to choose from including Facebook Advertising and Google AdWords. These two are probably the biggest mainstream advertising platforms and they are the most recommended for beginners. These two stand out because of the number of people that their platforms can reach. Google AdWords can be used to create ads for search engine result pages, websites using Google AdSense and apps that are using mobile AdSense ads. If your marketing message is better delivered using videos, you can also use AdWords to put up ads in YouTube.

You can target your ads based on the search terms used by people. Text and banner ads shown in website hosting AdSense can be targeted using the type of content in the said website and the information that Google has on the person using the website. For instance, you can make your ads appear only in financial websites to promote your financial affiliate programs. You can also make the ad target market narrower by targeting people only from specific countries.

With mobile becoming the primary way of using Google, the AdWords platform also allows advertisers to target users based on the type of device they are using. If the product you are promoting can only be used through mobile, you can make your ads show only on mobile devices.

Most importantly, Google has a variety of free tools that allows you to monitor and learn from your ad campaigns. For instance, you can use Google Analytics to track the number of visits you get from an ad campaign. With this tool, you can also use this tool to track how these people moved around your website and whether they clicked on any of your affiliate links or not.

Facebook Ads on the other hand standout because of the wealth of information that Facebook has about their users. Just like Google AdWords, Facebook ads can also be used to target people based on the device and the type of network they are using (Wi-Fi or mobile data). The primary types of information used targeting in Facebook though are the person's interests and basic demographics. Basic demographics refer to information like the person's age, gender, location and occupation. Facebook allows advertisers to use these types of information for ad targeting. Advertisers can then use the person's interests to make the targeting narrower. The interests of a person are based on the contents that they engaged with in the network. A person who follows basketball stars and teams for example, will be matched with ads that are targeted to people who are interested in basketball. That pretty much sums up the basic way of ad targeting in Facebook.

Tracking success and refining your campaigns

Your success in affiliate marketing will depend on how you adjust your ad campaigns to make them more effective and efficient. To do this, you will need to use two important tools. The first one is Google Analytics. This tool will tell you how people arrived in your website, what pages they viewed while they were there and on what page they left. If the visitor viewed more than one webpage, additional information like the average time spent on the website will be available.

You can use Google Analytics to decide whether your ads campaign is bringing enough traffic or not. You can also use it to track the movements of your users within your website. Most importantly, you can use this tool to check whether the users you've targeted click on your affiliate links or not.

The next best tool for tracking your ad campaigns is Facebook Pixels. Similar to Google Analytics, Facebook Pixels requires that you use a tracking code in your website. With this tracking code, you will be able to track the website users who come from Facebook. By tracking these people, you will be able to create a custom audience made up of Facebook users who go to your website. By using this feature, you will be able to create ads targeted towards people who are already visitors of your website.

For example, you could create a page that will redirect people to the landing pages of the affiliate link. You could then use Facebook Pixel to track this page. Next, you will need to distribute a link to this page around the website, which will serve as your proxy affiliate link. You should promote this link as you would promote your affiliate website. When people from Facebook click on that link, they will be redirected to the affiliate landing page. But before that, they will first pass through the proxy page, allowing Facebook Pixel to track their activity. Back in Facebook Pixels, you can create a Custom Audience made up of only those people who clicked on that link. This way, you will be able to create ads or boosted Facebook content specifically targeted towards people who clicked on your Facebook link in the past.

Another feature unique to Facebook ads is the ability to create a Lookalike Audience. This type of audience is created by using the qualities of a previous group you've created. Let's say you have a Facebook page with 100 likes. You want to increase the number of likes to your page using a Facebook promotion. You can create the Lookalike Audience feature to target people who are similar to the people who liked your page.

You could also make a Lookalike Audience group from the data you've gathered from Facebook Pixels. First, you will need to set up Facebook Pixels in the pages that you want to track. Next, you will need to create a custom audience made up of people who visited the page tracked by Facebook Pixel. Lastly, you can create a Lookalike Audience based on the custom audience group you've created. The people in the Lookalike Audience group will be new users who have similar characteristics of people who clicked your affiliate link. This type of audience is likely to click on your affiliate links in the future.

While this all sounds great in theory, the reality is that it will take you multiple tries to create the best type of audience group in your Facebook ad campaign. Even if you already have a successful campaign, you should not stop tracking. Keep tracking your campaigns and making adjustments. You should then test these adjustments to keep improving your ads targeting system.

Starting your first campaign

An ad campaign will only become successful if you do the necessary preparations before you start doing it. Follow these steps to increase the likelihood of success in your first campaigns:

Define your advertising goal

All your decisions and the actions you make should be based on one advertising goal. In most cases, your goal will be related to increasing sales. For instance, you could create a goal of sending more traffic towards a specific affiliate link.

Identify the target audience of your advertising

The next step is to identify the types of people you need to reach. You need to create a profile of your target audience based on the affiliate product that you are promoting. If you are promoting a high-end electronic shaver for example, your target will be men who are obsessed with grooming. If you are promoting luxury handbags on the other hand, your target will be women who are interested in fashion and luxury items.

To begin with, try to think of real people you know who are interested in the product you are promoting. Using these people as your inspiration, try to identify the defining characteristics of your target audience. You should include basic information like age, gender and location. You could also include specific information like interests and preferences of the people you are targeting. For example, you can target people with specific hobbies or with important responsibilities.

Identify the platform where you will put your ads

You do not have to create ads in all of the advertising platforms online. This will cost a lot of money. Instead, you should only look for the platform where your target audiences are found. If your target users are searching for the product online, you can choose to use Google AdWords so that your ad will be shown in the search result pages. On the other hand, if the product you are promoting is visually appealing, you can put your ads in highly visual social networks like Instagram, YouTube or Pinterest.

If you are targeting professionals, you could use networks that can target this kind of information. LinkedIn and Facebook for instance are able to group people based on their occupation. You could use these networks to target people of specific professions.

If you are just targeting anyone from a specific location, you also have the option to use CPM advertising. CPM or cost per mille is an advertising scheme where in the advertisers pay per 1000 impressions on an ad. With this type of advertising scheme, you will be able to show your ads to thousands of people. The targeting tools of this kind of advertising are less accurate than that used in Google and Facebook ads. This is more suited for affiliate marketers who are offering products with no specific target buyers in mind.

After choosing your advertising platform, you should learn as much as you can about it before making your first ad campaign. You could begin by reading about how others experienced creating their first campaigns. You can go online to learn about how to do a campaign.

After learning how to do it through people's blog posts, you can learn further by making a mock campaign. Go to your chosen ad platform, create an account and test out their interface on creating your first campaign. You will not be charged until the ad goes live.

Create a plan for the overall user experience

Before you make your first campaign, you should first plan what kind of user experience you will give your audience. In this step, you should draw up how you will make use of the traffic that you will get from the ad. If the affiliate program will allow you, you can make the traffic go straight to the affiliate link's landing page to minimize the chance that the visitor will bounce. Many affiliate programs allow this kind of traffic scheme however, they do specify not to use ad keywords that may compete with their own ads. An affiliate program for a website called ABC.com for example, will usually not allow you to use the words ABC.com. If you choose to use this path, you should use a redirect page to go between the ads and the affiliate landing page. This will allow you to track the number of users that your ad brings to the link. It also allows you to use Google Analytics and Facebook Pixel to track the users.

If the affiliate program does not allow ad traffic, you can still make use of ads. However, you will need to send them to your own website first. If the ad link goes directly to the affiliate landing page, the ad only needs one click for it to be successful. If you need to make them pass through your website on the other hand, you will need to get an extra click from the users to make the ad successful. First, they need to press the ad link and then, then will need to press the affiliate link on the website. To make this ad scheme successful, you will need to create a great landing page in your website that will receive the traffic sent by the ad.

Create your advertising creatives

Now that you have chosen the platform where you will publish your ads, the next step is to create the creatives or visual marketing materials. First, you will need to decide on the type of ad that you will use. Search result pages only allow text ads to show while Facebook allows a combination of image and texts. Ads for mobile are also mostly just text ads while ads published in websites are mostly in the form of banners.

After deciding on a type of creative, it is time make them. Text ads are the easiest to create because they do not need an image to become live. You only need to decide on what your ad will say and then input the statements in the ad creation process. Text ads in the internet usually come in a specific format. The biggest part of the ad is the title and it states what the ad is offering the online user. Below it, there is usually subtitle in smaller fonts. This part explains further the offer made in the title of the ad. Lastly, the last part of the ad is the URL or Domain name where the ad will go when someone clicks on it. Text ads are usually used by cost per click networks like Google AdWords.

Next to text, the second type of ad contains images. These are more commonly known as banner ads because they are usually square or rectangles in spaces around the content. You can create them yourself using Adobe Photoshop or any other image editing tool. You can also use free tools like Canva.com to craft it. If you do not want to make your own ad creatives, you can choose to have it made with websites like Fiverr.com.

When creating ad images, make sure that the offer is clear by adding text over the image. Remember to state a clear offer to the intended audience. With the fewest number of words possible, tell the target audience what you are offering or what problem you are trying to solve. You can use a straight statement that says what product or service you are offering or you can start the ad text with a question. Also include the name of your website. This way, you will be putting the name of your website out there.

With images, you can add whatever you want in the ad. However, ad images with people tend to have better click-through rates than those that only contain images of things. However, there is no way of knowing the effectiveness of an ad image for sure before launching it. The best strategy is to try out multiple images and track the methods of each.

Create a landing page

Next to the contents of the ads, the landing page is the most important part of the entire ad process. If the landing page is convincing, the entire user experience that comes with the ad will convert a high percentage of visitors. Otherwise, the ad campaign will lead to losses.

When creating a landing page, think of how you can convince the ad visitor to buy the product. This usually begins with a description of the product and statement of the benefits that comes with using the product or service. Ideally, you should also add features like testimonials from other users of the product as well as video reviews showing people using the product or service.

Throughout the page, there should be a call-to-action button with the affiliate link. The call to action button usually comes with a text component. Many affiliate marketers use words like "Buy Now" or "Visit Website". Make sure to modify the words that you use here so that they catch the eye of the visitor. You could also test different colors of the call to action button or link. Together with the call-to-action button, you should also include a short descriptive paragraph that tells the users what to expect when they click on the button. By adding this paragraph, you are making the process of going to the website of the user easier for the visitor. Most people try to avoid buttons when they do not know what it does. By explaining what the button does, you will be able to set the right expectations to the prospect buyer.

Just like your ad text and images, you should also try out multiple ad landing pages to see which ones are most effective. You could changes different factors to see how they perform when traffic passes through them. You can change the words that you use in the landing page. You could also change other factors like the images and color scheme of the page. After experimenting and getting enough data, stick to the landing pages with the highest success rate.

Remove distractions from landing page

The average webpage has between 30-40 links, going to various pages inside and outside of the website. You should remove these links from your landing pages. The only links in your landing page should be your affiliate link. You should also remove any other distraction that has nothing to do with the product or service that you are offering in the page.

By removing other distractions from the page, you will be able to prevent the user from doing any other action other than to click on the affiliate link in the call-to-action buttons.

Emphasize the benefits of your products by telling a story

The most successful affiliate marketers are master storytellers. They use their storytelling skills to establish the importance of the product they are using. Marketers like Darren Rowse and Pat Flynn for example, use the storytelling method to tell audience about their online projects. In the process, they also talk about what products they use and how these products help them in reaching their goals.

By using storytelling to talk about products and services, marketers are able to connect with the audience without sounding like they are selling something. You can also do this with the products you are using. Instead of just making a list of the benefits of the product for example, you could talk about how you discovered the product. You could also talk about your contrasting experiences before and after using the product. For example, you could talk about how bad your experience was before you discovered the product. You could then explain what the differences were when you started using the product. Your story will have more credibility if you show an image of yourself with the product.

When you run out of stories to tell, tell other people's stories

There will come a time when you exhaust most of your own stories. While they will still be in the internet for new fans to see, you will need to keep serving new content to keep people coming back to your content. To do this, you could discover other people's stories in your niche. Let's say that you have an affiliate website that promotes fitness products. You started your website by talking about how you personally lost weight and started a healthy lifestyle. A year after creating your website, you are running out of things to say about your personal journey. You know that if you stop making content, the traffic will begin to dwindle, decreasing the earning potential of your website.

To be able to create more content, you could look for other people who are undergoing the same journey. You could ask them if they would like to be featured in your website. You could do it in a form of an interview so that you will be able get answers for the important questions. For example, you could look for gym trainers and tell their story in their website. They could talk about their experience in the fitness industry and provide tips to people who are trying to lose weight. You could also talk about the products and services that they would recommend. You could then post an affiliate link of these products.

By creating the stories of other people related to your industry, you will be able to help them promote their own businesses. You will also be able to tap their market when the people you feature share the content about them in their personal social media accounts.

Do the math to check the profitability of an ad

Before you actually launch your first ad campaign, you should first check the cost and reward aspects of the ad. You will need to learn how many sales you will need to make in the particular campaign to break even. If you begin by creating an ad campaign with a $100 budget for example and you get $5 for each sale you create for the affiliate marketer, this means that you will need at least 20 sales to break even. You can lessen the required number of sales that you need to deliver by promoting products with a higher commission. Ideally, you want to increase the commission with products with better commission rates rather than promoting more expensive products. An ad with the same budget but pays out $20 per sale will only require you to make 5 sales to break even. All your sales after the fifth sale will go directly to your profits.

After learning how many sales you need to make, you can run a small scale campaign to test the conversion rates of your content. For example, you can start promoting an affiliate link with a $20 budget in your chosen ad platform. If the ad conversion rate in the $20 campaign looks promising, you could go on with a full scale campaign by increasing the budget or the duration of the ad. Let's say that a $20 campaign brought you 100 visitors and 2 conversions. If each sale makes a $10 revenue, then the ad campaign will just breakeven.

In this case, you need to make some changes to increase the conversion rate of your overall user experience. One thing you can do is to change the ad targeting. You will need to use the tracking tools discussed above to find targeting mistakes that may be affecting the success rates of your ads. You could also check the landing pages of your ads as well as the landing page of the advertiser. Some landing pages for example, use call-to-action buttons that are too small. Sometimes, these buttons may also be in the wrong color or the text included in them may not be inviting enough to click. These factors need to be changed to increase the likelihood of success. Make sure that the call-to-action button is always visible to the audience. Also make changes with the text in the button. Sometimes changing the call-to-action button from "Buy Now" to "Check Prices" may increase the click-through rate of your page.

Chapter 13 Quiz
Please refer to Appendix L for the answers to this quiz

1. How will you be paid for your guest posts?

    A) Guest posting does not pay
    B) Based on the number of words
    C) Based on the amount of traffic that your content gets
    D) Through affiliate sales generated by the guest post

2. What page should you use to contact a website administrator?

    A) Front Page
    B) Exit Page
    C) Contact Us Page
    D) Blog Page

3. What is one positive effect of guest posting?

    A) Positive SEO effects due to backlinks
    B) Increase in popularity
    C) Social Media popularity
    D) More sales

4. What do you call video journal entries in websites like YouTube?

    A) Vines
    B) Skype
    C) Vlog
    D) Blog

5. What tools can you use to become a vlog guest without going to the studios of vloggers?

    A) Skype
    B) Telephone
    C) Audio Recorder
    D) Text-to-Speech Technology

6. What is the biggest search engine in the world?

    A) Google
    B) Yahoo
    C) Amazon

D) Bing

7. What do you call the artificial intelligence software used by search engines to collect information about websites around the web?

   A) Search Engine Crawler
   B) Sear
   C) Search AI
   D) Search Engine Bug

8. What is one factor that establishes your website's identity to search engines?

   A) Social Media Profile Links
   B) Video Content
   C) Color Scheme
   D) Domain Name

9. What do you call the second phase of SEO wherein you optimize each article in your website?

   A) Page-level SEO
   B) Site-level
   C) Site Mapping
   D) Search Analytics

10. What do you call the practice of using keywords and phrases unnaturally in an article in the hopes of ranking higher in search engine results?

    A) Crawling
    B) Keyword Splicing
    C) Keyword Stuffing
    D) Search Engine Optimization

Conclusion

Before anything else, I would like to thank you for reading this book up to this point. That only shows that you are truly serious in pursuing opportunities that will earn you decent passive income. Being serious about it is a good start. It also prepares you in developing the right mindset. As I've mentioned in the beginning of this book, having the right mindset is crucial to your success. Most of the people who fail in this journey do so because they didn't have the right mental approach. They were lazy. They got discouraged too easily. They didn't have patience. If you truly read this book and follow it up by implementing the tips and strategies discussed within, I am confident that you are going to reach your passive income goals.

Furthermore, I want to share with you something that I find terribly sad. Once people start reading a book, they typically only read 10 percent of it before they give up or forget about it. Only 10 percent. What's sad about this is that from this statistic, we can see that very few people actually follow through on what they commit to (at least when it comes to reading). The reason for this is harsh but understandable: most people are not willing to hold themselves accountable. People "want" and "want" all day, but very few actually have the fortitude to put in the work.

So what's my point? First, I am trying to tell you that if you're reading these words, you are a statistical anomaly (and I am grateful for you). But here's the kicker: in order to become successful as a result of this book, you are going to have to be in the .1 percent. You need to take action.

So What's Next?

Now that you are fully aware of the various opportunities that you can explore in your attempt to generate passive income, what's the next step? Well, it's time to pull up your sleeves and get to work. It's time to take action. It's time to fire up that laptop and start getting things done. Many aspiring online entrepreneurs will never achieve their goals because they never get started. Don't be one of these dreamers. You have to take action.

I'll tell you right now that getting started is going to be difficult and often confusing. But that is part of the game. As the saying goes, the city of Rome wasn't built in one day. Generating a good amount of passive income takes time and hours of hard work. It can be weeks, months, or even years before you get to see some consistent revenue coming your way. This is why throughout this book, I've always reiterated the values of patience, determination, and discipline. If you don't have these attributes, your journey can be easily cut short by the smallest setback.

Others Did It, So Can You

There are a lot of people out there making decent passive income using one or more of the ways discussed in this book. Although most of them are doing it part-time, there are those who have turned it into a full-time gig i.e. they make 100% of their income from their online businesses. It's not uncommon for a blogger or affiliate marketer to be making six figures a year. Some even make six figures a month. The bottom line here is that it's really possible to create a comfortable income stream from a passive source. If others can, then you can as well.

My last piece of advice for you is this: "Set your goals and don't stop until you achieve them." Don't let anything or anyone try to discourage or bring you down. Just focus on those goals and keep on working and hustling towards them. That's what most successful entrepreneurs would do. Work hard, work smart, and be patient. These are the keys to achieving your goals. It doesn't matter if these are short-term or long-term goals. I wish you the very best of luck!

The End

Thank you very much for taking the time to read this book. I tried my best to cover as many ways to earn passive income as I could. If you found it useful please let me know by leaving a review on Amazon! Your support really does make a difference and I read all the reviews personally so can I understand what my readers particularly enjoyed and then feature more of that in future books.

I also pride myself on giving my readers the best information out there, being super responsive to them and providing the best customer service. If you feel I have fallen short of this standard in any way, please kindly email me at michael@michaelezeanaka.com so I can get a chance to make it right to you. I wish you all the best with your journey towards financial freedom!

Work From Home: 50 Ways to Make Money Online...
Michael Ezeanaka

Appendix A

Solution to Chapter 1 Quiz

Question Number	Answer
1	B
2	C
3	A
4	A
5	B
6	B
7	B
8	D
9	A
10	A

Appendix B

Solution to Chapter 2 Quiz

Question Number	Answer
1	A
2	C
3	D
4	A
5	A
6	A
7	D
8	A
9	A
10	A

Appendix C

Solution to Chapter 3 Quiz

Question Number	Answer
1	A
2	D
3	A
4	D
5	A
6	A
7	B
8	A
9	B
10	D

Appendix D

Solution to Chapter 4 Quiz

Question Number	Answer
1	A
2	B
3	A
4	B
5	B
6	A
7	B
8	C
9	A
10	D

Appendix E

Solution to Chapter 5 Quiz

Question Number	Answer
1	A
2	B
3	A
4	C
5	B
6	C
7	C
8	A
9	A
10	C

Appendix F

Solution to Chapter 6 Quiz

Question Number	Answer
1	C
2	A
3	A
4	B
5	D
6	C
7	B
8	C
9	B
10	D

Appendix G

Solution to Chapter 7 Quiz

Question Number	Answer
1	D
2	C
3	A
4	A
5	D
6	A
7	D
8	C
9	A
10	D

Appendix H

Solution to Chapter 8 Quiz

Question Number	Answer
1	D
2	B
3	D
4	C
5	C
6	D
7	C
8	A
9	C
10	C

Appendix I

Solution to Chapter 9 Quiz

Question Number	Answer
1	C
2	A
3	B
4	C
5	B
6	B
7	B
8	D
9	C
10	A

Appendix J

Solution to Chapter 10 Quiz

Question Number	Answer
1	B
2	C
3	B
4	A
5	B
6	B
7	C
8	B
9	A
10	A

Appendix K

Solution to Chapter 11 Quiz

Question Number	Answer
1	C
2	C
3	A
4	B
5	A
6	A
7	A
8	A
9	D
10	A

Appendix L

Solution to Chapter 12 Quiz

Question Number	Answer
1	C
2	B
3	D
4	A
5	C
6	A
7	D
8	C

9	D
10	A

Appendix M

Solution to Chapter 13 Quiz

Question Number	Answer
1	A
2	C
3	A
4	C
5	A
6	A
7	A
8	D
9	A
10	D

Printed by Amazon Italia Logistica S.r.l.
Torrazza Piemonte (TO), Italy